D1624875

THE MOSSAD AMAZONS

For Phyllis and Eddie
With my warm wishes —

November
2021

The Mossad Amazons

THE AMAZING WOMEN IN THE ISRAELI SECRET SERVICE

MICHAEL BAR-ZOHAR

and

NISSIM MISHAL

KTAV PUBLISHING HOUSE

The Mossad Amazons

KTAV PUBLISHING HOUSE
527 Empire Blvd
Brooklyn, NY 11225
www.ktav.com
orders@ktav.com
Ph: (718) 972-5449 / Fax: (718) 972-6307

Typeset by Raphaël Freeman MISTD, Renana Typesetting
Research and editorial coordination: Nilly L. Ovnat
Jacket design by Pini Hamou

ISBN 978-1-60280-446-3

Printed and bound in the United States of America

Amazon – a member of a race of
Female Warriors of Greek mythology.

(Merriam-Webster Dictionary)

CONTENTS

Liat to the Authors

A *Lohemet* Speaks

I AM A *LOHEMET* – A MOSSAD FEMALE WARRIOR.
I was born in Israel, in the Jordan Valley. I have been a Mossad warrior for the last twenty years. I am whole-hearted and enthusiastic about what I am doing. It is important that each of us warriors would feel a profound commitment to the defense of the nation, of our families and ourselves.

But one should also have a spark in one's eyes.

I have participated in undercover missions all over the world. I know how to change my identity and appearance at any given moment. When I am abroad you won't recognize me; I do not look like this, except when I want to attract attention [Liat is extremely beautiful, tall, blue eyed, with curly blond hair]. I get excited when I hear, on the loudspeaker system, that my squad is summoned to the briefing room. I know that something is going to happen. I know that I'll drink my morning coffee in Tel Aviv, but I do not know where on the globe I'll have dinner.

Women fulfill all the tasks in a Mossad mission, all of them. Exactly like the men. Sometimes there are missions where women are the majority. Men come from the army. They know the drill: Weapons – Intelligence – ways and means. I do not. I am in a gray area somewhere in the middle. Being a woman, I can pass beneath the radar.

When we, the Mossad Amazons, read in the papers about Mossad women, they always are described as "gorgeous and breathtaking". That is nonsense, we do not like it. What is much more important is that we are absolutely equal to the men. By the way, you wrote to me that among the women warriors there also are "technicians". You should have written "cyber experts, engineers, computer specialists."

You gave me the address of the café where we are meeting. Come on, let's be serious. Give me a name in Bangkok and I'll be there, on time. I do not need directions. I can find any place where I am told to be.

I must know how to think, how to act according to a detailed plan, but if there is a change in circumstances – be able to reach different decisions in a matter of seconds. This is not easy to learn and to execute. Of course, there are rules which I'd follow, when I am on a mission or not. For instance, I'll never sit in a café with my back toward the entrance. I'll always pay for my drink the moment I'm served, so I'd be able to leave at any chosen moment. When I'm abroad, and someone recognizes me and calls me by my real name, I'll never turn back.

When I return from a mission I have to be able to immediately adapt to my real identity, to life in my country. My biggest joy is when the Immigration officer stamps my passport. Already in the taxi home I return to my old self. It is a dramatic change. I can one day hold in my hand one of the most sophisticated devices that Israel ever has invented – and the following day find myself despairing, at my wit's end, in front of a washing machine that broke down.

I am divorced, mother of two daughters and a son. They do not know what I am doing. My little daughter spoke to me about spies and I said, "Perhaps I could be one?" and the three-year old said: "You? You're unable to switch roles…"

I used to date a very rich guy who was trying to impress me. He kept telling me that his dream was to become a Mossad warrior. "These guys know to change identities like this", he clicked his fingers, "they could stand under my nose and I wouldn't be able to recognize them for what they are."

Now, I looked at him, and he was very tall and I stood virtually under his nose.

TRIO

Nina, Marilyn and Kira

MARCH 7, 2007.
Ibrahim Othman got out of the elevator on the hotel's fourth floor and walked to his room, but a strange sight made him stop in his tracks. A young woman was sitting on the floor, by the room next to his, bitterly crying. Beside her lay a big silver suitcase. She kept pounding on the suitcase solid cover with her fists, or pressing its two clasps, trying to open it. In vain.

Othman hesitated a moment, then he approached her. "What happened?" he asked in English. "May I help?"

She raised her tear-streaked face. "The suitcase is locked," she sobbed. "I lost the key. I do not know how. I do not know what to do"

"Perhaps downstairs, at the reception", he said. "They may know…"

"They do not know nothing! I put inside my purse with all my papers, and the key to my room, I can't enter my room. And…my documents, and the money…"

"I can try helping you," he said again, awkward.

"No, you can't."

He kneeled down beside her and tried to release the clasps. Nothing happened.

"Perhaps we can call downstairs?" he asked again.

"It won't help." She hesitated. "Wait, somebody told me once... Perhaps you have some other key, a screwdriver...or a penknife I could use?"

He shrugged. "No, sorry." Suddenly he got an idea. "Perhaps my room key? Let's try."

"I do not think", she said. "But...let me try."

He gave her his room key. She bent over the suitcase, turning her back to him in a way that he could not see her hands. Deftly, she pressed his key in some plasticine-like material concealed in her palm.

She passed Othman's key in the narrow slit over the clasps, then she pressed the suitcase clasps again. A metallic click was heard. "God!" She looked at the suitcase in amazement. "It worked!"

"It worked," he repeated after her. She looked at him with a happy smile.

"Thank you", she said. "Thank you so very very much. You saved me. You really did!"

She gave him back his key and started digging in her suitcase. He saw her pulling out a big brown purse and opening it. "Here, here is my key!"

He stepped toward his room.

"Thanks again, Sir," she called.

He entered his room. And he did not know that when the young lady pressed his room key in the Plasticine, she actually duplicated it. In less than an hour the weeping girl, Nina, together with her Mossad comrades, would succeed to reproduce the key. And so, an operational team of the Mossad would be able to penetrate the room of Ibrahim Othman, the head of the Nuclear energy commission of the Syrian government.

*

The Mossad had been tailing Othman for quite a while, but without success. Bits and pieces of information from various sources, and mostly a report by IDF's major Yakobi, employed in the AMAN (Military Intelligence), had raised the suspicion that Syria, perhaps following Iran, Iraq and Libya, might be trying to develop nuclear weapons. Most Mossad experts rejected Yakobi's theory. One of their major arguments was that "this does not suit Bashir [Assad]." Suit or not, the debate went on; but finally the Ramsad [Head of the Mossad] Meir Dagan decided to examine Yakobi's hypothesis. At a meeting with the Mossad departments heads Dagan stubbornly brushed off all the objections and doubts, and ordered to use all possible ways to find out if Syria is building a nuclear installation. The "Keshet" department, that specialized in sophisticated intelligence gathering operations overseas, was charged with the task.

"Keshet" was the Mossad most active department. Its men and women carried out hundreds of operations a year. Its warriors were among the most creative and original in the service, conceiving cunning operations for obtaining intelligence, documents and devices; they also developed ways of subtly approaching leading enemy officials operating abroad. Sometimes these were individuals or delegations sent to Europe, Asia or Africa by enemy governments and were targets for penetration and investigation; sometimes these were the enemy allies, suppliers or even foreign army commanders that cooperated with Israel's foes.

The nuclear danger was on top of the list of the Mossad missions. And Iran was on top of the nuclear list. But Ramsad Dagan believed that if Iran was deeply involved in a nuclear project, and if Iraq had also tried to undertake a similar venture, his duty was to make sure that no other enemy country built nuclear weapons in secret. That was why he doggedly insisted to find out exactly what Ibrahim Othman, "Mister Atom" of the Syrian government, was doing.

According to foreign sources, it was Ram Ben-Barak, the head of "Keshet" who sent his warriors to tail Othman. The man used to travel a lot. "Dagan ordered us to find out if Syria had or did not have a nuclear project," Ben-Barak told a reporter years later. "You execute several actions all over the world during a few months until you get lucky. Somebody makes a mistake in one place – and somebody achieves a victory in another. Meir Dagan was a man of tremendous perseverance. Many people told him: there cannot be a reactor in Syria. All these expenses and the loss of time are for nothing. But we kept following his orders and did not let go."

Apparently, the various missions did not bear any fruit. The dispatch of "Keshet" teams on Othman's tracks cost a fortune and the results were nil. But lately the Mossad officers found out that Othman was coming to Vienna, for the annual conference of the International atomic energy agency. Othman had an apartment in the Austrian capital, but this time he had decided to stay in a hotel, and there he met the crying Mossad amazon.

Getting the key to Othman's room was the first stage of "Trio" – three stages, each one a mission by itself. And starring in all of them were three young amazons.

*

Second stage. The following morning, Othman came down for breakfast and entered the hotel restaurant. He looked around and saw that the restaurant was full to capacity, and all the tables were taken. He did not know, of course, that most of the guests were Mossad warriors who had occupied the tables and ordered breakfast. They had left him only one seat in the entire restaurant: an empty chair by a table, where a young woman was sitting. She was speaking on her mobile phone while sipping her coffee.

"May I sit down here?" he asked.

"Sure," she shrugged indifferently and continued her phone conversation, in English, and in growing anger. She raised her voice a few times, then looked about, fuming, and finally hung off, slamming her mobile phone on the table. "Bastard", she mouthed. "To do this to me!" She raised her eyes and looked at her new neighbor. "Sorry, I lost control, but he shirked off again, the bastard!"

Othman nodded sympathetically and the furious girl kept rumbling. She told him about her boyfriend, who could not be trusted, in anything. He already had canceled dates at the last moment, but now? Tonight? They were to celebrate the anniversary of their first meeting and had chosen Vienna as a romantic place where they would spend a weekend. She had arrived last night, and he was supposed to arrive today – and here he was, canceling again! Today of all days!

Othman kept nodding in polite agreement. "Apparently he doesn't realize what he is missing", he said.

She looked at him. "And who are you?"

He introduced himself by his name but did not mention his position in the nuclear energy committee.

"My name is Marilyn", she smiled. She asked some casual questions and found out that he knew Vienna well, and had traveled the world. Gradually they plunged in an easy, pleasant conversation. Othman liked her, and fully enjoyed talking to such a young and beautiful woman.

She was back at the failed date with her boyfriend. "I tried so hard to prepare a wonderful evening", she said. "I reserved a table at "Silvio Nickol". You have to reserve a month in advance. You know, it's the best restaurant in Vienna!"

"Yes, so I heard."

She suddenly raised her head, frowning. "Tell me, what are you doing tonight?"

He was surprised. "Why do you ask?"

"It would be a pity to cancel the reservation", she said. "Perhaps... perhaps you'll come with me and we'll have dinner there?"

"The two of us? Together? And if your boyfriend arrives..."

"He won't arrive and doesn't deserve this", she stated. "So, what do you think? We'll share, of course."

He looked at her and smiled. Not every day he was invited to dinner by such a gorgeous woman. "Why not?" he heard himself saying, "A great idea. At what time?"

*

At eight PM they met in the hotel lobby and took a cab to the restaurant. After they left a "Keshet" team spread in the lobby. Two amazons and a male warrior sat on armchairs close to the elevators. If Othman suddenly changed his mind and came back too early, they would delay him before he went up to his room. The team commander, Eitan, sat in a car parked outside, close to the hotel. After a few minutes he heard the voice of one of his men in his headphones. The officer used a code-word, to report that the couple had arrived at the restaurant and already were sitting by their table. Othman did not know, of course, that the neighboring tables were occupied by other Mossad warriors, who were there to make sure that the dinner was proceeding according to plan, and protect "Marilyn" if Othman misbehaved…

Everything was ready for the third stage – and the third Amazon – of the mission. Eitan sent the operational team – Eyal and Kira – to the hotel fourth floor. They had the key to Othman's room and got in easily. They started a search of the room. On the desk Othman had left a few personal effects – and his cellphone! Probably he did not want to be disturbed by phone calls during his dinner with Marilyn, that was why he had left the phone in his room.

The cellphone was protected by a password. Kira took it and, in a few minutes succeeded to hack into it, bypassing the password. She checked the contents of the smartphone, that was full of messages and documents, And all of a sudden…

All of a sudden they stumbled on a large file of photographs. One after the other, amazing pictures popped on the screen. They showed a huge building, and inside it a nuclear reactor in advanced stages of construction, large parts of the reactor's core, and Asian men – Chinese or Korean – standing beside it. Other photographs showed the site of the reactor, in a deserted area. There were about 35 photos. They could not believe their eyes. Othman had photographed the secret reactor and the Asian experts with his cellphone!

After overcoming their excitement, the two completed their mission. Eyal perused the documents spread on the desk but did not find anything of interest. Kira copied the photos from the cellphone with the instruments she had brought over. The two of them put everything back on the desk and slipped out of the room.

At the end of the gourmet dinner at Silvio Nickol, Othman and Marilyn returned to the hotel. They parted in the lobby and Marilyn warmly thanked Othman for the pleasant evening.

He deserved her thanks.

*

As the report goes, the "trio", the three Mossad amazons, accomplished one of the greatest achievements of the Mossad. The astonishing material that was obtained thanks to Nina, Marilyn and Kira was immediately presented to the Ramsad, the army Chief of Staff, and the Prime Minister. The images taken inside the building revealed a large cylindrical structure with thin but solid fortified walls. Other pictures showed an external scaffold designed to strengthen the reactor outer walls. There were also photos of a second, smaller building equipped with oil pumps; several trucks could be seen parked around it. A third structure was apparently a tower that supplied water for the reactor. The Ramsad Dagan placed on Prime Minister Olmert's desk a brown envelope containing the 35 photos that the Mossad had brought from Vienna. Ehud Olmert was stunned. "This is a plutogenic [plutonium producing] reactor", Dagan told Olmert. It was hard to conceive a more astounding discovery, that actually exposed a mortal danger for Israel. "The question marks are over," Dagan's assistant told Olmert. "Now we have only exclamation marks!" Dagan asked Olmert: "Mr. Prime Minister, what shall we do?" Olmert's answer: "We'll destroy it!"

The achievement was astounding indeed, but it also exposed a grave mishap of the Israeli intelligence organizations. During a few years, till the Vienna mission, attributed to the Mossad, a nuclear reactor was being built on Israel's doorstep, and nobody knew about it. If not for the erroneous behavior of Ibrahim Othman, Israel might have awakened to a grim reality – an atomic weapon in the hands of its most implacable foe.

The photos obtained by Keshet's amazons were transferred to the Mossad and Aman research labs. The analysts quickly discovered the reactor's exact location: Al Kibar, an isolated desert site in the Dir a-Zur province, East Syria. The site was close to the Iraqi border, and the Euphrates River. The building had the form of a large cube, 20 meters high, with a surface of 16,000 square meters.

Now that the photos were analyzed, the Mossad knew where to look, and the story behind the pictures took shape. The Asian men photographed at the reactor site were North Koreans. It turned out that the cooperation between Syria and North Korea had started with the 1990 visit to Damascus of North Korea's president, Kim Il-Sung. During that visit, he signed an agreement on military and technological cooperation with Syria's president Hafez el Assad. The agreement included a nuclear paragraph but concentrated mostly on the shipment of Scud missiles from North Korea to Syria; the first shipment of Scuds arrived in Syria in February 1991, during US Operation Desert Storm.

The nuclear issue was back on the agenda only in June 2000, when a North Korean delegation came to Damascus for the funeral of President Hafez el Assad, and met with his son and successor, Bashar. Their talks about constructing a nuclear facility in Syria were crowned, two years later, by a tripartite meeting in Damascus, where Iran joined the project. The three parties agreed that North Korea would build the Syrian reactor and Iran would cover the cost, two billion dollars. The Al-Kibar reactor would be a copy of the North Korean reactor at Yongbyon.

Construction started, but the US and Israeli intelligence organizations were totally unaware of it. Even the visit of Iranian nuclear scientists in Damascus in 2006 did not turn on any warning light.

But the new information the trio had brought from Vienna meant that dramatic decisions had to be taken. Copies of the photographs were rushed to the CIA; In June 2007 Ehud Olmert brought a detailed report to US President Bush, and suggested that the US bomb and destroy the reactor, that constituted a grave danger to the Middle East nations. Several administration figures, like Vice President Cheney, supported a military strike, but Bush hesitated. On the advice of Secretary of State Condoleezza Rice and some of his assistants, he refrained from action, arguing that bombing the reactor would be an attack on a sovereign nation. He preferred using diplomacy instead. In a phone conversation Olmert bluntly said to Bush: "Your strategy is very disturbing to me. I'll do what I believe necessary to protect Israel."

"This guy has balls," Bush later said. "That's why I like him."

*

In the meantime, the surveillance of the reactor was delegated to the US and Israeli space satellites. They reported that in order to avoid attention, the Syrian regime had refrained from placing anti-aircraft batteries around the reactor. The Syrians even spread garbage around the structure, to create the impression that it was not active. But the satellites also reported that the Syrians were building the facility at breakneck speed. Washington and Jerusalem believed that the reactor would be hot and operating by the end of September; any attack on it later would release lethal radiation with terrible repercussions, both on the environment and on people in and outside Syria.

Olmert decided to bomb the reactor. The operation was code-named "Out of the box".

September 4, 2007. According to the London Sunday Times, an elite commando unit, Shaldag [Kingfisher] had been sent with helicopters to the Dir A-Zur area and spent almost a full day in hiding close to the reactor. (Another version says the mission was carried out by the *Sayeret Matkal* commando.) Their task was to illuminate the reactor walls with laser beams the following night, so the Air Force jets could home in directly on the target.

The aircraft came indeed, the following night. At eleven PM four F-15 aircraft took off from the Hazerim airbase and six F-16 took off from Ramon runways. In order to prevent a war with Syria all possible measures were taken to conceal Israel's involvement in the forthcoming mission. The planes flew first to the north, over the Mediterranean, and when they reached the Syrian-Turkish border, turned south, as if they were coming from Turkey. They approached Dir a-Zur, flying at an exceptionally low altitude. IDF electronic warfare units, airborne and ground-based, disrupted the activity of the Syrian radar stations and the planes' approach was not detected. They reached the Al Kibar site, zeroed on the reactor whose walls were painted by laser beams, dropped their bombs and annihilated the cube-shaped structure.

The following days, banner headlines and sensational reports swept the world press, attributing the bombing to Israel, as seemed logical. Pundits prophesied in their columns that a war between Syria and Israel was imminent. But President Assad chose to avoid a war. Israel kept total silence and did not admit it had anything to do with the operation. Assad and the Syrian General staff understood, of course, that Israel's air force had bombed the reactor. But Israel's silence allowed them to avoid a retaliation; besides, Syria was not interested in revealing that the destroyed structure was a nuclear reactor, built by the North Koreans, of all people … After long hours of silence and confusion, the Syrian official news agency published a befuddled statement. Israeli aircraft had penetrated Syrian space at one AM, the statement said. "Our air force forced them to retreat, after [they had] dropped ammunition over a deserted area. There was no damage to people or equipment."

*

This mission had a last chapter, no less dramatic. The head of the Syrian nuclear project was General Muhamad Suleiman, the leader of the Syrian "Shadow army" – a small, secret unit, whose members were the best officers and military experts in the country. Suleiman, one of the most powerful men in Syria, also was the confidential adviser to President Assad, operating behind a thick veil of secrecy, far from media exposure. After the destruction of the Dir a-Zur reactor, Suleiman started planning another reactor; but before embarking on his next endeavor, he took a few days leave in his home at Rimal Al-Zahabiya, in the north of Syria. The house was on the beach of the Mediterranean Sea. Suleiman invited a group of friends who sat at the porch, facing the tranquil sea, and enjoyed a relaxed dinner. According to the media reports, they failed noticing two shadows that emerged from the lazy waves. Those were sharpshooters who had dived over a long way from their boat. They aimed their weapons at Suleiman's head and fired simultaneously. Suleiman collapsed on the table, while the two fighters dived back in the water and swam back to their boat.

The Syrian government published a press release on Suleiman's death, caused – so it said – "by a heart attack."

That was the end of the mission that had started by the trip of three young amazons to Romantic Vienna.

NOTE: *All the names in this chapter are fictitious, except for those of Meir Dagan, Ibrahim Othman, General Suleiman, Ram Ben Barak and the political figures involved in the affair.*

Part One

Vanguards

CHAPTER 1

Sarah Aaronson

Death on Mount Carmel

O N OCTOBER 5, 1917, A SINGLE PISTOL SHOT REVERBERATED in the small Jewish village Zikhron Yaakov, on the green slopes of Mount Carmel, in Palestine. The Turkish guards who rushed into the Aaronson house bathroom found a young woman, Sarah, lying in a pool of blood on the colorful tiles. She had shot herself in the mouth with a small pistol. But the bullet had missed her spinal cord; she was still alive.

Sarah was a prisoner of the Turks. At the time, Palestine was a part of the Ottoman Empire. In World War I the Turks were fighting on the side of Germany and Austria, against Great Britain, France and their allies. Sarah and her family belonged to the small Jewish community in Palestine. Sarah's brother, the world-famous scientist Aaron Aaronson, had discovered the emmer wheat in Galilee, the original wild plant from which derive the domesticated strains of wheat. American and European foundations financed Aaronson's laboratory at Atlit, a small port on the Mediterranean coast. Aaron Aaronson also was the proud owner of the first automobile and the first bicycle in Palestine. The Aaronsons were bitterly opposed to Turkish rule in Palestine. They believed that the only way to achieve Jewish independence in Palestine ["the Land of Israel"] was by helping the British Empire win the war. Risking their lives, they created an espionage network, "Nili." Nili agents supplied the British with intelligence about movements of the Turkish forces. At its peak, the network, led by Aaron and his 27-year-old sister, Sarah, numbered 40 spies and informants. Sarah's lover, Avshalom, had been murdered by Bedouins while trying to cross the Sinai Peninsula and the front lines on horseback, bringing vital information to the British High Command in Cairo.

At the end of September 1917, the Turks intercepted a carrier pigeon bearing Sarah's recent report to the British. Sarah and her father were arrested. After four days of beatings and savage torture the Turks decided to take Sarah to Damascus where she would be tried and hanged. Sarah asked permission to change her clothes. Once alone in the bathroom of her house, she removed a loose tile, pulled out her tiny pistol, and shot herself.

She died on October 9, 1917 the first Jewish *Lohemet* of the modern era. Her sacrifice was for the right cause: the British and their allies won the war, Great Britain became Palestine's ruler, and willingly or not, blazed the road to the creation of the State of Israel. And 30 years after Sarah's death, when the State of Israel was born, many other women dedicated their lives to defending their country as latter-day Mossad Amazons.

*

Out of Israel's turbulent history, a gallery of bold, creative and confident women has emerged. Many of them were recruited by Mossad or Army Intelligence, others volunteered and even conceived perilous missions, without asking anyone for instructions or training. Most of them were Mossad "warriors" [front-line operatives], others – Mossad officers in various functions; they also deserve to be considered as part of that unique community. Many paid a heavy price for their daring – torture and prison if apprehended, or painful solitude, both when on a mission or in their private life, having sacrificed their dreams of family and children to their calling. Out of the heaps of books on *the Mossad emerges a misleading picture – a shadow army of brave, strong and smart men, similar to James Bond or other master spies populating the movies, TV series and cheap fiction. Time has come to replace that imaginary picture with the real one where, beside the men, we meet the Mossad women.

We cannot describe all the hundreds of women who served in this secret army. We cannot even name all of them or tell their stories in full, as much of what they did and are still doing, will remain classified for years to come. And yet, the female warriors whose stories we have chosen to tell here, duly represent that secret and devoted order, equal to the men, that has often been ignored or overlooked.

*

At the beginning a Mossad woman was a secretary or a *bat-levaya* – a female escort to a Mossad operative, playing the part of his wife or girlfriend. A couple always was less suspicious than one or more men; the presence of a woman in a couple or a group always reduced the suspicions. A couple hugging in a car also did not seem suspect, and few would guess that the embracing couple might be watching or even commanding a covert operation nearby.

The Mossad warriors in those early years were tough and daring men, former underground fighters of the *Palmach* and *Irgun* organizations that had preceded the creation of the State. The best among them served in the operational unit of the Shabak (the internal secret service) that was also used by the Mossad in its early years; it was later replaced by the Mossad operations' department, "Caesarea". At first Caesarea employed only men; but the Mossad commanders found out that women sent to "target countries" [meaning enemy states] can clear immigration more easily and carry out missions without raising suspicions. As one Mossad amazon told us: "When you see a man standing alone at a street corner at night – you suspect him. When you see a woman alone – you want to help her." And so, gradually, women joined the warriors' community. At first, the women were trained in hotel rooms or apartments where they stayed alone, *incommunicado*, and the instructors came to train them there, individually. Later, they started participating in the Mossad basic courses together with men; often a course would include 15 or 20 men – and a single woman. It took a long time until the tough, confident men realized that the women at their side were not only secretaries and phone operators and coffee servers – but full-scale warriors, their equals in recruitment and training, and their partners in complicated and perilous missions. Most of the first amazons, however, suffered from a harrowing solitude. For many years they were trained alone, and alone participated in risky operations, at times in the company of men, rarely in the same team with other women. Today, that method has been abandoned. But even after they retire, they cannot speak about their past. Many of these amazons met each other for the first time in their lives – on the pages of this book.

In the world media the Israeli amazons were often described as "temptresses". That never happened. The founders of the Mossad established an iron rule – women would never be ordered to use their bodies for their missions. A Mossad *lohemet* was never ordered or asked to sleep with the "object" of her mission. Only once was an amazon instructed to establish partial physical contact with a man who was the target of a mission in the "Cindy-Vanunu" operation; that infringement of the rules had far reaching consequences (see chapter 17).

If a sexual contact was deemed necessary, in very rare cases, the Mossad officers hired prostitutes for the mission. The owner of a famous French restaurant, a former hooker, volunteered to help the Mossad and did not hesitate to use her physical attributes in order to fulfill her mission; but she was not a Mossad warrior and all what she did was by her own initiative. [In the Mossad there is a clear distinction between a warrior – an operative of the Mossad – and an agent, who is somebody foreign, recruited, but not belonging to the Mossad]. Yossef (Yos'ke) Yariv, a former commander of Caesarea, described the recruitment of an agent in Europe, "a respectable woman of forty known as very liberal as far as sex was concerned. . . . We wanted her to get intimate with a few important "targets" in some foreign countries. She worked for us for two years and the results were excellent. She found out who these targets really were, what were their functions and what was their cover; she also learned who were their contacts, where and when they were meeting. This was vital for us; but I wouldn't have recruited her as a warrior..."

"More than once I used my being a woman," said the warrior Yael in an interview. "But I never used my body in order to gain acceptance or trust in enemy countries. I felt that observing the limits was precisely the advantage of femininity. And that was the message I received from my superiors. They never expected me to 'go to bed' with someone in carrying out my mission. Quite the contrary, and more. That always was the policy."

One of the early "tempting" cases – within the authorized limits – took place in 1954. The Mossad operational unit was in Europe, chasing a traitor, Alexander Ivor. He was an IDF (Israel's Defense Forces) officer who had got into financial troubles and escaped to Italy, where he sold maps and secret documents to Egyptian diplomats. He then vanished for a while but emerged in Vienna, when a former schoolmate of his happened to run into him in the street. The chance encounter was reported to the Mossad, and several warriors rushed to the Austrian capital.

The unsuspecting Ivor boarded a Paris-bound plane; an attractive "Frenchwoman" took the seat beside him. They started a conversation that became very friendly, and the two decided to have dinner in Paris together. When the airliner landed, the sweet lady suggested that Alexander joined her in the drive to Paris. Friends of her, she said, were waiting for her at the airport with a car. Ivor agreed and they got into her nice friends' car. On the way to Paris the car suddenly stopped, and Mossad warriors kidnapped Ivor. The pretty lady disappeared; her mission completed. (Ivor died in a cargo plane on the way to Israel, after being injected with an excessive quantity of sleeping drug; by a questionable order of Isser Harel, the Mossad chief himself, his body was thrown in the sea).

That had been a rare case of a woman participating in a Mossad mission. A few more years would pass before women warriors would be sent to missions like the men. And yet, even before the State of Israel was created, some daring women appeared, refusing to wait until the Mossad would find them, and "recruited themselves" to the service of the nation. That was an era, when the secret services' structures and rules had not been established yet. And while the military and civilian organs were still to be created, young women appeared, who volunteered or were randomly recruited, and without any training set out to the shadow world of espionage.

CHAPTER 2

Yolande Harmor

Her Shoulders Were Padded with Secrets

Y OLANDE WAS DETERMINED TO ACT TONIGHT.
She had taken her time getting ready, memorizing her lines, inspecting her makeup in her small vanity mirror, smothering her fear. Her blond hair was coiffed in a perfect chignon; she was wearing a cocktail dress of gray silk that enhanced her figure. She was confident and self-assured and knew exactly what to do – but nobody had done that before. Sitting by her table, she surveyed the magnificent decorum surrounding her with a fixed smile.

That evening, in the winter of 1945, the Cairo high society was dining, as usual, in the elegant restaurant of the Shepheard's hotel. The dining room was resplendent – marble-paneled walls, sparkling crystal chandeliers, majestic columns, tall arched windows and a huge bell-like cupola. Around the tables covered with fine white linen and scintillating silverware gathered men in formal attire and women wearing expensive gowns, freshly shipped from the Paris and Rome fashion houses. Most of the diners were Europeans – British, French, Italian – with a minority of rich Egyptians – businessmen, members of the local nobility, senior public servants and cabinet ministers. A few patrons were wearing British Army uniforms. Arab waiters in long *galabieh* robes, embroidered vests and red fezzes moved like shadows between the tables, carrying silver trays laden with European food. Cairo, Yolande thought, was the last bastion of white European colonialism, and Shepheard's was one of its holy shrines. The orchestra, that had played Viennese waltzes and light pot-pourris had completed its concert a few minutes before, and the only sounds populating the vast hall were the clicking of the silverware on the china dishes, and the low-keyed conversations around the tables.

Suddenly, all noises stopped. A sepulchral silence settled in the dining room. The conversations faded away and all eyes turned toward a group of men who had entered the hall and made its way toward a long rectangular table at the far end of the hall. The head of the group, in a civilian suit and a fez, a thin mustache adorning his round, flabby face, was Egypt's King Farouk. A suite of aides, friends and bodyguards trailed in his wake. Yolande watched the king and his suite as they took their places by the table. The waiters unloaded plates, trays and drinks, and diners in the hall returned to their food and their conversations.

Now, Yolande decided. It was the unique opportunity and now was the right moment. She got up from her seat and darted toward King Farouk. Her move triggered a shock wave in the vast hall. What was she doing? Dashing between the tables, she noticed the diners' expressions of outrage and amazement. That impudent woman was interrupting the king's dinner! Unthinkable, no less than sacrilege! She ignored the angry looks and exclamations; at this moment she did not care about the local mores. Two of the king's bodyguards stepped towards her, but too late. She stopped in front of the king, bowed and flashed her best smile. "Excuse me, Your Majesty", she slowly said, "you can arrest me if you wish, but so far your people did not let me reach you. I asked the palace officials repeatedly for an interview with you, but I got no answer. I am a journalist – what shall I tell my editors in America?"

After a brief hesitation King Farouk got up from his seat and politely shook her hand. He produced a business card from his vest pocket and presented it to her. He then invited her to call the Royal office directly and get her interview with no further delay.

Yolande Harmor stepped back, delighted. She had done it! She would get her interview. But nobody here knew the real reason for her bold move. And nobody knew her secret: she was the head of the Zionist espionage network in Egypt and she just had established a close connection with the Royal Palace.

*

She never thought she would become a spy.

Born to the affluent Gabai family in Alexandria, outrageously spoiled at home, the mischievous, jolly teenager was dispatched to an expensive boarding school for girls at Saint Germain, in France. She liked France, but she expected her future in Egypt to follow the pattern of most Jewish girls of her age and her social standing: a life of leisure, a wedding of lace and roses, a beautiful home, children... It indeed started that way. At seventeen she was called back to Egypt where her father had arranged her marriage to a successful businessman, Jacques de Botton; then came a nice house, servants, and a child, Gilbert. But there the routine abruptly ended. Soon, the bright young woman decided she wanted a different life. She knew languages, history, literature, she was well versed in current affairs; she wanted to do something in her life. At 21 she also had grown to be, as a man told her, an "amazingly beautiful" woman. After four years of a dull marriage, she divorced Jacques, took the three-year-old Gilbert and the family car, and drove to Cairo. She decided to become a journalist.

In Cairo, her beauty, her charm and her intelligence paved her way. She started writing about the political scene in Egypt and soon established close contacts with leading figures in the country. Her articles were published first in the local papers, later in the Palestine Post in Jerusalem, then in American magazines. She got used to people staring at her when she would walk into upscale restaurants in company of ministers, politicians. high-ranking army officers and foreign diplomats.

Yolande liked the pleasures Cairo could offer. Cairo was an exotic city, with wide streets, green parks, and majestic buildings. These were great times for the rich, thriving European community whose life seemed a succession of decadent pleasures – morning sails on the Nile, tennis in the exclusive clubs of Heliopolis and Al Gezira, tasting delicatessen at "Gropi's", afternoon tea with music and dancing at the Continental hotel, cocktails at the Mina House bar, camel riding and red sunsets at the pyramids.

Yolande's parents took care of all her needs and wishes -a great apartment, a sleek boat at the Nile shore, frequent travels to Europe, mostly to her beloved Paris. Many regarded her as a lightheaded, careless hedonist, a party girl who was also a journalist on the side. She did not mind. She smoothly integrated in the Cairo social life; her beauty and personal charm enticed the local high society. Some called her "mysterious and tempting", others – *"femme fatale."* She often heard bits and pieces of what people said about her. One of her friends described her as "the one and only, a super-intelligent woman.... No woman In Egypt," she added, "could be compared to Yolande. Men fell in love with her and fell smitten at her feet." Her attraction, some said, stemmed from the warmth and the *joie de vivre* that she radiated. "When she smiles, she smiles not only with her face, but with her whole body", said her Italian friend, Dan Segre. "To see Yolande dance was a unique experience," a woman friend added with a hint of jealousy. "She seems totally enthralled by her partner, as if there is nothing but him in the whole world."

But there was. The world war that exploded in 1939, brought two major changes in Yolande's life. One was a broken heart; the second – an unexpected kind of solace. As the German armor of Erwin Rommel approached Cairo, she briefly moved with Gilbert to Jerusalem. At a party, she met a handsome and smart South African pilot, John Harmer, whom she found irresistible. Their passionate love affair led to marriage; but that marriage was short and ended in tragedy. Harmer was killed in action, and his death was a terrible blow for Yolande. Gilbert saw her in her most desperate hours. "She never overcame her grief" he will say one day. Yolande took her husband's name and hebraized it to "Harmor".

The second change was a lecture she attended in Cairo. The speaker was a young Italian-born Jew, Enzo Sereni, a rising star in the Palestinian Jewish community. A passionate Zionist, the young man was a pacifist and believed in Jewish-Arab co-existence. He spoke with deep conviction of the plan to create a Jewish State in Palestine after the war's end. With a group of influential Jewish leaders, Yolande listened, enthralled, to Sereni's speech. He offered her a noble cause, a challenge that could turn into consolation for her loss. That evening, she said later, was a turning point in her life. She walked out of the meeting a different person and fervently embraced the Zionist ideology. In the young man's words, she found a new meaning and a new goal for her life – help create a Jewish State in Palestine.

But after Germany's defeat she heard that Sereni, too, had met a grisly fate. During the war he had organized a team of Jewish-Palestinian paratroopers who were dropped in occupied Europe as part of the British Special Operations Executive (SOE). 33 men and women, all of them volunteers, were sent on a mission impossible, a pathetic attempt to rescue the doomed Jewish communities. Some of them reached Yugoslavia, Hungary, Romania and Czechoslovakia, Sereni himself was parachuted in Northern Italy, captured by the Nazis and murdered in Dachau concentration camp.

*

Sereni was dead, but his dream lived in her heart. She engaged in intensive Zionist activity, writing, speaking, meeting with influential Jewish-Palestinian figures. Many Zionist leaders, like future Prime Minister Moshe Sharett, future Mayor of Jerusalem Teddy Kollek and others, often visited her office in Cairo, run by a smart woman, Ora Schweitzer. After the war, a romantic affair developed between Yolande and Moshe Sharett, and lasted till the creation of the State of Israel. During that time, Yolande was not only Sharett's lover, but also his close confidante, and he shared with her his intimate thoughts and plans.

Yolande also met with the legendary David Ben Gurion on several occasions; once she picked him up at the Cairo airport, but on their way to the city her car broke down; she drew pleasure and pride from the long conversation of Ben Gurion with her son, nine-year-old Gilbert, while they leaned on the immobile vehicle, in the middle of the desert, waiting for the tow truck.

The *Haganah*, the major Jewish underground against the British in Palestine, sent many of its commanders on secret missions to Cairo, which was the nerve center of the British Empire in the Middle East. One of them, 37-year-old Levi Avrahami, who dealt with weapons in the organization, came in 1944 on a top-secret assignment, but Yolande quickly put two and two together. "Come, sit beside me," she quipped with a naughty smile when he walked into her office, "and I'll tell you why you came to Egypt."

He stared back at her, confused.

"You want to collect the huge quantities of weapons that the Germans have left in the desert battlefields, and smuggle them to Palestine, right? For this you need a large warehouse, but you do not have one. So, let's find you one."

Avrahami was amazed. "And I am not easily amazed", he confided in a friend later. The next morning Yolande took him to the outskirts in her car, and they looked for some isolated "Lovers' nest". She finally found a big villa, surrounded by a wall and a cactus fence, and rented it on the spot. "That was an ideal place", Avrahami admitted, and used the villa for a long time. He was later appointed head of the *Haganah* organization in Cairo and stayed there for a long period. Wearing a British Army uniform, he would also accompany Yolande to that dinner at the Shepheard's in 1945, and witness her impudent assault on King Farouk's table.

But by then Yolande was not just a Zionist activist anymore; she had become the *Haganah* major spy in Egypt.

*

In March 1945 Yolande learned that the leaders of Egypt, Jordan, Syria, Iraq, Yemen, Saudi Arabia and the Palestinian Arabs were about to meet in Cairo. Some Egyptian politicians whispered in her ear that the meeting would be focused on the creation of "The Arab League".

The League's offices would be based in Cairo; its major goal would be to prevent the establishment of a Jewish State that Ben-Gurion was promoting in the last three years.

Yolande brought the detailed information to Reuven Shiloach, Ben-Gurion's major Intelligence adviser. She liked the suave, soft-spoken gentleman who kept popping up in Cairo without warning. Slim, balding, bespectacled Shiloach was born in Jerusalem, spoke Arabic as a mother's tongue and was already a legend in Zionist circles. This future founder of the Mossad, a former spy in Baghdad, Beirut and Damascus, was said to have close connections with the American OSS, the precursor of the CIA. He also was Ben-Gurion's secret advisor.

When Yolande showed him the Arab League documents she had obtained, Shiloach was impressed. "Can you help us?" he cautiously asked.

"You mean, create an espionage network in Egypt? I have everything ready."

Indeed, she had prepared everything, even before being asked. In her home she had already installed a dark room for the development of photographs. She had transformed her office into an intelligence center and established a list of dedicated informants, who worked for her wholeheartedly, convinced that they were supplying her with information for her work as a journalist. They had no idea that they were working for the Zionists. The devoted Ora Schweitzer paid some of them a monthly fee. High on Yolande's list was a "Muslim Brotherhood" leader; several high-ranking government officials; editors of Al Ahram major daily; Mahmoud Mahlouf, the son of the Great Mufti (the top Egyptian religious authority). Another frequent visitor to Yolande's office was Taq-al-Din al Sulh, a future Minister of Refugees at the Arab League, who was desperately in love with her. Azzam Pasha, Secretary of the Arab League, and the Lebanese Statesman Riyad Al Sulh were also close friends. Two major informants were "the two colonels", one of them a senior officer in the political department of the Police, the other – a well-connected military physician. Each of them received 50 Egyptian pounds every month from Yolande's manicured hand.

And when the Swedish ambassador, Widar Bagge, fell in love with her, she made him a devoted informant and later – a fervent Zionist.

Shiloach established communication channels for Yolande with his headquarters in Palestine. She received a radio transceiver, but did not use it, claiming that she was "not technical". Most of her material was dispatched to addresses in Europe, but that critically delayed the reception of the intelligence in Tel Aviv. For a while, for emergency transmissions, she could use the clandestine *Haganah* radio station which exchanged messages with Tel Aviv at least once a day. She was also instructed in writing messages in invisible ink and passing written reports by other means. And she signed her reports with the codename "Nicole".

A codename, she thought, me with a codename! I would have never believed that...And she felt very proud of her new assignment.

She also was very proud of her contacts with the Arab League. Always glamorous and nonchalant, often playing the role of the dumb blonde, she was the last person that one could suspect of cloak and dagger activities. The League secretary, Azzam Pasha, said to her once, with a mixture of admiration and jealousy: "You see the minutes of the League deliberations even before they reach my office!"

Indeed, she was informed regularly of the secret deliberations of the Arab League. Those reports became crucial as the creation of Israel approached and the Arab nations had to decide if they were going to war against the 600,000 Palestinian Jews. On November 29, 1947, Yolande sat with Gilbert by the radio at home. They followed with bated breath the vote at the General Assembly of the United Nations on the motion to partition Palestine into two independent states – Jewish and Arab. The partition plan was adopted by a majority of two thirds, and was immediately embraced by the United States, the Soviet Union, and the Jews of Palestine. As Yolande had reported beforehand, the Arab nations and the Palestinian leaders angrily rejected the plan. The date for the departure of the British and the creation of the Jewish State was set for May 14, 1948.

The Egyptian government, a Yolande report read, was still hesitating like some other Arab countries, if they should go to war against the tiny Jewish community in Palestine. But long before they reached a decision, Yolande got a surprising offer.

A Syrian military chieftain and former colonel in Hitler's Wehrmacht, Fawzi el Kaukji, had raised a "Salvation Army" in Syria and planned an attack on the Jewish community in Palestine. That project profoundly worried the Jewish leaders, as they had not created an Israeli army yet. The British were still in Palestine, and no regular Jewish army could be created before their departure. In late January 1948 one of Yolande's agents approached her with an unusual offer: he could supply her with Kaukji's offensive plans, for the sum of 300 Egyptian pounds.

"That is a lot of money," Ora said to her. But Yolande could not wait. She rushed to the *Haganah* secret radio station and dispatched an urgent message to Ben-Gurion.

She returned to her office, exuberant. "Ben-Gurion said," she told Ora, "that one drop of blood of our young men is worth more than 300 pounds. He authorizes the payment."

The deal was done. Beside Kaukji's maps and logs Yolande obtained a few drafts of the Arab League invasion plans. But how will she transfer them to Tel Aviv? She decided to fly to Palestine and bring the papers to Ben-Gurion herself. There still were flights to Palestine, as long as it was still under British army control. Yet, the Egyptian military control on the flights to Lydda airport, near Tel Aviv, was very strict. Egyptian officers thoroughly checked and perused every bag and every document of the rare travelers.

Yolande found a way. She removed her shoulder pads from her elegant jacket. Ora spent the night sewing the folded maps and documents in the shoulder pads, then had the pads stitched back in the garment.

Yolande smoothly passed the controls. Concealing her emotion and her accelerated heartbeat, she joked with the Egyptian officers while they checked her bags and found nothing. Her excitement grew as the plane approached Lydda. Suddenly, the pilot's voice resounded in the loudspeakers. The captain informed the passengers that because of the daily clashes between the *Haganah* and bands of

Arab irregulars, the traffic between Lydda and the Jewish cities may be very hazardous.

But when she landed, Yolande discovered that Ben-Gurion had thought about her arrival, A *Haganah* armored vehicle had been dispatched to Lydda to pick her up and bring her safely to Ben-Gurion's office. "The Old Man" as he was called, was dressed in a khaki quasi-military uniform. Yolande knew that this great admirer of Winston Churchill was trying to emulate him in many ways, and wearing an army uniform was one of them... Ben-Gurion and the taciturn, poised Shiloach were waiting for her, with a few other officers; but they all were rather taken aback when her first demand was for a pair of scissors...

Once the maps on Ben-Gurion's desk, Shiloach examined them closely and vouched for their authenticity. With Yolande listening, the officers and Ben-Gurion plunged into a strategic debate.

There was something strange in their conversation. On hearing some hints and remarks exchanged between the officers, Yolande deduced that they possessed some additional information about the planned attacks from the north; she guessed that they had another source of intelligence in Beirut or Damascus, but when she asked about it they fell silent.

But on that day, when her debriefing ended, Ben Gurion and Shiloach thanked Yolande warmly. "You do not know how important your work in Cairo is for us," Shiloach said, and asked her to take all necessary precautions to protect herself. "The day of the creation of the State approaches," the master spy said, "and with every passing day the vigilance and the suspicions of the Egyptians will grow. Please, beware!" She also met with Teddy Kollek, one of the Intelligence chiefs. "You are assuming too many risks," he said openly. "I advise you not to return to Egypt."

"I have no value for you in Palestine," she retorted, "but I have still a lot to do in Egypt."

The following morning Yolande was back in Cairo. The mission had been very successful. But the jacket was ruined.

*

Yolande returned to Cairo while in Palestine the clashes between Jews and Arabs had turned to a civil war. But the real danger, of course, was the invasion of Palestine by the armies of the surrounding states. "My main effort", Yolande reported, "was focused on those targets in Egypt that already were directly involved in the fighting in Palestine – the Arab league, the Palestinian leadership in exile, the Muslim Brotherhood, and the "Misr el Fatat" [Young Egypt] party. We monitored the Arab League meetings in Cairo, activated sources in foreign embassies and the British military command, who supplied us with intelligence about the secret British designs for Palestine and the Jordanian "Arab Legion" [at the time, the strongest Arab army in the Middle East]. Our agents even penetrated the Egyptian volunteer brigades that intended to set out for Palestine and take part in the fighting."

Yolande, indeed, still had a lot to do in Egypt as she told Shiloach and Kollek. But as May 14, 1948 was approaching, the tension in Cairo was rising. And then, barely a couple of days before the State was proclaimed, Yolande received a disturbing message from her friend Moshe Sharett, Ben-Gurion's deputy in the leadership of the Jewish community in Palestine. She knew that on May 8, in Washington, Sharett had met with The US Secretary of State, George Marshall; but she did not know that Marshall bluntly had warned Sharett not to create a Jewish State. Marshall had warned his guest that a bloodbath was going to take place in Palestine, the Jews would be massacred and the United States wouldn't help them, come what may.

Sharett, shaken to the core, sent Yolande a message that she and Ora read with trepidation. "I am returning to Palestine with my daughter Yael," Sharett wrote, "and I fear that we are about to make a big mistake." Yolande and Ora were devastated. Was Sharett, Ben-Gurion's closest partner, going to oppose the establishment of the State, the dream of the Jewish people for two-thousand-years? What Yolande was about to learn later, was that the faithful Shiloach, aware of Sharett second thoughts, waited for him at the airport, literally whisked him off the tarmac and drove him to Ben-Gurion's house, where Sharett meekly surrendered to his leader's pressure.

And on May 14 the State of Israel was born. Yolande followed with apprehension the news about the armies of all the surrounding Arab states, Egypt included, converging upon the nascent nation, to smother Jewish independence at all costs.

But danger loomed not only for Israel. In her undercover work Yolande kept taking utterly perilous risks. Now, for the first time, she felt she was being followed, and feared that her arrest was imminent. "... Yet, because of the crucial importance of my mission" she wrote, "I kept working." On May 20, she wrote to Shiloach: "My situation here is very shaky. I am still "outside" [she meant outside of prison] thanks to the influence of some friends. If you think I might be more useful somewhere else, I'll not object to a change of air." She learned that the Cairo police interrogated quite a few Jewish leaders and repeatedly asked them the same question: "Who is Yolande?"

"Who is Yolande?" Dr. Joseph Michael, a banker and Yolande's fervent suitor, told her that he had been warned bluntly by the police: "Beware of your friend!" He realized that Yolande was in danger.

Her fears were well-founded. In July, Yolande was arrested and thrown in jail. A strange jail, though. Every day she ordered gourmet meals from Cairo's best restaurants; she received morning papers and had free use of the telephone. She could call whoever she wanted, and she did. The other women in the prison assailed her with questions about her special treatment, but she kept silent. In the meantime, though, her spy network started to crumble down. The agents besieged her office and demanded their pay. One morning Yolande heard her name shouted, over and over again from the street, beyond the prison walls. She managed to climb to her cell window and saw a stout Arab woman, clad in a black *galabieh*, her head covered with a *hijab*, standing in the street outside. A teenage boy stood beside her. Gilbert! The woman in the black robe disguise was Ora. "What should I do?" Ora shouted in Arabic. Yolande shrugged, helpless. "Do what you can," she said.

All that time, Yolande was not interrogated or indicted. After a few weeks she was transferred to a pleasant villa, that was used as a special jail for foreign women. Yolande fell sick, lost weight, and almost could not get up from bed. The authorities apparently did not want her to die in their prison; so they hastily released her and put her and her son on the first flight leaving for France.

In Paris, Yolande could work for Israel without fear. She formally joined the Israeli delegation to the UN plenary session, held that year at the Palais de Chaillot. She wore a name tag embossed with the Israeli flag. And yet, she kept meeting with Egyptian diplomats, who respected her and treated her with warmth and friendship. On a visit to the Israeli embassy, a friendly clerk showed her a telegram, that the embassy secretary Shmuel Divon, had sent to Jerusalem. "When one needs to establish contacts in real time," the enthusiastic Divon wrote, "there is just nobody like Yolande." Beside the Egyptians, she established firm connections with French leading figures and foreign diplomats.

But she created all those contacts because she had her own agenda. Yolande staunchly believed that peace between Jews and Arabs could be achieved. While Israelis and Arabs were shedding each other's blood all over Palestine, she kept meeting with Israel's enemies and writing memoranda to the newly appointed Foreign Minister, Moshe Sharett, insisting that the Egyptian government wanted to reach an agreement with Israel.

In Paris she also met Sharett, Shiloach and other Israeli friends. When Israel's independence War ended, and armistices were signed with the Arab countries, it was obvious that Yolande would come to Israel. But her decision stunned everybody. Against all odds, despite frantic calls and telegrams from Israel, even angry orders from Shiloach – she decided to return to Egypt!

For many that was an act of madness. In Egypt she had been arrested and jailed, suspected of treason and espionage. Returning there was for her like sticking her head in the lion's mouth. But she felt that Cairo was her place, and she could revive her private enterprise.

It turned out that she was right. Cairo welcomed her with open arms, as if nothing had happened, as if she never had been thrown in jail. She got back to her old home, Gilbert got back to his school; her friends and relatives, and even Egyptian high-ranking officials treated her with renewed trust. "It was all so very strange", Gilbert would tell her one day, "and the strangest, of it all – was that nobody thought it was strange…"

Yolande tried to return to espionage, and again spun her connections with the Cairo *Who is Who*. One evening she entered a renowned restaurant with the head of The Egyptian Secret Services (*the Mukhabarat*) in Cairo, Shusha Bey, and two of his lieutenants. At a nearby table she saw an Israeli intelligence officer, Eliahu Bracha, who operated in Cairo under cover. He stared at her, stunned; she figured out that he thought she had been arrested by Shusha. She excused herself and went to the Ladies' room. When she passed by Bracha's table, she dropped her handkerchief, which he deftly pocketed. Inside the handkerchief she had concealed a note with her phone number. That night he called her, the two of them met, and she gave him a full report of her activities. From him she learned that a former Haganah envoy, Shmuel Antebi, was leaving Egypt by boat, on his way to Israel. In the dead of night, she came to Antebi's house, and gave him a toothpaste tube; instead of paste, the tube was stuffed with papers. "When you get aboard the ship," she said, "give the tube to the captain. He'll know where to deliver it."

This strange situation continued for two more years. Finally, Yolande realized that she was living on borrowed time. Egypt was changing, politics were becoming more turbulent, criticism of the king and his corrupt regime was rising. Yolande realized that the merry days of Cairo were gone forever. In 1951, together with her son and her old mother, she immigrated to Israel. She settled in a small apartment in Jerusalem, so small that she and her mother had to pile the carpets they had brought from Egypt one on top of the other.

But it was not the modest apartment that bothered Yolande. It was the fact that in Israel there was no use for her talents and qualifications. In Tel Aviv she met Colonel Benyamin Gibli, the Head of Military Intelligence, who had shared her reports from Cairo with the Mossad. Gibli was very nice and grateful for what she had done but did not offer her a position in his department. The State of Israel was extremely grateful to her for what she did – but did not know what to do with her. She had foreseen that situation – and this had been one of the reasons why she had delayed so much her departure for the Promised Land. Leaving Cairo was the beginning of Yolande's end.

In Jerusalem she finally was given a job in the Ministry of Foreign Affairs, but it was a minor position in the Protocol Department. Her friend Reuven Shiloach just had founded the Mossad but did not invite Yolande to join him there; only seldom she was sent to Europe on missions for the Mossad or the Research department of the Foreign Ministry.

Her rare visits to Paris brought her immense joy. And it was the old Yolande who was coming to life. One day she would have lunch with her friend Rene Mayer, a future Prime Minister of France, the next day dinner with Pierre Mendes France, also a future Prime Minister, the third day with a group of Egyptian diplomats. She loved the pleasures Paris could offer and often invited Betty, Reuven Shiloach's wife to "Parisian breakfasts" of oysters and champagne. But back in Israel she failed to integrate in the political and social texture of the Ministry. She was an extremely talented woman, and yet, nobody tried to find a position where she could really be of service. She stayed smiling and pleasant but deep in her heart she felt lonely and disappointed. "Look. they do not know what to do with you at the office," told her a ministry co-worker. "You are not a typist who can sit by her desk from eight in the morning to four in the afternoon. They know they owe you a lot, but do not know what to do."

She sensed, though, that they looked at her as somebody foreign, not belonging. The Ministry staffers did not like the way she dressed and her European manners. "She was a coquette when the Israeli girls were wearing shorts", said her friend Dan Segre, "she was elegant in a country where elegance was regarded as decadence, she was refined and pleasant in a society where people were tough pioneers." The diplomats and their sweet wives used to ridicule her behind her back and to call her "Lady Levantine" – a spiteful term for the manners, the language, the clothes and the culture of that "frivolous" woman, who was – God forbid – Levantine, not even European but from Cairo, from the Middle East! A rare exception to that disdainful choir, was

Minister of Foreign affairs Moshe Sharett, who remembered the pretty and intelligent heroine from Cairo, and often invited her to official dinners at his home.

Historic events took place around her, but she was excluded of even giving her advice. In Cairo, a military junta deposed King Farouk. The aggressive colonel Nasser became president of Egypt and the whole *ancien regime* was swept away. Nasser then acquired huge quantities of weapons from the USSR, swore to destroy Israel, and nationalized the Suez Canal. Israel launched a victorious offensive in the Sinai, in secret collusion with France and Great Britain. Yolande's intimate knowledge of Egypt could be priceless in the shaping of the Israeli policy, but nobody thought of asking her. Closer to home, Shiloach resigned from the Mossad, actually forced out by the ambitious Isser Harel, head of the internal Secret Service. Harel did not know Yolande and her connection with the Mossad faded away.

She profoundly suffered for being relegated to a backwater while she could still be of service. Her friends and commanders from the Cairo days had forsaken her. She was pained and frustrated. "It isn't fair!" she kept repeating to her few friends. "It isn't fair."

She lived alone with her mother in Jerusalem. Her sister lived far away, in Australia. Since 1954 she had not seen Gilbert, who was studying in the United States. She fell sick again, this time with cancer, and was urgently moved to the hospital. Her situation quickly deteriorated. Even while she was struggling for her life, her frustration haunted her thoughts and feelings. She yearned to receive at least a diplomatic grade, but the Foreign ministry rejected her application. She lay, helpless, on her deathbed in the hospital, but the Ministry bureaucrats refused to give her the diplomatic grade, pettily arguing that "she might demand a pension from the ministry . . . " Only under the pressure of some influential leaders, the ministry heads finally agreed and bestowed the diplomatic grade on the dying Yolande.

Of course, it was too late. The cancer invaded her whole body and she died. She was only 44 years old.

CHAPTER 3

Shula Cohen

Monsieur Shula,
codenamed "The Pearl"

W HEN IN 1947 YOLANDE BROUGHT TO BEN GURION AND
Shiloach the invasion maps, she guessed, by their questions,
that they had another source in Lebanon or Syria. She asked them if
they did, but they abruptly fell silent. Yolande's question remained
unanswered.

Well, did they have another source?

They did.

*

Young, blue-eyed, pretty and elegant, already a mother of five, and
bored to death, Shula Cohen was standing in her husband's store in
Beirut. It was a cold afternoon in December 1947, the store was almost
empty, and Shula overheard the loud conversation of two Lebanese
merchants who had just walked in. The creation of the State of Israel
was approaching, and the two Arabs exchanged valuable information
about the invasion of Palestine from the north. They spoke about the
efforts to recruit young fighters from several villages along the future
Israeli border, and the planned invasion of Galilee from Syria and

Lebanon. All this was very important, Shula thought and shuddered. In her mind she could visualize Israel being consumed by fire and death. That was the first time in her life of comfort and plenty that she felt real worry, a worry about the fate of Israel. She pulled her husband aside. "We must do something, Joseph!" she said, "we must alert the Israelis!" Joseph, a rich trader in Imported fabrics, agreed with his fiery wife, as always. "I know an Arab smuggler from Adissa village," he said. "He is a friend of ours. He would take a letter across the border."

Shula hurriedly wrote a letter, reporting in detail what she had heard. She used a rudimentary "invisible" ink, that she had learned to prepare at a girl-scout camp in Jerusalem; and her message was dissimulated in a seemingly innocent inquiry about a sick relative in Jerusalem. She wrote her report of the Arab merchants' conversation with invisible ink, in the spaces between the innocuous words. According to her husband's instructions, the smuggler delivered the letter to an address in the Jewish town of Metula, across the border.

Would she get an answer? Sending the letter was a fateful act for the young woman. All of a sudden, a lofty goal took shape before her eyes – help the nascent nation of Israel. She lived in Lebanon, where she was called "Um Ibrahim" – Mother of Abraham – by the name of her oldest son, Abraham. But she considered herself an Israeli and felt a deep commitment to Israel.

*

Shula was the fourth of Meir and Allegra Cohen's twelve children. She was born in Buenos Aires, Argentina, where her father, a well to do businessman from Jerusalem, had a commercial enterprise. Her mother did not like Argentina and the family returned to Jerusalem; but her father had to spend a large part of the year in Buenos Aires for his business. Every time he left for Argentina he took with him one of his children, to dispel his loneliness. Shula spent a year with him in Buenos Aires, learned Spanish, sang and danced the Argentinian trademark tangos. And liked them.

But she grew up in Jerusalem and studied at the prestigious girls' school Evelyn de Rothschild. When the teenager emerged on the

Jerusalem scene, everybody agreed that she was one of a kind – intelligent and attractive, romantic but practical, gifted with a fine sense of humor and an avid book reader. She spoke Hebrew, Arabic, Spanish, French and some English, and belonged to an amateur drama club. Rather vain, she cared a great deal about her looks – fashionable dresses and expensive jewelry, hair style and manicure, matching bags and shoes. Adventurous and charming, that slender, auburn haired and cheerful girl knew to captivate people and easily made friends. But most of all – she had fire in her belly, a consuming ambition to do "something important, something of value."

She was happy in Jerusalem, until disaster hit. When she was sixteen, her parents decided to marry her to Joseph Kishik, a rich Jewish merchant from Lebanon, a man twice her age. Kishik and his family arrived from Beirut, and Shula's parents announced her betrothal. Shula was devastated, for being "sold" as merchandise for a bride price. But in those days that was the custom and she could not do a thing. "Never in my life did I cry as on that night" she said later. "I was sixteen, I had dreams..." Jerusalem was for her "the top of the world, the closest place to heaven", and she felt she was falling to a dark and lonely place. Shula locked herself in a small room and wept.

The young bride arrived in Beirut, bitter and miserable, despite the pleasant life that awaited her – a nice home, servants, a highly regarded position in the Jewish community that clustered in the Wadi Abu Jamil neighborhood. But her pain slowly dissipated as time went by, and she found out that her husband was an intelligent, loving man, who respected her and would do anything to please her. Without batting an eyelid, he paid for her expensive dresses and coats, and even bought her a very high-priced diamond brooch, "The dame with the Camellias", that every woman coveted those days. Yet, he was immersed in his business and in the community life, while his mother and sister tried to control his young bride. Shula gave birth to her first baby, then another one and another, and spent days and nights taking care of the children; during the next fifteen years she was to have seven children. But neither taking care of the children, nor reading heaps of books, could satisfy the young woman. Shula needed a goal in life, a purpose that would be a worthy challenge for her passionate character.

*

The letter that she entrusted to the Arab smuggler in December 1947 reached the Haganah Headquarters, and a few weeks later an unknown Arab knocked on her door. He introduced himself as "Shukri Mussa". He told her that her letter had reached its destination and described the first mission that "those you wrote to" wanted her to carry out. "They want you to get a passenger named Winkler off the ship 'Transylvania' that arrives in Beirut port tomorrow and smuggle him to Palestine."

She immediately went to work. On her husband's advice she rushed to the home of a Jew named Abu Zik, who had shady connections in the port. For a bribe of 800 Lebanese pounds, that came from Joseph Kishik's pocket, Abu Zik's friends found Winkler on the "Transylvania", whisked him off the ship in a docker's garb, and a few hours later he was across the border, in Palestine.

Shula's first mission was a success, and she felt pride and satisfaction that finally, besides breast-feeding and changing diapers, she was doing something important. The following day Shukri Mussa knocked on her door again. He congratulated her for her successful mission and added: "The people in Palestine ask if you'd agree to keep working for them. They want to meet you. I can take you across the border."

She agreed, her heart pounding. Crossing the border could be dangerous. But if she wanted to help her people, she had to take risks. She decided to leave the following morning, a Monday, because she had to be back on Wednesday, to prepare the house for the Shabbat [Saturday] dinner. Before leaving Beirut, she dropped – as usual – in the beauty salon, put on flat heeled shoes for climbing the border hills and a voluminous coat, to conceal her advanced pregnancy. A devoted, close-mouthed neighbor, Linda Belanga, took charge of the children.

A car took her to a desolated gully in the hills. A black night had fallen, and cold winds whirled from the Northeast. She shivered. Even her heavy coat could not protect her from the brutal cold. From afar she could see the flickering lights of two villages. Suddenly, out of the dark, emerged a few Arabs – the smugglers. She recognized Shukri Mussa and followed him uphill without a word. The walking was hard and painful. For the first time she felt a surge of fear; Lebanese army patrols were crisscrossing the area, and she was afraid of a disastrous encounter. But she had to cross the border at all costs.

They kept trudging in the blackness, when suddenly Shukri Mussa stopped and pointed at some scattered lights in the distance. "Metula", he said.

Half an hour later they were in the Jewish town of Metula, across the border. She walked right to the "Arazim" [Cedars] hotel, where Grisha, a member of the nearby kibbutz Kfar Giladi, was waiting for her. He identified and debriefed her, then a jeep with an Haganah armed escort took her southward. On their way, she saw the silvery lake of Tiberias for the first time in her life.

Late that night, they reached the town of Kiryat Haim, near Haifa. She never had been there before. The office of Haganah Intelligence was located in a small house, in a side street. Two intelligence officers questioned her, at length, about the invasion plans of Kaoukji that she had described in her letter. They made her repeat every word she had heard about the forthcoming offensive. One of the officers told her that they already had sent a copy of her letter to headquarters. Once the invasion subject exhausted, they started asking personal questions: how was her life in Beirut, who were the close and distant members of her family, what were her connections with the Muslim and Christian communities.

She spoke about her yearning to help Israel despite the danger of covert activity in Lebanon. The Haganah officers warned her, over and over again, of the terrible risks in such activity.

"Do you understand," one of the men, Cherbinsky, quietly asked, "that if Lebanon joins the war against us when the state is created, and if you are caught – you'll be tried as a traitor?'

"Yes", she said.

"And you know what they do to traitors?"

"Yes."

"You know it's the gallows."

"Yes."

"And you still are ready to help?"

"Yes."

He vaguely described to her the Haganah main subjects of interest in Lebanon: information about the Lebanese army and mostly about the units trained for the attacks on Israel, their bases and their weapons. He established some secret channels of communication she could use, promised to cover all her expenses and offered her a salary.

"No," she said. "No salary. My husband covers all my needs." She only agreed that her expenses, if any, will be paid to her family in Jerusalem.

And that was it. That night, in a small house in a small town she never had heard of, without any training or initiation, without clear instructions and well-defined goals, Shula was recruited to the Intelligence community of the future State of Israel.

The following morning, she was back in Metula; late that night Shukri Mussa led her back to Lebanese territory by his tortuous paths; on Wednesday morning she was back in Beirut. On her way home, after the obligatory beauty salon, she stopped at the market, to buy fruits and vegetables for the Shabbat dinner. In her room she found a surprise gift from her husband – an ensemble of silvery angora wool that they had seen in an upscale shop window. That was, she understood, Joseph's way to welcome her back and express his delight that their life was returning to normal.

Well, not exactly. The Independence war raged in Palestine and Shula devoted her energy to two goals: The first – obtaining vital intelligence and passing it to Israel, and the second – smuggling multitudes of Jews from Syria and Lebanon to Israel.

"Nobody recruited me to the Israeli Intelligence services," she proudly would say one day. "I recruited myself."

*

On May 14, she heard on the radio the voice of David Ben-Gurion reading the Declaration of Independence of the State of Israel. During the bloody war that ensued, she did her best to supply the Israelis with reliable intelligence; but her main efforts were to smuggle thousands of Jews into Israel. She recruited a virtual army of Arab smugglers who were at her pay; they kept crossing the border at moonless nights, followed by long columns of Syrian and Lebanese Jews. A constant stream of European Jews came as well, via the Balkans and Turkey. A few months before, she had been seized by dread at the approach of the border. Now she often joined the illegal immigrants and supervised the passage into Israeli territory.

An Israeli officer in charge of the immigration told her once that "her" immigrants added up to several thousands. Two of those were her own children, Abraham (Bertie) and Meir, aged 7 and 10. During the car trip to the border, the Arab smuggler told her later, the children were talking and shrieking in loud voices; he feared that their shouts might endanger the entire operation. He then made them drink a few spoonfuls of Arrack, an anise-flavored liquor with a high content of alcohol. The children fell asleep right away and woke up in Israel. That mission was very important to Shula as she wanted her sons to grow up in Jerusalem. Her oldest daughter, Yaffa, reached Israel by air, flying to Turkey and changing planes in Istanbul.

The breakthrough in Shula's career as a spy, happened almost by chance. One morning, while passing by the "Maccabee" sports club, she heard the teenagers trying to sing a Hebrew song, "Etz Harimon" [the pomegranate tree] and failing to pronounce the Hebrew words properly. She walked in, and taught the right pronunciation to the youngsters. The principal of the Jewish school heard that Shula knew Hebrew and invited her to join his staff, which she readily accepted.

At the end of the year, the school planned a graduation ceremony. The principal asked Shula to go to the Prime Minister's office and invite him to be the guest of honor at the event, as in previous years. Shula put on her best dress, made up her face, and went to Prime Minister Riyad a-Sulh's bureau. Sulh's secretary, though, treated her with contempt and refused to let her see the Prime Minister. She felt humiliated and turned to go. At that moment the door of Sulh's bureau opened and the Prime Minister stepped out. He saw Shula, greeted her politely and invited her to his office. He immediately agreed to her request, and they engaged in a relaxed conversation on the current political situation. Sulh liked the young Jewess and invited her to his home.

The following evening Shula was ushered to the Prime Minister's residence where she met his wife and his three daughters. The youngest, Huda, was of Shula's age, and the two were to become close friends. Starting that day, Sulh started inviting Shula to official events, ceremonies, and receptions, where he introduced her to all the political and military elite in Lebanon – ministers, members of Parliament, generals, visiting dignitaries, mostly from Syria. The gates to the governing spheres were wide open – and Shula walked through with confidence.

"There is nobody in the world that you can't reach", said Shula to her son Isaac. And indeed, the new reality was amazing. The young woman became overnight a guest at the official and private meetings of the Lebanese leaders. All his life Isaac will remember the huge bouquet of flowers that he received from Lebanon's President, Camille Shamoun, for his Bar-Mitzvah; the thirteen-year-old boy was also invited for a private visit to the President's palace. Another leader who Shula charmed, was Pierre Gemayel, the head of the Phalanges, the powerful paramilitary organization of the Christian community. Gemayel was the father of the future Lebanese presidents Bashir, who was assassinated shortly after his election, and his brother Amin Gemayel.

Friendship with presidents and ministers was fine, but Shula was interested in connections with the shadow world as well. She succeeded to develop a rapport with the much feared "King of the robbers" or as other called him, "the Gang Baron", Bulus Yassin, who controlled a dark empire of casinos, night clubs, prostitution, drugs and gold smuggling. Many in Beirut loathed him, many more were afraid of him, but Shula did not hesitate to befriend him, for the simple reason that he controlled most of the smuggling in and out of Lebanon. With his help she could smuggle thousands of Middle East Jews into Israel. He spread a veil of immunity over her actions, and in return she would serve as his interpreter, would write his letters, and would stand beside him at the receiving line at his glitzy parties and greet the important guests.

Shula's connections reached the nerve centers of power. She laughed a lot one night in 1950, when Sammy Moriah, one of the greatest Israeli spies, popped up at her door. He had arrived in Beirut, he said, on his way to Damascus. A cheeky and exceptionally bold operative, he walked straight to the Beirut Headquarters of the *Mukhabarat* – the Lebanese internal Secret service and introduced himself with his false identity. He was an Iranian businessman, he said, and had to meet the Secret Service head "about something extremely important and very urgent." The head of the *Mukhabarat*, Farid Shehab, agreed to meet him. As soon as the two of them were alone in Shehab's office, Moriah said: "I bear you greetings from Robert Lustig."

Shehab paled, and froze in his seat.

Moriah knew that in the past Shehab had been a member of the Lebanese – Israeli armistice commission, that held some of its meetings in Tel Aviv. Shehab had met there an Israeli police officer, Robert Lustig, and the two of them had nightly enjoyed some of the unholiest pleasures Tel Aviv could offer. "They wildly partied at all kinds of places," Moriah told Shula later, "and what they did there was to remain under wraps."

Shehab apparently realized that if his Tel Aviv adventures were exposed, that would be the end of his career. "You come from Tel Aviv?" he anxiously inquired. "Are you Israeli?"

"Yes and yes", Moriah answered, then he asked: "Where is the Jewish neighborhood in Beirut?

"Why do you ask?"

"I have some relatives in Beirut, they probably live there."

Shehab smirked. "Nonsense. You want to see Shula, right?"

Moriah did not answer.

"Don't go there during the day," Shehab advised him. "Go at night. It's safer."

The two parted with a meaningful handshake. Shehab's Tel Aviv gallivanting would remain a secret and Moriah would be free to fulfill his mission.

On his way to Wadi Abu Jamil, Moriah mulled over the strange meeting with Shehab. The head of the Beirut *Mukhabarat* knew Shula Cohen; not only he knew her but tried to protect her and the envoy of the Israeli Intelligence...Moriah indeed visited Shula that night, enjoyed her cooking, debriefed her on the political and military situation, then left Lebanon without any hindrance.

*

Shula 's secret crossings of the Israeli border became a routine. Her handlers, the officers of Military Intelligence, used to summon her to Metula and she would arrive at night, guided by her faithful smugglers. From Metula she was driven to Jaffa and admitted to the "Kishleh", the old Turkish jail in the Clock-tower Square, that was now the command center of IDF unit 504, in charge of spies and agents in enemy countries. Her children even did not know about her trips, that were disguised as short absences with the discreet connivance of Shula's friend Linda. Her son Isaac was ready to swear – years later – that his mother hadn't left Beirut even once.

In one of her trips Shula was taken to "the Green House" in Jaffa, a splendid building surrounded by a tall fence, the former home of a rich Arab merchant who had escaped during the Independence War. The Green House was now the Headquarters of Military Intelligence. Shula took the stairs to the second floor, and was escorted by a couple of soldiers to an office where she met the Head of Intelligence himself – Colonel Benyamin Gibli. He was a tall, ruggedly handsome officer, clever and knowledgeable. They engaged in a long and thorough conversation. Shula felt, for the first time, that she was a part of an official, well-structured organization. Still, Gibli warned her that Israel was officially at war with Lebanon, and if she was apprehended, it would mean certain death.

The risk did not scare her.

During the meeting Gibli asked her to collect information especially about the Syrians, their army and their regime; Syria regarded Lebanon as a kind of vassal state, supervised its army, and Syrian generals and officials were always present in Beirut. Gibli stressed that the Syrians were more dangerous than the Lebanese. His assistant gave Shula invisible ink and directions how to use it, and a special code for their correspondence.

And they gave her another thing: a code name. "The Pearl."

Back in Beirut, the Pearl spread a vast network of informants, in military and civilian spheres, who supplied her with precious intelligence and got well paid. She met senior officers, including the Syrian Army Chief of Staff at Riyad-a Sulh's parties and tried to make them talk about their occupation; but she did not know that the Syrians mistrusted her and started suspecting her.

She reported her talks with the Syrians in letters written in invisible ink and sent to Israel with the smugglers. Her instructions from her handlers arrived by several ways. Often it would be Shukri Mussa bringing her innocent-looking letters, written in a secret code and containing questions and instructions. It also could be the neighborhood pharmacist, who would call her to come fetch "her medicine" that had just arrived from abroad. The poor man did not suspect that the messages from Israel were written with invisible ink on the *Directions* labels fastened to the vials of medicine. And another channel: every Friday, at noon, the entire Kishik family would gather around the big table in the dining room, for a festive lunch. Shula would turn on the radio, and the family would listen in absolute silence to a program of Hebrew songs broadcast from Israel. The children knew that they were not allowed to say a word during the program. Only years later would Isaac find out, that many times the songs broadcasts contained secret instructions for his mother.

Shula was not alone. She often asked her husband's advice, or his help. When she was instructed by her handlers to fly to Istanbul for an urgent meeting, she needed a logical pretext for the journey. Joseph suggested that she visit his Turkish supplier in Istanbul market, and get from him the new samples of lace and broderies for the Kishik business. That was an adequate reason for her trip. Joseph treated her with respect, and never asked where she was going and whom she was meeting. And she did not tell him…

But once in a while he tried to revolt and put his house "in order".

He complained that she spent very little time at home, the children did not see their mother, most meals were cooked by Linda, and so on. After all, he said to her, he was one of the leaders of the Jewish community, and he knew that people were gossiping about him and his wife. But Shula stood up to him and bluntly told him that this was her life and she wouldn't change a thing. Finally, the good Joseph capitulated, and at the end of the day, on his return home, he would ask her: "Well, Shula, should I take a valium pill before you tell me what did you do today?"

*

Shula was aware that her position in the Beirut high society was quite unusual. Lebanon, indeed, had been modernized during the French rule; half of its citizens were Christians, educated in Western values and customs. And yet, the Lebanese nation was mostly a traditional Arab society. The woman's place was at home, in the kitchen and with the children. The Lebanese men were not used to face an attractive, elegant woman, who spoke with them as equal, smoked cigarettes in public, went everywhere alone, without fear, without restraint. She also was a rich woman, who was ready to pay a lot for military and political information. The rumor spread in Beirut and quite a few officers and senior civil servants were tempted into becoming Shula's agents.

Shula was very proud of the rising smuggling of Jews through Lebanon's porous border. What had started with Winkler, a lone immigrant aboard the Transylvania, had turned to a large and intensive enterprise. Shula used to host the immigrants overnight at the synagogue or in several Jewish homes including her own; she rented buses that brought the immigrants to several departure points close to the border, where her smugglers were waiting. She often sent her daughter Carmela to a public payphone, gave her a phone number and told her to call and read numbers to the party at the other end of the line: "twenty... Fifteen... thirty-two..." These numbers actually were reports about the number of immigrants who had crossed the border that day. Sometimes Isaac would call his mother and tell her: "The goods have arrived", meaning a group of Jews has set out on their way. *Mukhabarat* detectives who had been listening to Isaac's calls assailed him with questions, but the boy played dumb. "I help my dad at the store, and I use to call my mother and let her know that a shipment of goods has arrived…"

Sometimes groups of immigrants were captured by the local police but released after Shula bribed the officials. Still, sometimes she needed to improvise. That was the case when she planned the departure of seventy children to Israel. Everything was ready. The children were waiting in the synagogue, the bus was parked at the corner of George Picot Street, smugglers waited by the border. Suddenly a youngster, member of the local auto-defense organization, knocked on Shula's door. "They got us!" he managed, breathless. "The *Mukhabarat* apparently found out that something was happening. Detectives have deployed by the synagogue. You can't send the children!"

Shula recalled that at one of her visits to Israel she was taught a chapter in secret warfare, called "cases and reactions." Every Intelligence warrior sent on a mission, had to answer several questions starting "What to do if…" meaning, how shall he or she act if during the mission something unanticipated went wrong. What to do then?

Shula had to act quickly. She told the bus driver to leave the place right away and wait by the beach. She then hurried to Hassan's grocery store and bought seventy-two colorful candles. "Why do you need so many?" the Arab merchant asked. "For the festival of Hanukkah", Shula said and rushed to the synagogue. On her way she met Rabbi Heski who was on his way to the kosher slaughterhouse, to oversee the proceedings.

"Forget the slaughterhouse and come with me," she commanded. "This is a matter of life and death."

She entered the synagogue with him, ordered the children to form two lines, lit the candles and gave each child a burning candle. Then she and the rabbi took their place at the head of the two lines, also holding burning candles. "We are going now on a march, to celebrate the Hanukkah festival", she announced. [The Hanukkah festival that lasts eight days takes place in December, and the Jews light candles in a traditional candelabrum]. "We shall march in the streets and sing the Hanukkah songs we learned at school."

And indeed, the procession left the synagogue and advanced through Beirut's Streets, with the children singing Hanukkah songs at the top of their voices. Surprised Jewish faces popped at the neighborhood windows; Hanukkah was supposed to take place only in a fortnight! While the singing group advanced, some detectives approached Shula and asked what that march was all about. "We are celebrating Hanukkah", Shula answered. The detectives did not know much about the Jewish holidays, but they had heard that Hanukkah was a festival observed shortly before Christmas. They trudged for a while behind the singing children, then had enough of the songs and the shouts and left. When the procession reached the beach, all the *Mukhabarat* officers had gone away. The children put off the candles, got on the bus, and the operation continued as planned.

*

Yet, the situation worsened when Colonel Gamal Abd-el Nasser seized power in Egypt. He initiated a very hostile policy toward Israel. He had heard about the illegal immigration from Lebanon and pressured the Lebanese authorities to tighten their border controls. Shula had to find an alternative to the crossings by land, so she started organizing crossings by sea. She hired several fishermen and started filling their boats with illegal immigrants; far away, in the open sea, Israeli navy vessels were waiting to take their human cargo to Israel. In the cat and mouse game between Shula and the Lebanese secret service, she tripped once in a while. Once she was spotted while directing the loading of immigrants into the fishermen's boats; the police arrested her, she was sentenced to 38 days in jail, but soon was released thanks to her contacts, and was back at work as if nothing had happened.

A few nights after her release, a visitor surreptitiously slipped into her house. It was an older man, Haim Molkho, who had participated in Shula's smuggling operations. Deeply disturbed, he told Shula that one of the smugglers had been captured by a Lebanese army ambush on his way back from Israel. He was frisked and searched, and the soldiers found in his pocket a note addressed to Shula. She was deeply troubled, but concealed her fear and calmly coordinated with Molkho the answers they would give the police if arrested. Molkho indeed was arrested on his return home; the following morning a black police car stopped in front of the Kishik house; an officer and two soldiers entered and took Shula to the *Mukhabarat* headquarters. She was brought to the office of a Christian-Maronite officer named George Anton. He treated her with courtesy, called her "Madame Cohen" and released her after a short interrogation; yet, he asked her to come back to his office in a couple of days; he then repeated his demand several times. She started coming to his office twice a week, coiffed, made up, wearing her best. He would ask her a couple of routine questions and then they would have coffee together and discuss every possible subject.

It dawned upon her that Anton, a handsome and sophisticated man, had fallen in love with her. He canceled all charges against her (Molkho was sentenced to several months in prison and then expelled to Israel), invited her to dinner in a posh restaurant in Bahamdun, a nearby town, and confessed his feelings. "You and I, we both act in the same sphere," he said frankly. "But you have more cheek, and I – more experience. Together we can be a perfect couple." Shula, too, liked him. He told her that the Syrian *Mukhabarat* was very interested in her, and had sent him a demand to investigate her and her activities. He added that he had answered the Syrians that no evidence against her was found. He told her, however, that he knew she was working for Israel. He even drove her to an area where the main arsenal of the Lebanese army was going to be built, and went as far as saying that he would like to meet her handlers. When he drove her back to her home in Beirut, he kissed her on the cheek. "We are the perfect couple" he shyly repeated.

Shula controlled herself. She wouldn't let her feelings interfere with her mission. Anton's courtship could be a trap, but she was convinced he was sincere. She immediately dispatched to Jaffa a request for a crash meeting. A few days later she was back in the Green House, and Gibli welcomed her with a warm embrace. In his office she also met some officers of the Mossad. She described to them her meetings with Anton. They were stunned, and immediately charged her with a new mission: bring the enamored Anton to a meeting in Istanbul. Back in Beirut, she convinced her suitor to fly with her to Istanbul and continue the following day to Rome, where Anton was to meet some Mossad officers. On their way they spent a night in the Palace hotel in Istanbul. At dinner, he spoke of his love for her. He escorted her to her room. They were both tense and uneasy. What happened that night? According to Shula they slept in separate rooms...

In Rome, Anton met the Mossad people and became their agent. Shula did not participate in the meeting. On their return, they kept meeting at least once a week, for many years. She never spoke to her family about Anton.

*

At the end of 1954, disturbing news arrived from Egypt. The newspapers reported that the police had uncovered an underground of young local Jews, who had carried operations of sabotage in Cairo and Alexandria. Eleven young men and one woman, Marcelle Ninio, were brought before a military court and sentenced to long years in jail. Marcelle got 15 years in jail. Two of her comrades were hanged. The heavy sentences were an ominous reminder for Shula that her secret career in Beirut might end the same way, in gruesome death.

More than once indeed, she ran a mortal danger.

Like that morning, soon after the birth of David, her seventh child.

The day had started well. At dawn, Shula hurried to the home of her friend Abu Zik, to plan together the departures of two groups of immigrants, Syrian and Lebanese, to the border. Then she hastened back home, to a second meeting. She bathed and breastfed the baby and was ready for the conspiratorial knock on the door. That was Suleiman of Kleia, a seasoned smuggler, who was about to lead the immigrant groups across the border. Shula served him some Turkish coffee, and a dish of cookies that he liked. While they were talking, they heard loud pounding on the door. Suleiman knew that he should not be seen in that house, so he swiftly sneaked to one of the back rooms and hid there.

Shula opened the door. In front of her stood one of her most important agents, Abu Alwan, a man of high position in the government administration. Shula invited him in, and quickly prepared for him his favorite drink – sweetened tea, with sage leaves. He drew out of his pocket a top-secret document that he had stolen from the Prime Minister's office and triumphantly handed it to Shula.

He then savored his tea, and was gone. Suddenly Shula heard the shouts of the young men of the Jewish auto-defense organization. She understood – the *Mukhabarat* people were coming to search her house, as they had done so many times in the past. She was badly scared. They had come in the past and found nothing, but this time she was holding a stolen secret document,

She had to act quickly. She ran to the room where Suleiman was hiding and made him leave the house right away. Then she dashed to her room, the document still clutched in her trembling hand.

Where would she hide it, she feverishly thought. She knew that if the detectives found it – she was doomed. She looked about her. A heap of diapers lay on her bedside table. She stuck the document between the diapers. She suddenly felt that her elbow was touching somebody. She turned around – and saw, in front of her, a Druse *Mukhabarat* officer whom she knew. He had entered the house stealthily and entered her room without asking permission. Behind him appeared two Syrian officers, seven Lebanese soldiers and Dib Saadia, the Chairman of the Jewish neighborhood. They all forced their way into her room and surrounded her. The Druse officer pushed her aside and grabbed the diapers. He apparently had seen her pulling her hand out of the stack, she thought, horrified. She froze. She felt that her life was hanging on a thread. If they found the document, that would be the proof that she was a spy, and spies were hanged in this country. She could feel, already, the hangman's noose choking her throat. In her heart, she started praying God to save her.

The officer pulled his hand from the stack of diapers, His hand was empty! Did God answer her prayer? She felt a surge of confidence and started yelling at the officer. "How dare you," she shouted, "break into the room of a woman, who just had a baby, who has to take care of the child – and mess up her things! And to bring with you officers and soldiers as if she were a common criminal!"

The officer did not seem impressed. "Where did you hide the document?" he shouted.

"What document?" she shouted back. "I have not hidden anything!"

The officer barked an order to his soldiers, and they spread all over the room, turning over furniture, bed pillows and blankets, throwing clothes on the floor. One of the soldiers swept away the objects on the bedside table, and doing so, tossed the pile of diapers on the floor. Once again, the document did not show up.

This is a miracle, she thought, a miracle from heaven. Thank You, my God, thank You! But her troubles weren't over. The next threat exploded in … the good words of the Jewish chairman, of all people. He courteously turned to the soldier: "Ya Habibi [Dear guy], do not you see that the lady is exhausted of nursing the baby? Show some consideration and put back the diapers in their place."

Good God, she thought, not again! Why did this moron have to open his mouth just now? But the soldier bent down, scooped the diapers and cast them on the bedside table. She bit her lip. And for the third time – the document did not surface.

The Druse officer was beside himself. "Where did you hide the document?" he roared again.

She confronted him furiously. "You should be ashamed of yourself! That's the way you treat an innocent woman? With all your soldiers and all your guns! There is no fear of God in your hearts?"

"You're coming with us to headquarters", the officer said. "You haven't found anything here," she retorted, "and you do not have the right to arrest me as a criminal. I am ready to take a cab and come to headquarters later, but first I must bathe and feed the baby."

The Mukhabarat officers did not know, of course, that she had done that already. They had no choice, so they got out of the room and left her alone with the baby. She then thrust a shaky hand in the diapers heap and immediately found the document! She folded it, stuck it into her brassiere, and when she went to the bathroom to dress, hid it in a concealed crack over the window.

An hour later, wearing a sleeveless green dress, she arrived in the Secret Service Headquarters. She walked in, smiling and confident, but she did not know what was in store for her. The officers who were waiting for her, first tried the sweet talk. "Um Ibrahim, we respect what you are doing for your people and your country. If you just give us the document, we shall not bother you anymore. We know you've got it. Just tell us where you have hidden it or deliver it to us – and we'll part as friends."

She denied everything. The officer then nodded toward one of the soldiers in the room, who violently hit her in the face with his rifle butt. Shula screamed in pain. Another question – and another blow. She almost fainted. The soldiers pounced upon her, beat her up, extinguished burning cigarettes on her arms and legs. She kept shouting but did not break.

The awful interrogation lasted thirteen hours. Finally, lacking evidence, the officers let her go. At 4:00 AM she plodded her way home, beaten and bruised.

Her life was saved, but whenever she recalled the Druse officer sticking his hand into the diapers, she would start trembling. She was to learn later that she had been arrested on the order of the Syrians, who suspected her of high-level espionage.

And yet, a few days later, she was back in Jaffa. Major changes had taken place since her last trip. Colonel Gibli was not Chief of Military Intelligence anymore, and her unit had been disbanded. She had been transferred to the Mossad, and met her new handlers and the *Ramsad* himself. He was Isser Harel, a short, bald man, nicknamed "Little Isser". She heard rumors that Gibli had been fired because of his connection with the colossal failure in Egypt that had resulted in the Cairo sabotage trial a short while ago. Shula could not help thinking of Marcelle Ninio, the only woman among the accused, that was now rotting in an Egyptian jail.

Back in Beirut, and despite the *Mukhabarat* suspicions, she resumed her secret activities. For a while, the police and the Secret service left her in peace. But once again, a few years later, she had to face mortal danger.

That night in May 1958 eleven Jews, who were participating at the funeral of a friend, were abducted by the Muslim militia in Beirut and taken to a hiding location, deep in the Muslim part of the city. Those days Lebanon was torn by a bloody civil war between Muslims and Christians; the Jewish community at Wadi Abu Jamil was threatened by the Muslim militias commanded by a charismatic and cruel chieftain, Abu Mustafa, nicknamed "the Tiger". He was known as a criminal and a murderer, and also as the top Syrian agent in Lebanon. When the eleven Jews were kidnapped, the community was terrified, and some assumed they were dead already.

A group of women came to Shula's house and implored her to activate her contacts and save the hostages. She smiled at them but clenched her teeth. Most of the time these women – and with them most of the Wadi Abu Jamil community – gossiped about Shula's way of life, her activity for Israel that "endangered the community", her friends and suitors, her "lovers", her open and secret connections with nefarious people... To the point that when Bulus, the 'Robbers' King', was taking her back home in his black Chevrolet, she would ask the driver to stop at the street corner and not by her house, and walked home by foot.

And now, the same women who vilified her were running to her, begging for her help.

Shula agreed. She realized that if she did not help, the eleven hostages may be doomed. Right away she started calling her contacts. She succeeded to get an Army jeep with a driver, and traveled in the dark to the Tiger's headquarters, deep in Muslim Beirut, between ruins and roadblocks, to the incessant reverberation of gunfire. Fearsome militiamen, stunned to see the beautiful woman in the jeep, shouted threats at her, while wielding their weapons, but let her through. Her driver, a young recruit from a northern village, was almost paralyzed with fear.

Shula finally met the Tiger in his headquarters – a filthy pharmacy that had been transformed into a field hospital. There she stood in front of the Tiger, amidst dead bodies, torn body parts and bleeding wounded. The Tiger, a handsome and fascinating man, surrounded by armed bodyguards, could not believe his eyes: a pretty young woman, in European clothes, and a Jewess on top of that, dares to come alone to his command post!

"How did you dare?" he asked, and she explained she wanted to free the hostages. He added with wonder: "You so much cared about their fate, that you took the risk to come to this place, alone? I've never seen something like that, I've not seen any man who would have dared doing what you're doing, and as I can see – you're a woman!"

A woman . . . Not only she succeeded to talk him into releasing the hostages, but he took her to meet his mother, who treated her with affection. When she returned to Wadi Abu Jamil, safe and sound, with the liberated Jews, her friends could not believe she had met the Tiger himself; that nightly venture, they said, could have ended with her death.

Following that horrible night Shula's Arab friends started calling her "Monsieur Shula" – Mister Shula – and not Madame Shula anymore. Because, they said, she indeed seemed to be a pretty and charming woman – but actually was tough and brave like a man!

*

One of Shula's best agents was Muhammad Awad, a senior official at the Ministry of Finance. He was 55 years old, but looked younger, a handsome, charming and elegant man. Persistent rumors maintained that he was closely connected with Syrian Intelligence, but also worked for the Egyptian services and for anybody who would pay well. Shula indeed recruited him, but actually he was the one who contacted her. At first, she was reluctant, but after he brought her the highly classified list of all the government secret agents in Beirut, she started taking him seriously. He became a frequent guest in her house, grew to be friendly with her husband and children, helped Isaac in math studies, and often dined at their table. He openly admitted that he would like to work for the Israeli Mossad, and with Shula's help he secretly flew to Israel, via Istanbul, met with the Mossad experts and became their agent. Hence, a monthly salary was deposited by the Mossad to his numbered Swiss account.

Awad revealed to Shula that the Egyptians also would like to employ her, for a lot of money. She refused. But one night two strangers came to her house and tried to recruit her to the Egyptian services. She vehemently rejected their offer and even threatened to call the police.

They left indeed, but late one night, when she came home from Bulus' casino, she was attacked with automatic fire, from a car parked by the curb. She succeeded to escape to a nearby courtyard and was only lightly wounded from ricocheting stones. The shooters' car darted forward and disappeared. Shula alerted Anton. He reported that the attackers probably were members of the Egyptian services, that wanted to retaliate for being rejected so bluntly.

Some months later George Anton told her that he had decided to leave Lebanon with his family and find a new homeland, He had reached his decision, he said, because the Syrians, whom he hated, achieved control over Lebanon and her secret services; he had no future there. Shula was devastated. Anton advised her to leave Lebanon too, with her family, as the situation was becoming utterly dangerous.

She refused. She was at the peak of her activity. She had recruited army officers and senior officials to her network and had brought quite a few of them to Israel by indirect flights, via Istanbul. Others had met Mossad officers in Rome or Lucerne in Switzerland. In Beirut she had powerful friends, among them the President and the Prime Minister, business tycoons, the commanders of the Christian phalanges and the Muslim militias. When she parted with George she told him she was not leaving Lebanon.

That was a fateful mistake.

*

In the spring of 1961 Shula flew to Israel via Istanbul, as usual. The procedure was simple. she would fly from Beirut to Istanbul with her Lebanese passport, and would continue to Tel Aviv with an Israeli *Laissez Passer* [a passport substitute]. As so many times in the past, she had her passport stamped with an entry visa at Turkish immigration, then flew to Israel with her Israeli certificate. She returned to Istanbul a week later, but the Turkish immigration officer was surprised. He remembered her arriving a week before, but when he leafed through her passport he did not find any exit stamp. That was strange. If she had left Istanbul a week ago and returned today – where was the exit stamp? After a long discussion he stamped her passport with an entry and exit stamp for that same day.

Shula realized that those stamps could be troublesome. If her passport was thoroughly inspected in Beirut, the immigration officers wouldn't understand where and how she had disappeared for a week. At the very last moment, when the passengers were already boarding the flight to Beirut, she changed her mind. She invented some pretext about a family emergency, that compelled her to stay in Turkey. Nervous flight attendants and furious porters unloaded her suitcase from the plane; she immediately called Shadmi, the Mossad agent in Istanbul and explained the problem to him. "Don't worry", Shadmi said, "we have experts who will 'iron out' your passport, and expunge the suspicious stamps. But that will be done in Rome, where we have a bigger station."

Shula flew to Rome, delivered her passport to the local Mossad resident – but was told that the "ironing" can be done only in Israel, and she would have to wait a while in the Italian capital. The wait lasted a couple of months. Shula was not prepared for that. She missed her family, but she also missed her activity. She feared that her networks might collapse, if she was not in Beirut; still, there was nothing she could do but wait. Shula spent all this time alone, in depressing solitude. She had a lot of time to think, and her instincts told her that she should not return to Lebanon. Perhaps it would be better if she flew to Israel and brought her family too? But she finally decided to return to Beirut. She received a perfectly ironed out passport, and flew to Beirut with a guy named Milad, whom sweet Muhammad Awad had sent to Rome, to assist her.

At last she was back home, with her family.

*

August 9, 1961, 12:30 AM.

Heavy pounding on the front door awakened the Kishik family at Wadi Abu Jamil. Isaac, in undershirt and short pants, wearing a gold chain with a Star of David, opened the door. In front of him stood a large group of armed soldiers and policemen. "Where is Shula Cohen?" an officer asked.

Shula was at home. There was no escape. " Our entire street was blocked by soldiers and tanks," her daughter Arlette recalled. "As if my mother had wings and could just fly away and escape." The policemen handcuffed Shula and took her to a local jail. Two days later they arrested her husband as well. In her cell, Shula had a lot of time to think; she reached the conclusion that she had been betrayed by an insider.

Shortly after, it turned out that the snitch was no other but the suave Muhammad Awad. His deposition against Shula filled 319 pages. He and Milad became the main witnesses for the prosecution. Some Mossad officers, who heard about Shula's arrest, even claimed that Awad had been planted by the *Mukhabarat* from the beginning. but that claim wouldn't hold water. The information he had supplied to the Mossad in the past was credible, and he could not have been a double agent all those years. One of the Secret Service officers who arrested Shula, Sami El-Hatib, disclosed that an audit in Awad's office had found out very incriminating financial evidence. Awad's telephone was tapped, and the detectives discovered many calls to a certain woman – Shula Cohen. When the police informed Awad of their findings, he broke down right away and made a full confession about Shula and her espionage network. Perhaps he expected that he would save himself by that. He was mistaken. He was thrown in jail and died of a heart attack a year later.

Sami el Hatib also revealed that the *Mukhabarat* had rented a few apartments around Shula's home. Her phone line was tapped as well, and the incriminating evidence was meticulously collected.

The news about Shula's arrest literally shook Lebanon. Huge banner headlines screamed from the newspapers' front pages. Breathless radio pundits described Shula's missions. The world press published sensational articles about "Mata Hari of the Middle East." Mata Hari was a famous spy, an exotic dancer born in Holland, that operated in the First World War and was executed as a German spy in France. The name Mata Hari had become a symbol for a female master spy. Shula had read once an obituary of another woman, whom the press had named "Mata Hari" – a woman who had been the head of an espionage network in Cairo and died in Israel in 1959, Yolande Harmor.

She had worked for fourteen years in the dark, Shula thought in her cold cell. She did not know if the material she had obtained had served for any purpose; she did not know if she were a good agent, reliable and important or just a weakling. And now, all of a sudden, they called her Mata Hari.

At the *Mukhabarat* cellars the nightmare started at once. The prisoner was brutally, systematically beaten and tortured. At the first brutal flogging she screamed, but then fell silent. She decided not to break down, not to give her inquisitors the pleasure of watching her collapse. She did not scream anymore, biting her lips till her mouth filled with blood. Facing her, on a wooden stool, sat her torturer, "fat Sammy". and seemed to delight in her suffering. She remembered her grandfather's words: "Shula, you're one of a kind. You always get up on your feet!"

Her situation slightly improved only when Pierre Gemayel, now Minister of the Interior in the Lebanese government, came to the jail and ordered the inquisitors to stop hurting her. "The Tiger" also paid her a surprise visit, and made the staff provide her with kosher food.

But even when her grilling ended, the female jailers kept beating her, and the Arab prisoners kept her distance. "I was the only Jewess in two thousand female prisoners, and I wanted to prove to the whole world that I am a proud woman and I won't give up."

Isaac and his sisters did all they could to save their mother. They hoped that with the family money and Shula's connections they would be able to obtain a mild sentence for her. On the advice of her attorneys she only admitted helping smuggling Jews to Israel, which was not considered a major crime. But the prosecutors accused her of treason – and that implied a death sentence.

Her lawyers tried to outsmart the prosecution. Shula carries a Lebanese passport indeed, they said, but she was born in Argentina and she is actually Argentinian. She can't be accused of treason in a country that is not her motherland. The military court, indeed, agreed to change the charges from "treason" to "espionage".

The trial started on November 5, 1962, in the Beirut Military Court. Shula appeared in court as always – made up, perfectly coiffed, wearing a beautiful but modest dress. While walking to the box of the accused she met with Isaac and Arlette who whispered that everything was going to be all right. She indeed was led to believe that with the right bribes to the right hands she would get out with a light sentence. But during the break, before the sentence was read, a policeman told her: "Your son asked me to let you know that what was promised cannot be achieved."

And indeed, the sentence was terrifying. "Shula Cohen", the president of the military court said, "This court has found you guilty of espionage on behalf of the Zionist enemy. You are therefore sentenced to death by hanging."

Shula's husband was sentenced to ten years in prison. On hearing Joseph's sentence, Shula fainted. When she recovered and was taken out of the courtroom, she passed by Isaac and shot him a silent look, as if saying: "That's all that you could do for me?" That look, says Isaac, haunted him for the rest of his life.

*

Shula did not give up. When she returned to Sanaya Women's Gaol, with the death sentence hovering above her, the warden told her maliciously: "Well Shula, the sun has set down for you, hasn't it?"

His words reminded her of her childhood in Jerusalem, when her father would return home from work, and ask her mother to turn on all the lights in the house. Her mother would always answer with the same words. And today, in her most horrendous hour, Shula recalled those words and whispered: "Don't turn on the lights, it ain't dark yet."

So she said, and was led to her cell, to await her execution.

CHAPTER 4

Marcelle Ninio

Better death than torture

MARCELLE WANTED TO DIE.

Her nightmare started on the night of July 25, 1954 when police officers broke into her apartment and dragged her to the Cairo *Mukhabarat* headquarters. Marcelle, a 24-year-old brunette, delicate and soft-spoken, was shoved into a small windowless room, and there several men pounced upon her and savagely beat her up. While hitting and slapping her, they hurled at her questions about bombs, names, and addresses. Dazed and hurting, she did not answer. Then her torturers started punching the nape of her neck, whipping her heels, pulling her hair, tearing her nails from her bleeding fingers, all this accompanied by vile curses and menaces. She fainted and they woke her up and started again. She fainted again, and again the torture resumed. Finally, they left and she sank in fitful sleep on the stone-paved floor.

For a moment, while lying on the filthy floor, she recalled Jean-Paul Sartre's words in his play *"Les Mains Sales"* [Dirty Hands] – Happy is he who sleeps in his bed. God, she thought, I will never see my bed again. Her tormentors interrupted her thoughts and threw her in a prisoners' van that took her to the *Mukhabarat* Alexandria offices, and there the beatings and the torture started again.

I can't stand this anymore, the wretched girl said to herself. I want this nightmare to end, I do not want to live! The moment her torturer reached for his hellish instruments, spread on a table in the back, she darted toward the open window and jumped, crashing on the stone-paved yard two stories below.

She woke up in the prison hospital. She had crashed but she did not die. The doctors told her that she had been brought over unconscious, with broken legs, arms and pelvis, 11 fractured ribs, internal bleeding and cerebral concussion. Half her body was immobilized, in cast, and the doctors had hung weights on her legs, to reduce the pressure on the shattered pelvis. The doctors, and most of the nurses, members of the Christian Coptic minority in Egypt, treated her with devotion and sincere compassion; but she was a wreck. For three months she lay motionless in bed, in excruciating pain.

In her bed Marcelle recalled her life and times, and the events that brought her to her present vicissitudes. Marcelle Victorine Ninio had been born in Cairo to a Jewish family, a Bulgarian-born father and a Turkish-born mother. At home, with her parents, she spoke *ladino* [the ancient Spanish dialect of the Sephardic Jews], at school – French. In the Catholic School for girls "Saint Clair", the nuns taught her English. Out of home she spoke Arabic.

Her father stuck to the tradition and on Saturdays took his family to the synagogue. He died when Marcelle was ten, and she grew up with her two half-brothers, her father's sons of a previous marriage. She passionately embraced Zionism and joined the *"Hashomer Hat'zair"* [The Young Guardian] a Zionist left-wing youth organization. Her boyfriend was a member of the Young Guardian as well, but he immigrated to Palestine and joined kibbutz Ein Shemer. Marcelle, a fervent Zionist, had heard the whispered stories about a woman called Yolande Harmor, who recently had disappeared from Cairo. According to the rumors, Harmor had been a great spy for Israel, had risked her life, and had escaped to Jerusalem at the very last moment. She had become a role model for Marcelle and many of her friends, although they never had met her.

Marcelle, too, wanted to help the State of Israel, that had been created four years before. But how? After graduating from high school, she studied shorthand, and got a job as assistant to the manager of a business company. So far, she thought, nothing special. Her life was similar to that of thousands Jewish, Muslim and Christian young women. But then things changed. She was twenty-two when her friend from the Young Guardian, Mira, came to see her. "Marcelle," she said, "we need someone to help us." She understood this was for Israel and agreed at once, without even asking what exactly "they" needed. Mira introduced her to a young Jewish doctor, Victor Saadia, and he took her to a meeting with a secret envoy from Israel, "Martin". The skinny, swarthy Martin actually was Shlomo Hillel, a senior intelligence officer. Only later she would learn that "Martin" had a long record of daring missions, including operating in Baghdad under false identity and organizing the mammoth immigration of the Iraqi Jews to Israel. He seemed to Marcelle to be a knowledgeable, authoritative man, and yet, modest and calm. "Martin" told her she had to carry out certain tasks, like "carrying packages and things", but warned her: "This is risky business. You may end up in jail." Jail? Well, that did not scare her. The Egyptian regime was rather friendly to the Jews, and there was nothing to fear; her friend Mira, who had recruited her, had been arrested and had spent three months in prison. That hadn't been so terrible.

That was how she was recruited to the fledgling Israeli Intelligence. Like Yolande Harmor and Shula Cohen, she did not go through any training. And even worse – she was not provided with any escape plan from Egypt, in case of emergency.

A short while later, Dr. Saadia asked Marcelle to meet a representative of a European electrical equipment firm, a curly, thin-faced Englishman from Gibraltar, named John Darling. Once alone with her in his office, he revealed his true identity: Avraham Dar, a former member of the *Palmach* elite battalions, a member of Kfar Yehoshua, a collective village, and an agent of the Israeli Intelligence. Marcelle was overly impressed by the young agent. He told her she would be working with him in his apartment. To avoid any suspicions by the government services about their connection, he posted an ad in the "wanted" sections of the newspapers, announcing his search for a half-time secretary. Marcelle "got the job" and started working with Dar.

Occasionally she would type a business letter for him. But most of the time she focused on undercover work. Dar had put in place an underground organization of young Jews. She knew that the underground would be engaged in a secret mission for Israel. That was enough for her. In those days Zionism was the inspiration of the young Jews in Egypt, and Israel was for them a lofty symbol, a sublime achievement, and they were ready to defend it and even sacrifice their life for it.

The organization was divided in two cells, one in Cairo and the other in Alexandria; Marcelle was going to assure the liaison between them, carry packages and letters, and deal with financial and administrative issues. Dar taught her to use codes and invisible ink and charged her with writing reports and mailing them to a secret address in France. She got the code name "Claude". Dar promised her a passport for crash escape in case of clear danger. But this did not happen.

Marcelle visited the safehouses in Cairo and Alexandria and knew where the secret hiding places were situated. She met with the members of the two cells. Dar wanted all of them to get together and get to know each other in order to work together as a team. That, for the first time, angered Marcelle: "What is this, a kibbutz general assembly? No compartmentalization, no separation between the cells, the members? That's how we're building a secret organization?" She believed, till her dying day, that this was a fatal mistake.

The underground members flew to Paris and there secretly boarded flights to Tel Aviv. In Israel they were sent to military camps and underwent basic courses – handling weapons, gathering intelligence, sabotage, operating radio transceivers, coding and decoding messages. After completing the course, they returned to Egypt, again via Paris. Marcelle did not participate in that trip for several reasons. She still did not have a passport, was not a member of the operational cells, and had to take care of her ailing mother who contracted a vicious strain of cancer.

In the meantime, a political earthquake shook Egypt. The "Free

Officers" junta carried a coup, King Farouk was exiled, and after a short presidency of moderate general Naguib, the charismatic colonel Gamal Abdel Nasser assumed power. Egypt's attitude toward Israel became utterly aggressive. Winds of war swept Cairo, and the bellicose Nasser emerged as Israel's major enemy. The two cells of Dar's underground were buried under deep cover, ready to be used behind enemy lines, if a conflict erupted between Israel and Egypt.

In 1953 Avraham Dar returned to Israel and Marcelle got a message summoning her to a meeting with his successor "Emil" at Groppi's café in Cairo. "Emil" turned to be an IDF intelligence officer, Max Binneth, who was sent to Cairo under German cover, as an importer of artificial limbs. He was Marcelle's handler for a short while, and then was delegated to another position, while the underground got a new commander: a blond, handsome German businessman named Paul Frank, whose real name was Avri El'ad. Marcelle did not know that El'ad's past was marred by a long criminal record of thefts and impersonation. She maintained her contacts with the members of the underground and almost did not work with El'ad. She kept traveling between Cairo and Alexandria, carrying secret messages and coded letters. In all her moves, she diligently observed conspiracy rules, and was certain that the *Mukhabarat* did not suspect her. The Egyptian secret services actually were much more interested in her brother, a communist, whose main activity was to print flyers on a stencil printer he kept at home. "And with that printer," Marcelle chuckled, "he was going to save Egypt."

In Cairo's newspaper "Al Ahram" Marcelle read about a dramatic political event: Great Britain had decided to reduce her military presence in several regions throughout the world, that included the Middle East. The cabinet in London signed an agreement with Egypt, agreeing to evacuate the 80,000 British soldiers based in Egypt, mostly along the Suez Canal. Great Britain delivered to Egypt many bases, airfields, and equipment belonging to the British army.

That agreement stirred deep anxiety in Israel. The transfer of the bases to the Egyptians was a formidable booster to Nasser's military power; besides, the British military presence in Egypt had been a moderating factor. Britain's departure was like giving a free hand to the extremists. The "fig leaf" in the agreement was a paragraph stipulating that in case of war, Great Britain would recover her bases in Egypt.

Marcelle did not know, though, about an ultra-secret plan that was ripening in Israel Defense Minister Pinhas Lavon and the Military Intelligence chief, colonel Binyamin Gibli, concocted a stupid and dangerous plot to prevent the British from leaving Egypt. They decided, in utmost secrecy, to carry out a wave of sabotage operations against British, American and Egyptian institutions. The media would certainly attribute the bombings to a local dissident underground, perhaps "the Muslim Brotherhood". That would prove to the British that Egypt was unstable, and Cairo's promises could not be trusted; and then, Lavon and Gibli thought with amazing naiveté, the British would cancel the agreement and decide to stay in Egypt.

The bombings were to be carried out by Avri El'ad's underground. El'ad informed the young men in the two cells about the plan, and they obeyed. They believed they were defending the very existence of Israel. El'ad appointed Shmuel Azar as head of the Alexandria cell, and a physician, Dr. Moshe Marzouk, as head of the entire operation. Marcelle knew Dr. Marzouk only from the hospital, where he treated her sick mother. The underground members, following instructions from Israel, prepared their "incendiary bombs": eyeglasses' cases in which they stuffed a condom full of acid; the acid would quickly eat into the condom rubber and get in contact with another chemical which had been placed in the case beforehand. That contact would produce a small, short flame. After they set several targets on fire, Lavon and Gibli assumed, the British Empire would have to think again.

Prime Minister Sharett was not notified about the plan. But how could Lavon and Gibli, two senior political leaders, believe that because of some rudimentary home-made bombs Great Britain would cancel its strategic decision? And the plan. beside its stupidity, was tainted with tremendous danger. If the young Jews, charged by the bombings, were captured, they might pay for the plan with their lives!

On July 2 and 14 the first bombings took place. The young men planted their spectacle cases in the post office and the American and British libraries in Alexandria. The small fires they produced were easily extinguished by the police. On July 23 El'ad sent his boys to five targets: two cinema theaters in Cairo, two in Alexandria and the luggage depository of Cairo railroad station. That evening, while a large crowd was entering the Rio cinema in Alexandria, a police officer noticed a young man writhing with pain, as smoke came out of his pocket. This was Philip Nathanson of the Alexandria cell. His bomb had gone off prematurely. Nathanson was arrested, and after him – all his comrades. The underground crumbled down as a line of dominoes.

When the news about the arrests exploded on the front pages of the newspapers, Marcelle was out of town with friends. She hurried back to Cairo, wrote a letter with invisible ink, and dispatched it to the secret address in France. "The children are very sick," she wrote, "this is a contagious disease and we can't visit them." The message was clear – the boys had been captured. A few hours later she, too, was arrested. One or several of her comrades had talked under torture and disclosed the names of the underground members, including her own. Marcelle never found out who had given her name and address *to the Mukhabarat*; but all the underground members knew her, thanks to the "kibbutz meeting" that Dar had organized a while ago.

And then, the nightmare started.

Marcelle later heard that Max Bineth had been arrested as well and committed suicide in his cell. Another Egyptian Jew, Carmona, was found dead in his cell and the rumor was that he had been assassinated by the Egyptians. Strangely, El'ad was not bothered, sold his car and left Egypt easily. Another member of the Alexandria cell was not arrested; warned on time, he destroyed all incriminating documents, disposed of his handgun, and was let go by the police. His name was Eli Cohen, who was to become Israel's most famous spy, and hang in Damascus eleven years later.

*

On December 11 1954 the "Zionist spies" trial started in Cairo. General Fuad el Digwi presided the Special Military court. Marcelle, still in pain, was brought to the courtroom, and felt lonelier than ever. All the boys were kept together in a kind of cage; she was alone, in another corner, flanked by two police officers. Every move of hers was watched by police and army officers; they feared she might try to kill herself again.

Marcelle was shaken by some horrible moments during the trial, especially when Dr. Marzouk confessed: "I am responsible for everything that happened!"

General Digwi started. "Did you hear?" he boomed, turning to the court stenographer, "underline what he said, – I am responsible." At that moment, Marcelle understood: Moshe Marzouk's fate was sealed.

The trial made headlines throughout the world. It ended on January 27, 1955. Two of the accused were acquitted, but six others were sentenced to long terms in prison, from seven years to life. The two leaders of the underground, Shmuel Azar and Dr. Moshe Marzouk, were sentenced to death. Israel turned to statesmen, famous intellectuals, writers, philosophers, religious leaders, the Pope; all those tried to intervene with the Egyptian authorities, begging grace for the condemned men, but in vain. On January 31, 1955, Azar and Marzouk were hanged in the yard of Cairo Central Jail.

Marcelle, stunned, heard her sentence – fifteen years in jail. Fifteen years, she thought. I will spend fifteen years of my life in their prisons. For what? I even did not participate in the bombings, never touched a spectacle case! Her frustration grew when she was brought to the Cairo women's jail and found herself in company of prostitutes, drug smugglers and thieves. "Sit down on the floor, with the others!" ordered the warden,

Marcelle clenched her fists. "I'm not sitting on the floor!"

"Sit!"

"No."

She did not care. Let them do with me whatever they want, she thought, I am not sitting down. She felt a new kind of stubbornness, a refusal to yield. And in a way it made her feel stronger.

The warden hesitated, finally turned away, as if ignoring the obstinate prisoner and Marcelle remained standing. A first, small victory. When they started assigning the prisoners to different cells, she rebelled again. She was not ready to share her years in prison with hookers and criminals. "I'm not staying here," she said. "Move me to some other place, and if not – I'll start a hunger strike." The guards did not know how to deal with that unruly woman; they insisted, yelled, threatened – and she stood her ground. The frail, gentle young woman had metamorphosed into a bold fighter. The trial, the solitude, the harsh sentence, instilled in her strength and resilience, and a feeling of total indifference. She wouldn't give up, and let them do what they want.

Finally, the warden told her that she would be moved to Al-Antar prison, outside Cairo. She landed in the juvenile delinquents' section, and got a big cell in the hospital wing, all for herself.

The fifteen years started. Her life here was more bearable. The hospital staff, again mostly Copt, treated her courteously. One of the doctors would smuggle her sandwiches under his coat, for her to eat something different from the disgusting prison food. But her solitude was terrible and at night she kept reliving the nightmare of those first days of pain and degradation.

During the first year she almost had no contact with the outside world. For a long time her communist brother could not visit her. She also could not receive books and newspapers. Her brother and his family finally received visas for France. Before their departure, her brother was allowed to visit her; he brought her a very original present: a sink! A real sink that he installed in her cell. She was delighted. Here is something that made me happy, she thought, something people in the outside would never understand. After a while, the regime at the prison softened a bit, and "the boys", the underground members who were incarcerated in another jail, were allowed to send her books and magazines. That was how she learned that in Israel Minister of Defense Lavon was forced to resign after a "nasty business" in Egypt. The military censorship wouldn't allow publication of any details on that subject. Well, she bitterly thought, I know exactly what the nasty business was. She also remarked that the Chief of Army Intelligence had been replaced.

Marcelle did not know that an unprecedented, top-secret crisis was shaking Israel's governing circles. Prime Minister Sharett and his cabinet ministers had learned only during the Cairo trial that the bombings had been carried on orders from Israel. The debacle in Egypt resulted in one question: Who had given the order for that catastrophic mission? Lavon and Gibli hurled accusations on one another; a board of inquiry failed to find who was responsible. Lavon had to resign, Gibli was transferred to a minor position and never promoted. The question "Who gave the order" was to poison the Israeli political life for years and even trigger the process that would bring Ben-Gurion down in the future.

Another enigma surrounded the unperturbed departure of El'ad from Egypt. Marcelle would learn later that El'ad's smooth departure had raised suspicions in the Israeli Intelligence community. The Ramsad, Harel, believed that El'ad had betrayed the underground and delivered its members to the Egyptians. No proof of that allegation was ever found. El'ad would be arrested in Israel on unrelated charges and spend 10 years in jail.

*

On October 29 1956, war erupted between Egypt and Israel. From bits and pieces that reached her Marcelle learned that Nasser had blocked the Straits of Tiran on the Red Sea to Israeli shipping. The straits were the only approach to Israel's southern port of Eilat. Nasser had also bought great quantities of weapons from the Soviet Union and finally, he had nationalized the Suez Canal. Israel had retaliated to the Straits blockade by launching a lightning offensive against Egypt, named the Sinai Campaign. According to the Egyptian press, France and Great Britain supported the Israeli assault. Israel won, and in seven days conquered the Sinai Peninsula and reached the banks of the Suez Canal. The war ended on November 6.

A few days later, the prison warden himself, wearing a freshly pressed uniform, appeared at the door of Marcelle's cell. He was bringing wonderful news. "Marcelle, you're being released" he said, all smiles. "Very soon there is going to be an exchange of prisoners of war with Israel. We have captured only one prisoner, an Air Force pilot. The Israelis are certainly going to request your liberation. General Digwi himself is among our prisoners." The warden told Marcelle that Israel had taken more than 5,000 prisoners of war; among them, indeed, was General Fuad Digwi, the Governor General of the Gaza strip.

The very same Digwi had been the President of the Military court that had sent Marcelle's friends to the gallows and her to fifteen years in jail. That was a kind of poetic justice, Marcelle thought. The man who had sent her to that damned prison – will be the one to take her out of there. Very soon, she imagined, she would be on her way to Israel.

She was swept by overwhelming, intoxicating happiness. The nightmare had ended. Very soon she would be in Israel. Now she waited for the key turning in her door and for the voice inviting her to gather her things and be ready to go. But a day passed, a week, and a month. She read in the papers that the prisoners of war were returning, she saw photos of General Digwi, in Israel, boarding a United Nations plane bound to Egypt, and enjoying a hero's welcome in Cairo. Finally, the last Egyptian prisoner returned to Egypt, The Israeli pilot was in Tel Aviv.

And no key turned in her door.

Her distress was terrible. Her entire world, her admiration for Israel, seemed to crumble down in one black moment. She learned that in the negotiation for the prisoners' exchange Israel hadn't even mentioned the "nasty business" prisoners. They had been forgotten, or abandoned, by Israel.

She did not know that during the Sinai Campaign her former commander, Avraham Dar, had planned a common operation with the French, who were Israel's allies. The plan was to carry a raid on Cairo's jails by Israeli and French paratroopers and rescue the underground prisoners. That was supposed to be a part of a French-British invasion of Egypt, simultaneously with the Sinai Campaign. But the French-British invasion failed, and the mission was aborted.

But when Dar returned to Israel, he found out that his country hadn't done a thing for the underground prisoners. He asked the military secretary of Ben-Gurion for the minutes of the negotiations between Israel and Egypt concerning the prisoners' exchange. To his amazement he found out that Israel did not demand the release of the nasty business prisoners. Nobody could explain how such terrible mishap had occurred.

Marcelle remained in her cell, her hopes and dreams evaporated. Israel she admired, the same Israel, for whom two of her friends had sacrificed their lives and the others – their best years, had turned her back to them. Marcelle realized that for many more years she'd see only the four decrepit walls of her cell in al Natar. She felt she was living in another planet, in a world totally different from the one where most -people live.

Her only contact with the "other planet" were the bits and pieces she heard from her jailers. From them she learned about the death of Yolande Harmor, in Israel, that was reported in the Egyptian newspapers; her jailers also showed her a copy of "Al Ahram" daily, that had printed the photograph of a friend she knew well, Eli Cohen, hanging from a gallows in a Damascus square. She was dumbfounded. Eli had been a junior member of the underground, and she had met him several times in Alexandria. In 1954 he had succeeded to elude arrest when the network collapsed; but eleven years later he had been arrested in Damascus by the Syrians and sentenced to death as a Zionist spy. Another Israeli spy that made the banner headlines of "Al Ahram" was a woman, Shula Cohen, sentenced to death in Beirut for espionage. But Marcelle's jailers did not know when the sentence was carried out.

Shula Cohen, Eli Cohen, Shmuel Azar, Dr. Moshe Marzouk… all these names of young Jews who had sacrificed their lives haunted Marcelle's nights and populated her nightmares. Like them, she had dedicated her life to Israel; she had not lost her life, but her youth.

And the future, even after she would be released, looked gloomy and uncertain. One day she learned that her former boyfriend had married a girl from his kibbutz. She felt deep pain, but there was nothing she could do, that's only natural, she said to herself. But at night, when she was turning and tossing in her bed, she thought of the other life she could have had, a family, a husband, children... And yet she did not give up. She struggled to preserve her sanity, her smile, to be ready when the day came to return to that other world where she used to live. She decided to act; she organized the other inmates into a sewing and embroidering team, and they got a remuneration for their work.

The events and the emotions took their toll. Marcelle fell gravely ill, and from the prison hospital she succeeded to smuggle a few letters to her brother in Paris. "Don't worry," she wrote, "I'll hold fast". In another letter she added: "If you have any good books, please keep them for me. I intend to read all of them." The letters, that she signed "Marianne", were the proof that she did not break, and was determined to overcome all the obstacles in her solitary journey. "One can only imagine what she had to cope with", said her underground friend, Robert Dassa.

Thus, she lived through another ten years.

One day three communists, sentenced to five years in jail, arrived in her section. Two of them (one Jewish) hated her cordially, for political reasons. The third one, even though a supporter of the Palestinian refugees, treated Marcelle with warmth and compassion. She was of Greek origin and her name was Mary Papadopoulos. Marcelle and Mary became bosom friends. The young communist became the only person in whom Marcelle could confide and bare her most intimate feelings. They spent long hours together, speaking about their lives, their failures, and their dreams.

Mary was discharged from jail but did not forget her friend. One morning the jail doctor, a Christian, entered Marcelle's cell and took out of her bag a tiny transistor radio that Mary had sent. Marcelle realized that the miniature radio was the product of a complicated operation, and had probably followed a Via Dolorosa, strewn with risks and obstacles. The doctor had also taken a risk by bringing her the radio. But this was not the only risk the warmhearted Copt had taken; the radio functioned on batteries, and once a month the good doctor sneaked into Marcelle's cell and brought her fresh batteries for the little radio, that became Marcelle secret friend and companion, day and night.

After thirteen years of prison, Marcelle's solitude abruptly ended. Her cell door opened, and the guards ushered in a beautiful, blond German girl.

"She will share your cell", one of the guards said.

The blond woman turned to Marcelle and smiled. "My name is Waltraud", she said, "but my friends call me Teddy."

CHAPTER 5

Waltraud

The Mysterious Mrs. Lotz

JUNE 1961, IN THE AFTERNOON.

The "Orient Express", Europe's most luxurious train, was snaking its way in South Germany's breathtaking scenery. Teddy got out of her compartment, annoyed by the hungry looks of the old man, sitting in front of her. She approached the passageway window. Two men were standing there, speaking in English.

"When are we arriving in Munich?" one of them asked.

The other shrugged. "I do not know exactly,"

"The train will arrive in Munich at six", she volunteered.

They turned toward her. One of them smiled. "Are you going to Munich?" He was slim, blond, handsome, wearing a suit and a tie. She was fascinated by his blue, limpid eyes.

"No," she said. "I am bound for Stuttgart."

"You live there?" he asked. The other man moved away.

"My parents live in Heilbronn, outside Stuttgart. I am going to visit them. Later I'll go see a friend. She lives in Fischbachau."

"I do not know this place."

"It's a small town, about sixty kilometers from Munich. I haven't been there for years."

"So where do you come from now?"

She smiled. "From sunny California."

They exchanged some casual remarks, and he gave her a long look, a look that she knew well. She was pleased, knowing that there was a lot to look at. She was twenty-nine years old, tall, slender, blond, and beautiful. She was used to men staring at her, and she liked it.

"Instead of standing in this corridor," he said, "why do not we go to my compartment? We can speak there, at ease."

She thought of the lecherous old man in her compartment. "Why not?"

They settled in his compartment. She told him about her life, her childhood in Silesia, in East Germany, her father's brutal persecution by the Secret police, the Stasi, then the escape of her family to the West, and her moving to America, first to Georgia and later to California. For a while she worked there as a hotel chambermaid, later as rooms' supervisor in a big hotel in San Francisco. "And you?"

He told her that he was living in Cairo now, where he owned a horse ranch. He described the exotic Egypt, the pyramids, the desert, the ranch with its thoroughbreds, the Egyptian elite, from the military and political spheres, who came to the ranch for riding – and to his home for dinners and cocktail parties. The exotic and glamorous world he painted captivated her imagination. She made a few amused remarks and he complimented her for her wit.

The conductor entered the compartment and asked for their destinations. To her surprise, her host answered in perfect German. "You speak German?" she asked, intrigued.

"Of course," he said. "I am German. Sorry for not introducing myself earlier. My name is Wolfgang Lotz. My friends call me Rusty,"

"And my name is Waltraud Neumann. Teddy for my friends."

The locomotive let a short whistle. "Well, I am leaving at the next station. It was a pleasure meeting you."

He seemed to hesitate a moment, then said: "Perhaps we'll meet again? In Munich?" He took a small notebook out of his pocket, tore a leaf and scribbled on it. "This is my phone number in Munich. Call me if you would like to go to dinner one evening, and I'll come to pick you up. I have a car over there."

She shook her head. "No chance. I'll be busy with my parents and with my friend." She knew she did not have neither the time nor the will to go to dinner in Munch with a stranger, yet she took the note with his phone number. Who knows, she thought. He seemed charming, and these blue eyes…

The train slowed down. They politely shook hands and she went her way.

*

Her friend in Fishbachau welcomed her with hugs and kisses and effusions of joy, as expected. She enjoyed the warm reception, the serene atmosphere in the small town, the beautiful sights all around. But very quickly her enthusiasm waned and was replaced by growing boredom. She had nothing to do, there was nowhere to go in the sleepy town. She had enough of the wonderful calm in the Bavarian nature. She told her friend that she had met "the man of her dreams" on the train, picked up the phone receiver and called Rusty's number.

That same afternoon he arrived in his big car, and they drove to Munich. She enjoyed the dinner in an exquisite restaurant, then – the tour of bars, night clubs, discotheques, with music, champagne, and a charming companion who behaved as the perfect gentleman. She saw that he, too, enjoyed her company; so much, that as the evening progressed, he proposed to her to join him in a "vacation". In ten days, he said, he was going to sail from Italy to Egypt. But in the meantime, they could travel to Austria, afterwards to Italy, to some of the most beautiful parts of Europe where she had never been before. She politely refused; she did not want to get involved and fall in love with a man who soon was to leave, and she'd never see again. Besides, he seemed to be a seasoned Casanova, who certainly had women all over the place and definitely in Egypt.

Still, the temptation to spend ten days with this charming man was overwhelming. When he brought her, after midnight, to the hotel room he had rented for her, he escorted her to the door; he bent over, to kiss her cheek good night. At that very moment, something happened to her, and she spontaneously hugged him and kissed him on the mouth. "I'll come with you, Rusty," she whispered.

That kiss was to change her life.

*

Since that evening, they were inseparable. Their relationship soon turned into a passionate love affair, that swept both of them. Two days later he amazed himself – as he later revealed to her – and asked her to marry him. And after a few more days, Rusty revealed to her his biggest secret. He was not only the owner of a horse ranch in Egypt, he said, he was also there on a secret mission of intelligence gathering – in short, spying. This confession only fired up her imagination and did not diminish her love for him. On the contrary, it looked like in the movies! One question, though, bothered her. Who is he spying for? She loathed the communists and the Eastern bloc countries, and even her own country, West Germany, was not her favorite. Rusty hesitated for a while, and finally he revealed this secret too, He was spying for Israel.

"Israel?" She liked that. She had heard a lot of good things about Israel.

"Yes," she said. "I'll marry you."

And so, when Wolfgang Lotz returned to Cairo, he told his friends and acquaintances that in two weeks his young fiancée would join him. Her name is Waltraud, he added, but everybody calls her Teddy.

Teddy knew that her fiancé had been born in Mannheim, in Germany, as he had told her. She did not know, however, that he was not a German – but an Israeli called Ze'ev Gur Arie, an IDF officer serving in unit 131, a special unit controlled by both the Army Intelligence and the Mossad. [131 would soon become 'Caesarea', the operational unit of the Mossad]. Waltraud did not know either that he had been born to a German father and a Jewish mother, who had escaped with him to Palestine when Hitler rose to power in Germany. The boy grew up in Palestine, volunteered to the British army during the Second world war, later fought in the War of Independence and was discharged from the IDF with the grade of captain. After the war he had tried – and failed – to find a suitable occupation. He had been looking for an intriguing and challenging job, and finally had approached the IDF Intelligence and volunteered to become a spy in an enemy country. His handlers and the 131 unit commander, a burly, easygoing colonel named Yosef Yariv, discerned Gur Arie's weakness for women and alcohol, and concluded that he was not stable enough; but they were impressed by his confidence and sangfroid, and finally decided to send him on a mission. One of the veteran Mossad officers, Motti Kfir, trained him in a secluded Ramat-Hen villa, and taught him the art of secret warfare – weapons, transmission, codes, invisible inks, communication channels, surveillance and evasion, composing intelligence reports. His handlers called him "Wulfi" but his code name was Samson. At the end of his training the unit commanders decided to infiltrate him in Egypt under German cover. He was first sent to Germany, to build his cover as a former Wehrmacht officer, and after several months arrived in Cairo.

He did not tell all of this to Waltraud. She also did not know his other big secret. Her lover and fiancé, who had recently celebrated his fortieth birthday, was a married man. He had a wife, Rivka, and a son, Oded. His family temporarily lived in Paris, which was the Mossad advanced headquarters abroad. When he had met Waltraud he was returning from a briefing by his Paris handler, Arie Sivan; and only a few hours before boarding the Orient Express he had parted from his family.

But in this entire tapestry of lies that he had weaved so diligently, there was one genuine truth: he had really fallen in love with Waltraud, an overwhelming, passionate love; he was "crazy for her" as a Waltraud friend described him; and he sincerely wanted to erase from his past all his former lovers, and the name of any woman who had shared his life, ever.

She also told him about herself, and about the man in California [He knew there must have been a man in California . . .]. But she did not tell him her biggest secret. When she was almost a child, at thirteen, she had been assaulted and brutally raped. She hadn't told a living soul about it. All she remembered about her rapist was his beard and his disgusting breath over her face. In her fuzzy memory, that she had tried to suppress, the rapist was a Russian soldier – or a priest. That was a terrible memory – and the source of terrible nightmares, recurring over and over again with maddening precision. She recalled the man, the pain and a big metal cross that he laid between her breasts.

And yet, today she was happy as never before. She was young, beautiful, and in love. She was going to get married to the most charming and loving man. She was of humble origin – and here he was, offering her an exotic, glamorous and dangerous life. What an adventure!

*

A few weeks after Wolfgang, a passenger ship brought Waltraud to Alexandria. None other, but the commander of the local police was waiting for her on the pier. A government car took her to Cairo. Everything enchanted the young woman – the Egyptian landscapes, the flat in the upscale Zamalek neighborhood in Cairo, the welcome party that Rusty threw for her on her arrival. A few weeks later, they moved to a beautiful villa in the Giza neighborhood, not far from the pyramids. Waltraud was stunned by the network of connections with senior officials and army officers that Lotz had put together. The most prominent dignitaries of the German colony were his friends as well. Some of them were Nazis, former officers in Hitler's Wehrmacht, exactly "like" Lotz, who proudly posed as a former Captain in the German army. She hated the Nazis but understood that Rusty had to play his part.

The horse ranch excited her as well, and she started riding daily. She spent the evenings with her lover in the best restaurants and night clubs in Cairo. She also became his devoted assistant in his secret occupation; she hosted officers and government officials at their home, easily charmed them and made them talk, and contributed a lot to Rusty's spying. Actually, the twenty-nine old woman who had never been trained or even briefed, became Rusty's full partner, She would sit beside him when he coded and transmitted his reports to Israel; she helped concealing the radio set and the incriminating documents, and blocked the visits of undesirable guests while he was carrying out his secret functions. She became Lotz's right hand and was very proud of it.

A year later the two of them traveled to Europe and got married in a genuine ceremony. The happy couple posed for photographs by the home of Waltraud's parents at Heilbronn, then departed on a long honeymoon before returning to Egypt.

Teddy did not know that her husband had not reported to his handlers that he had got married. His marriage actually had made him a full-fledged bigamist, married simultaneously to two women.

At the Mossad headquarters in Tel Aviv Lotz's superiors were convinced that he lived and operated in Cairo by himself. But one day, when Lotz transferred to the finance department an envelope with the receipts for his expenses, an officer named Eitan Ben-Ami discovered something strange. Those days some people used a brand of expensive envelopes, their inside padded with brown silk paper. On the silk paper in Lotz's receipts' envelope an inscription was printed: "Mr. and Mrs. Wolfgang Lotz". Mrs. Lotz? In Cairo?

A quick inquiry confirmed the existence of a Mrs. Lotz, and Wolfgang was immediately summoned to Israel. In the Mossad headquarters he was harshly reprimanded. He had to choose one of two possibilities: to be fired and recalled to Israel or ordered to cut off any contact with "the German". Mossad's regulations strictly prohibited any such relationships.

At the last minute, however, Yosef Yariv changed his mind. Lotz was now an employee of the Mossad, and Yariv was the head of Caesarea, the operations department. "Very early," Motti Kfir recalled, "Yariv realized the importance of female officers," Yariv also believed that the wife or fiancée of a Mossad warrior in an enemy country can be of tremendous importance, by helping him, carrying out missions by herself, and instilling confidence and stability in his work. He had done that with another officer, Shlomo Gal, whose smart and bold wife Dafna, a former beauty queen, had joined him in long stays in enemy countries, with excellent results.

Yariv understood that the new wife of Lotz had become his loyal and efficient partner, a solid support for his mission. He therefore decided: Waltraud should remain in Cairo, Mr. And Mrs. Lotz would continue their activity as in the past. This was a crucial, unprecedented decision. Nobody said a word about it to Lotz's Israeli wife and son. They were intentionally kept in the dark.

Waltraud, too, was unaware of the other woman. Rusty came back and their life continued as before – horse riding, parties, espionage, secret activity under a perfect cover. Lotz used to send and receive radio messages at dawn, always from the bedroom on the second floor of their villa. Afterwards he would decode the message from Israel, burn the paper in the toilet and conceal the radio set, the microphone and the headset in a Weight-Watchers' scale he had brought from Europe. Waltraud knew that the scale was booby-trapped with an explosive charge, and wrong handling of the machine could result in a deadly explosion. She took great care in extracting and concealing the transceiver in the scale.

And all of a sudden – a drama!

*

On July 21, Waltraud and Wolfgang heard a special broadcast on Radio Cairo, proudly revealing that a few hours before, the Egyptian army had launched new rockets to a distance of hundreds of kilometers. This was a total surprise for them.

On July 23, the National Holiday, they watched the traditional military parade in Cairo's streets. At the head of the parade, carried by enormous trucks, they saw two huge rockets, wrapped in Egyptian flags. They were amazed. a short while later, in an arrogant speech, President Nasser declared that the two rockets, "Al Zafer" (the Victor) and "Al Kaher" (the Conqueror) could reach "any target south of Beirut". Which meant – Israel. Al Zafer, Nasser said, had a range of 280 kilometers, and Al Kaher – 560.

Urgent messages from Tel Aviv alerted the Lotz couple. Israel had been struck with shock and anxiety. The Mossad had no prior knowledge of the Egyptian rockets. The Ramsad Isser Harel became the target of harsh criticism for his absolute ignorance of the Egyptian rocket project. He immediately radioed instructions to all his agents in Egypt to get intelligence about the rockets, at once and at all costs.

Lotz was called to Europe and met his handler in Munich. He then rushed to Paris, for a meeting with a nervous, grim Yosef Yariv. He had to return to Cairo right away, Yariv said, and get as much information as possible from his German friends,

All the Mossad spies in Egypt got similar instructions. Lotz and Waltraud soon found out that in the last few years, in utmost secrecy, Egypt had recruited hundreds of German scientists, engineers and technicians who had worked in the past in Hitler's "Wonder Weapons" plants and factories, producing superb aircraft and deadly v-1 and v-2 rockets. These scientists and the Egyptian army had erected three secret factories: "Factory 36", where German engineers were building a jet fighter on the instructions of Willy Messerschmidt, the father of the fighter aircraft of the World War Luftwaffe; "factory 135" where engineer Ferdinand Brandner assembled jet engines for the new plane; and the most secret of them all, "Factory 333", where the scientists were developing medium range missiles.

Mossad agents also discovered several companies in Switzerland and Germany, that carried advanced research for the Egyptian projects and supplied them with equipment and spare parts. Some of the scientists often shuttled between their base in Egypt and the laboratories and research institutes in Europe. Dreadful rumors spread in Israel: the Germans in Egypt were going to arm the missiles with atomic, radioactive or chemical warheads; they were buying huge quantities of Cobalt and Strontium gas, intended to poison the air over Israel for many years; they also were working on death rays, that could annihilate all living things on their path. Most of the rumors were pure fantasy, but to the Israelis it seemed that the extermination of the Jews by the Germans was resuming and the swastika was resuscitating, this time in Egypt.

Some of the German experts often took part in Rusty and Teddy's parties at their home, or used to ride at their ranch. The Lotz couple succeeded to get from them precious intelligence about the missile project. The two of them, as well as other Mossad agents in Egypt, succeeded to find the location of "333" in the middle of the desert, north of Cairo. But in the spring of 1963, Waltraud and Wolfgang heard a rumor about missile launches in a new area, where a secret missile base had been built recently. The base was said to be located in the Shalufa region, close to the Suez Canal and the Great bitter lake. Waltraud and her husband had scoured the area before, and had found nothing. But this time Lotz had received an urgent coded message demanding to find out that base without delay.

"I must go again to Shalufa," Lotz said to his wife after decoding the message.

"Can't you get some info from one of your generals? Perhaps one of the German experts?"

"No", he said. He had to drive to that area and see for himself.

"Okay," Waltraud agreed. "I am coming with you."

They perused a map of the region, that they knew well. If there is a base in that area, Lotz said, there must be a road leading to it. It must branch off the main highway.

They recalled two side roads that branched off the desert road. "One of them," Waltraud said, "is a dirt road, probably unimportant, and the other is paved. No signs."

"And if that area is closed?" Wolfgang asked. They spoke about the danger of entering a closed military area, and Wolfgang insisted to drive over there alone. But Waltraud revolted.

"Oh no! Not without me. In an emergency situation, two are better than one," She immediately invented a cover story; they will take, in their Volkswagen car, bathing suits and towels, as well as a basket full of delicatessen, and they would pretend to be on their way to "a picnic by the water", on the bank of the bitter Lake.

They set off on their way toward the lake. Waltraud was driving and Wolfgang was navigating by the maps he had compiled. An hour later they reached a crossroads; an asphalt-paved road split from the desert highway. A sign by that road announced: "Entry forbidden. No photographs." Beside the sign stood a guard's booth manned by a lone sentry, who seemed bored and apathetic.

"That's new", Wolfgang said.

The Volkswagen bypassed the junction, and after a few hundred meters made a U-turn and returned to the bifurcation. They were lucky. The sentry had left his booth and gone to relieve himself in the desert. This was their chance. The Volkswagen sped past the booth, down the forbidden road. The sentry, holding his pants, tried to run after them, shouting, but they were far already.

The road had been recently enlarged and cut a straight line through the desert, flanked on both sides by sand dunes. after a few hundred meters they saw a military jeep coming in the opposite direction. It passed by them, stopped, turned back and drove after them, honking. Lotz looked for a way to stay in the area despite the chase. He told Waltraud to stray off the road, head for the dunes, and get stalled in the sand. She did so, very deftly. The Volkswagen sharply veered to the right, left the road and got stuck in the virgin sands.

The military jeep reached them. Waltraud and Wolfgang played the role of innocent tourists, and asked the soldiers – in English and German – for their help to haul out their car. But the soldiers brandished submachine guns, arrested the couple, took their passports and drove them down the road in their jeep. After a long drive they passed through two armed roadblocks and arrived at the base. At the very moment of entering the base, the two spies saw exactly what they were looking for: big missile launchpads built in a half circle, bunkers, storerooms, and low administration buildings. That was the secret missile base!

They were taken at gunpoint to the base commander, a slim colonel wearing a bushy mustache. Waltraud felt that her presence embarrassed him, and he awkwardly offered her a seat. Then he turned to her husband and started threatening the two of them with jail, court martials, and all kinds of scary punishments; but Lotz convinced him to pick up the phone and make a few calls to Cairo, to some generals who were his close friends. After they heard Lotz's cover story about the romantic picnic by the lake, the generals ordered the base commander to release right away the two Germans. The confused colonel apologized to the two of them, sent his soldiers to haul their car out of the sand, and…even invited them to lunch. On their return the couple reported their findings to Israel.

But the Ramsad, Isser Harel, was not satisfied. He decided to launch a campaign of intimidation and even assassination against the German scientists. In Munich, the manager of a Munich company, "Intra", Dr. Heinz Krug, was reported missing. Intra was the major buyer of equipment and raw materials for the Egyptian project; Krug was never seen again. Persistent rumors in Cairo claimed that Krug had been assassinated by the Mossad. Another scientist. Dr. Hans Kleinwachter, was shot outside his research lab at Lorach, in Germany, but survived. Explosive packages and letters were sent to many of the major scientists in Egypt. The major part in that operation was entrusted to the Lotz couple.

Wolfgang Lotz received explosives concealed in Yardley soaps, and tiny detonators, that he and Waltraud packed in envelopes and packages, stuck Egyptian stamps on them, and addressed them to the scientists, many of whom were their friends. The results were grim: at a package explosion five Egyptian employees at factory 333 were killed. In another blast a German woman, Hannelore Wende, lost her sight. She was the secretary of Professor Wolfgang Pilz, a former rocket engineer in Hitler's Wonder Weapons project. The manager of a post office in Cairo was wounded, when he opened a suspicious package.

Soon, the instructions from Israel were modified, and Lotz sent threatening letters to the scientists, warning them of fatal consequences if they did not halt their infernal work. The letters were signed by "the Gideons". Quite a few scientists were frequent guests of the Lotz parties, but nobody suspected this charming couple, the darlings of the Cairo German colony.

Many of the scientists finally left Egypt, some out of anxiety, others tempted by better jobs offered by the German government. The Egyptian project collapsed.

*

And on February 16 1965 Lotz threw a lavish party for Waltraud's birthday. Her parents flew to Cairo for the party, and the enamored

Rusty slipped on her finger a huge diamond ring. Two of the guests at Waltraud's party were the German scientists Stengel and Vogelzang, who had received threatening letters mailed by their sweet hosts, only a few days before.

Three days later the Lotz couple and Waltraud's parents set out for an excursion in the Western desert. On their return, on February 22, they found their house surrounded by soldiers and policemen. There was no way out. *Mukhabarat* officers handcuffed Wolfgang and Waltraud. Her parents were also arrested but released after a few days. Waltraud was separated from her husband and transferred to the woman's wing of Cairo prison.

The Lotz couple's arrest stunned all those who knew them. Their friends in the Army and government distanced themselves. The media reported the arrests in banner headlines. The news made headlines all over the world, especially in Germany. The *Mukhabarat* investigation produced grave findings. Wolfgang and Waltraud were accused of sabotage and espionage for Israel. Waltraud was brutally interrogated, undressed, beaten and tortured. The inquisitors punched her belly with their fists, kicked her bare back, used other torture practices, kept her whole nights in a bathtub filled with ice cold water. But she held on, and did not confess.

In another interrogation wing, her husband confessed that he had been spying for Israel and even had sent explosive packages and threatening letters to the German scientists by order of the Israeli intelligence. He was an enemy spy indeed.

Still, according to a different version, Lotz hadn't been unmasked by the Egyptian Secret service, and the reason for his arrest had been totally different. Those days, the Egyptian government was preparing to host East Germany's President, Walter Ulbricht, and the authorities had decided to arrest about 40 German citizens living in Cairo, whom they deemed capable of organizing protests. Lotz and Waltraud were among them. That was nothing but a preventive arrest; they were to be incarcerated only during Ulbricht's visit, and freed at his departure.

Lotz, apparently, did not know that, and believed that he and his wife had been uncovered by the *Mukhabarat*. He then decided to tell everything. He took the Secret Service officers to his home, dismantled the scale in the bathroom, and extracted the radio transmitter. He also agreed to expose everything he had done in a television interview; but he firmly kept repeating that he was German and was spying for Israel only for money. An attorney, hired discreetly by the Mossad, arrived from Germany and joined the Egyptian lawyers who were to defend the couple in court.

Waltraud and Wolfgang did not know that the current Ramsad, Meir Amit, had urgently flown to Germany and met Reinhard Gehlen, the head of German Intelligence. He asked him "to take those 'two'" and Gehlen agreed right away. His envoys to Cairo reported to their Egyptian colleagues that "those two", genuine Germans, were also connected to German Intelligence. The Egyptians accepted the version about Lotz's German identity, and even decided to ignore some detailed accounts published in Germany and maintaining that Lotz was an Israeli officer, and a Mossad spy.

The couple was allowed to meet for a few minutes. For the first time in her life, Waltraud saw her husband lose his self-control when she told him about the torture she had endured. This was the worst moment for her. She realized that they would be put on trial and either hanged or jailed for the rest of their lives. For the first time in her life the optimistic, confident woman broke down. "Why should we give them this pleasure?" she asked her husband. "Let's get all this over!"

She whispered to the stunned Lotz that she had found a razor blade in the washroom and had hidden it in her shoe sole. "I'll pass you half of it" she offered. "Tonight, at exactly the same moment, we'll slash our veins."

Lotz was dumbfounded. Waltraud wanted to commit suicide! He furiously objected and finally succeeded to make her abandon – temporarily – that idea. He promised her that their situation would improve and in some months they might be released from jail. She pledged in return, that she would not do anything without his accord.

And indeed, their situation improved. The Lotz couple was allowed to meet almost every day during their incarceration, and order meals in some Cairo restaurants. The two of them were also invited to the office of the jail warden, General Munir Horolos, who served them coffee while press photographers were clicking their cameras. Waltraud drew energy and calm from short poems Lotz wrote to her in English, to ease her suffering. He even added to the poems tiny drawings and caricatures. In his verses Lotz expressed his everlasting love for her, and described the wonderful life they'll have in the future, somewhere far away, in the lush countryside. He ended his poems by a forceful and solemn declaration: "The happy Lotz couple will ride again!"

Their trial, before a special military court, started on July 27, 1965, The two of them entered the courtroom holding hands, she in a white dress and black sunglasses, he in a light summer suit. They were formally accused of espionage for Israel, and of sending explosive packages to the German scientists.

Waltraud was summoned to the box of the accused. Standing there, alone but self-assured, Waltraud spoke. She expressed her profound love for her husband and her dream that one day they will resume their life together. In her testimony, that had been previously coordinated with Wolfgang, Waltraud stated: "I was only an ordinary housewife. I did not spy for Israel and did not send explosive packages to the scientists. Wolfgang and me, we are two people in love, who sincerely hope to continue our life peacefully." She denied any knowledge about her husband's covert activities and claimed that she only knew he was on a secret mission for NATO. "I know that my fate and the fate of my husband are in your hands," she said to the judges. "Whatever happens to me or to my husband, I want to declare publicly that I love him today more than ever, and I hope that one day we'll be reunited."

The audience in the court was captivated. But the prosecutor immediately dispelled the emotional impact of Waltraud's words.

He demanded the death penalty for the two of them.

Waltraud was terrified.

But on August 21 the court ruled that Wolfgang Lotz was sentenced to life, and Waltraud to three years in prison.

CHAPTER 6

Freedom!

"MY NAME IS WALTRAUD", THE BLOND WOMAN SAID TO Marcelle, "but my friends call me Teddy."

After her trial, Waltraud had been jailed in Al Antar. She and her husband got a special treatment in prison. They could exchange letters and messages, and to spend one hour a day together. After a while, Waltraud asked her jailers to let her wash her face daily and was led to the cell of a prisoner who was no other but Marcelle Ninio. "One day in 1967," Marcelle recalled, "a young woman appeared at my cell door, tall, blond and pretty, and introduced herself as Waltraud, also known as Teddy."

At first, Marcelle did not like to share her cell with another woman. She had another year and a half of jailtime left, and had got used to live by herself. But step by step, she and Waltraud got to know and like one another. Waltraud suffered from nightmares and would wake up, terrified. She revealed the story of her rape to Marcelle and described her recurring nightmare. Marcelle learned to calm her down and put her back to sleep.

Marcelle also learned to appreciate her cellmate. "We were so different from each other," she said to a friend later, "but I got to know her. She was strong, level-headed, she loved her husband and knew how to reinforce him." The two of them listened together to Marcelle's small radio, and in May 1967 they heard Nasser's threats to eliminate

Israel; the radio reporters also described the anxiety that affected the Israeli nation.

The two women learned that on May 15, 1967 an unexpected crisis had shaken the Middle East. President Nasser had suddenly sent his armor to the demilitarized Sinai Peninsula, expelled the UN observers who were stationed at Israel's border and along the Straits of Tiran, closed the straits to Israeli shipping, and signed military pacts with Jordan, Syria and Iraq. Electrified crowds wildly danced in the streets of the Arab capitals, after Nasser announced that the end of Israel was near. And the Israelis felt that the very existence of their state was at stake.

Finally, on June 5, Israel attacked the Arab armies massed on her borders. Marcelle and Waltraud heard about the eruptions of hatred and fury against the Jews and the foreigners in Cairo streets; they were mortified by the fake news on the lightning advance of the victorious Egyptian army, soon to conquer Tel Aviv. But a few days later the small radio revealed the truth. In six days, Israel had defeated the armies of Egypt, Syria and Jordan, and conquered huge territories: the Sinai, the Gaza strip, the Golan heights, the West bank and the Old City of Jerusalem. This was a tremendous victory that would change the Middle East.

Israel had captured thousands of enemy soldiers. Marcelle and Waltraud heard of the forthcoming prisoners' exchange between Egypt and Israel, and their hopes surged. Soon they would be exchanged for the multitudes of Egyptian prisoners and will be sent to Israel! They imagined their liberation: they would be taken by car to Kantara, on the bank of the Suez Canal, then they'll get on a boat, cross the canal – and in front of them, they'll see the Israeli flag, waving in the wind!

But this did not happen. The war ended and again – silence. The last Israeli prisoner, Air Force pilot Yair Barak, was returned to Israel and the prisoners' exchange was completed. Marcelle and Waltraud listened to Barak's interview on the Israeli radio. Marcelle thought: "Well, that's it. Again." And Waltraud, who was so strong till that moment, collapsed and burst in tears.

Marcelle bit her lip. She had a feeling from the start, that she and her friends of the underground would not be set free. But she did not know that the Israeli Ramsad, General (res.) Meir Amit, had suggested to Defense Minister Moshe Dayan to turn directly to President Nasser and ask for the release of the "nasty business" prisoners, as a part of the war prisoners exchange. Dayan had reacted with skepticism. Nasser wouldn't agree, he kept saying to Amit. But Amit wouldn't let go. Over and over again, he would pester Dayan with his idea. Dayan and Amit were very close; Dayan, a lonely man, said once that Amit was his only friend. Finally, after one of their never-ending discussions, Dayan gave up. "Okay", he sighed. "Write to Nasser. But remember what I told you. He won't agree."

But he did.

Meir Amit wrote a letter to President Nasser, "as a soldier to a soldier" and asked for the release of the Jewish underground prisoners. He guaranteed that nothing would leak to the press and Nasser would not find himself in an embarrassing situation. Amit's letter was entrusted to a senior Egyptian officer, who also was released in the prisoners' exchange.

This time, unlike in 1956, the "nasty business" prisoners were not forgotten; neither were Waltraud and Wolfgang Lotz. In early 1968 all of them were liberated, in small groups, and secretly flown to Europe and Israel.

Waltraud and Wolfgang were transferred to Cairo International airport, and boarded an Athens-bound plane on February 4, 1968. There they got on a Lufthansa plane flying to Frankfurt and then to their last stop, Munich. But while their plane was in the air, the Mossad officers who were expecting them, suddenly had second thoughts. The Lotz couple risked being arrested in Munich and face trial for attempted murder! In the past, complaints had been lodged with the German judicial authorities about the explosive packages Lotz and his wife had sent to German scientists in Cairo. That was a good enough reason for their arrest.

The handler of the Lotz couple, Motti Kfir, had to find a solution and fast! He and his colleagues got in touch with the German attorney who had defended the couple at the Cairo trial, on Reinhard Gehlen's instructions. He immediately got to work. When the plane carrying the Lotz couple landed in Frankfurt, the Israeli and German services made them leave the aircraft, even without taking their luggage; they got new passports, and boarded a flight to Brussels.

That was a Caravelle plane, with two seats on each side of the aisle. Kfir, disguised with a mustache and a wig, was sitting close behind the couple. They did not recognize him. Suddenly Kfir heard somebody humming the song "Jerusalem of Gold" by Israeli composer Noemi Shemer, that had become the unofficial hymn of the Six Day War. He got up and walked up and down the plane, looking for the source of the singing. He was amazed to discover that Waltraud was the one who softly sang the Israeli tune. Stirred, he removed his disguise and approached the couple. Lotz jumped from his seat and embraced him warmly. Kfir turned to Waltraud: "How do you know this song?"

She smiled. "When I was in the cell, with Marcelle, we heard that song on the radio from Israel." The two of them stood in attention in their cell and listened to the Shemer song. Now, on her way to freedom, the emotional Waltraud remembered the song that had given her hope in those dark hours.

From Europe the couple flew to Israel. In the plane, Rusty handed Teddy a love letter, more passionate than anything he had ever said or written to her. But the same letter also revealed the truth that he had concealed for years– he had a wife and a son. He was about to leave his wife, he wrote, because his life had been bound to Teddy's forever. When she heard that he had a son, Teddy told Marcelle later, "she was in a state of terrible shock!"

*

When their plane landed in Israel, there was one person missing from the welcoming ceremony: Ze'ev's (Wolfgang Lotz's) wife, Rivka Gur Arie.

How long had she expected and imagined this moment! After years of anxiety and danger, of trial and imprisonment, her husband was coming home. Their son, Oded, who admired his father, was as thrilled. Rivka prepared for his homecoming, bought new clothes, made up her face, prepared the house for Ze'ev's arrival. But barely an hour before the plane landed, her doorbell rang, and she had an unexpected visit. A distant cousin, Avraham Shalom [a future head of the Shabak, the Internal secret service] and his wife were at the door. They revealed to Rivka the terrible secret, and gently advised her not to come to the airport.

Later that evening, Ze'ev's Gur Arie met with his son. Afterwards he came home and faced Rivka.

"That was a terrible meeting," Oded said, years later.

There are no words that could describe the pain, the shame, the humiliation that Rivka Gur Arie felt that night; these feelings returned to haunt her repeatedly for the rest of her life. She felt betrayed and cheated – not only by her husband but also by the Mossad, by Ze'ev's commanders, handlers and friends. Not only did they conceal the truth for years, but they also accepted it, espoused it and used it for their designs. Yes, the Mossad would take care of her needs, pay her Ze'ev's salary, find a job for her at the Ministry of Tourism; but nothing would heal her wound, and she wouldn't forgive the Mossad people for what they did to her, a wife and a mother, who was sacrificed on the altar of an Intelligence achievement.

She continued her life, wounded and torn, while not far from her Ze'ev Gur Arie rebuilt his life with Waltraud. They set up a horse ranch at Ganot, near Tel Aviv; Waltraud renewed her friendship with Marcelle who also arrived in Israel. When Marcelle got married, Gur Arie was one of those who held the four rods of the "Huppa", the traditional canopy of a Jewish wedding. Waltraud did not come to the wedding. She got sick, after the beatings and torture in Cairo, and died soon after.

Without her, Gur Arie was a lost soul. After Waltraud's death he married his third wife, Noemi, but she left him after he cheated on her with his future fourth spouse, a German journalist. He wandered between Israel, the United States and Germany, wrote his book, "The Champagne Spy", tried various jobs and died, lonely and poor in 1993.

The light in his life had been the passionate love story with Waltraud, the shadow – the tragedy and the pain he brought upon his wife and son.

*

In February 1968, after 5,000 days and nights in jail, Marcelle arrived in Israel. Her underground comrades arrived with her. Their release was kept in deep secrecy. Marcelle received the grade of Lieutenant Colonel in the IDF; she learned Hebrew, studied art and literature, and won the biggest prize – love. At 42 she met a businessman, Eli Boger, they fell in love and decided to marry.

Nasser died in 1970. And only two years later, at the wedding of Marcelle and Eli, the Israelis learned that the" nasty business" prisoners had been released and lived now among them. Prime Minister Golda Meir was the guest of honor at the wedding and hugged Marcelle, beautiful and radiant in her white dress, as she entered under the canopy, raised by her former jail mates.

After their arrival in Israel, Marcelle and her comrades were invited to a long succession of events, meetings and receptions. "They did not know what to do with us", Marcelle said. "Many wanted to see us." All that she and her comrades wanted was to shake off the unsettling memories. Only in Israel did they learn about the terrible rift in the leadership caused by the question:" Who gave the order?" Lavon or Gibli? Did Avri Elad betray them and did he deliver the underground to the Egyptians? There were quite a few senior officers and politicians who thought that Marcelle and her friends knew the answer to the questions that divided the nation. It turned out that they did not know a thing. "Once they took us to a discotheque," Marcelle recalled, "with all this earsplitting noise and the dancing music. We had nothing to do there. Somebody told us that Avri Elad was there. We left at once, we did not want to meet him. I also remember a party at Avraham Dar's house, when a man came to me and said: "Shalom Marcelle, I am Benyamin Gibli." I told Avraham – If you had told me that Gibli would be here, I wouldn't have come."

And yet, her life became more or less normal. She lived in Germany for five years with her husband, who represented an Israeli company there. In Israel she hosted her beloved friend Mary Papadopoulos several times. The two of them spent hours reminiscing their past together. Only with Mary did Marcelle feel free, relaxed, open, for Mary had been at her side in that "other planet", the Egyptian prison, living through a dark experience that others do not and can't understand ever.

Marcelle died in October 2019. She was the author's close friend. The Ramsad Yossi Cohen spoke by her open grave. "Marcelle was a heroine", he said, "like a lioness she sprung back from the terrible misery of the prison."

*

In Beirut, Shula Cohen also lived through a long nightmare in a Lebanese prison. For seven years she was humiliated and tortured; she fell gravely ill, but even on her hospital bed, when promised a better medical care, she never broke and never said a word. The Syrians exerted harsh pressure on Lebanon, to hand over that woman, who had penetrated the highest level of their government and befriended ministers and generals, but the Lebanese refused. They only allowed some Syrian *Mukhabarat* officers to interrogate her in Beirut.

In the meantime, in a 1963 appeal, Shula's death sentence was commuted to twenty-one years in jail. Joseph, the loyal husband, was released from prison. He came home a broken man. In jail, his head was shaven, the other prisoners and the guards abused and insulted him – and after his release he was not the same man anymore. His honorable status in the community had crumbled down, his wife had been taken from him – and he had lost his fortune.

But the earthquake that shook the Middle East during the Six Day War was also felt in Beirut.

Shula Cohen, the Pearl, was released after the war, as part of a prisoners' exchange between the IDF and the Lebanese army. Shula and an Air Force pilot were exchanged for four hundred and ninety-six Lebanese soldiers and civilians. Early one morning, after seven years in jail, Shula was hurriedly ordered to gather her things, was whisked out of prison, and placed in a car that sped southward, toward the

Israeli border. The car brought Shula to the border passage at Rosh Hanikra. This time, for the first and last time in her life, she crossed the border to Israel legally.

The *Mukhabarat* officer who had arrested her seven years before escorted her to the border barrier. "Shula", he said, "Now you're already with one foot in Israel and one foot in Lebanon. Tell me – all what they said about you and all the findings of the investigation – is it true or not? You did not do anything for Israel? You're leaving, so why not tell me now?"

"I thought to myself," Shula said later, "seven years I did not say a word. In seven or eight minutes I'll be with both feet in Israel. We'll see then." She did not answer the Lebanese officer. On the Israeli side, by the roadblock, an IDF officer was waiting for her, colonel Dan Hadani. He welcomed her and signed a "receipt" of one Shula Cohen, which he handed to the Red Cross representative. For years Hadani had strived by every possible means to get Shula released. And here she was now. She got into his car, that headed for Haifa and Jerusalem. On the way, looking by the car window, she felt a surge of pride. "Now I have a part in the State of Israel, even if the size of a match!"

But Shula was Shula. On the way, she turned to Hadani. "We are approaching Nahariya [a town on the Mediterranean coast]", she said. "Can we stop at a beauty salon over there? I do not want to get to Haifa like this."

*

Shula was fifty years old when she returned to Israel. Her family also left Lebanon. Arlette, Isaac, Carmela, David and Joseph flew to Cyprus, and took a flight to Tel Aviv.

After surgery and a long treatment, Shula recovered and received an apartment in Jerusalem. Shortly after, she was appointed manager of the Antiques shop by the King David Hotel in Jerusalem. The honors and medals rained upon her nonstop: The Intelligence Community Secret Warrior Award, Notable of Jerusalem, Begin Award, Donna Grazia Medal, Wiesenthal Institute Medal, etc.; and when she celebrated her ninetieth birthday she was invited to light one of the twelve torches in the official Independence Day ceremony, as "a tribute to the bold acts of a Jerusalem woman for the people and the nation of Israel."

And so, she lived fifty more years – half of her life – surrounded by her children, grandchildren and great-grandchildren. "Monsieur Shula" died at one hundred, a girl from Jerusalem that had become a symbol of boundless daring, ingenuity and self-sacrifice for her people.

Part Two

Little Isser Is Recruiting Amazons

CHAPTER 7

Yehudit Nissiyahu

Flamenco in Buenos Aires, A Girl from Jerusalem

Mₐʏ 8, 1960.

M AY 8, 1960.
She entered the Ramsad's (Initials for Head of the Mossad) office, where his energetic secretary, Malka Braverman, was waiting for her. "Are you ready to travel abroad?" Malka asked.

"Yes", she said.

"We got a telegram from the Ramsad. He wants you to set out right away."

"Good."

"You do not ask where you're going?"

"I'll be told."

"You're going to South America. You must be in Buenos Aires at the latest on May 10, in the evening."

"Okay. What should I tell my family?"

"Tell them that you're sent to an international conference in Europe."

Malka gave her a flight ticket to Madrid on her real name, Yehudit Friedman. In Madrid she met a Mossad officer, Ronni (Fictitious name) whom she knew vaguely. He took her Israeli passport and gave her a Dutch passport with a fake identity, but with her real photograph. He also gave her a flight ticket to Buenos Aires, Argentina, with "Iberia" airlines. She was very excited but tried not to show it. She was thirty-five years old, and this was her first mission overseas as a Mossad warrior.

She had officially joined the Mossad only lately. Born in Holland to a Zionist-religious family, she immigrated to Palestine with the last ship that left the port of Marseille in 1939, when World War II broke out. In Palestine she joined an orthodox youth movement, taught the Bible to girls her age, fought in the Independence War, then studied history and philosophy at Hebrew University in Jerusalem) And on October 25, 1955, her life changed forever, when she received a secret letter from her brother, Ephraim.

"My dear Yehudit –

"I am on an important mission for the Jewish Agency in an enemy country and I need help in a momentous undertaking for the people of Israel. I need a person that can be trusted a hundred percent, so I chose you. In a few days you'll be contacted by an Agency official. Please do not say a word to Mother, I'll update her at the right moment. Take care, Ephraim."

The Jewish agency official came indeed and told her that Ephraim was in Morocco, participating in a huge endeavor – bringing the Moroccan Jewish community to Israel. The operation was carried out by a secret organization, called "The Framework." The Framework also controlled a self-defense outfit, "Gonen" charged with protecting the community against possible pogroms by extremist Muslim groups. Yehudit immediately agreed to take part in the mission, and in 1956 was sent to Morocco with a Dutch passport. In her luggage she smuggled weapons and paperwork. She was thrilled by the mission – bring thousands of Jews to Israel!

That was the first time she adopted a false identity. She was no more Yehudit Friedman from Israel but a rich Indonesia-born Dutch woman who had moved to Casablanca because she could not stand the climate in Holland. In a Casablanca café she met Shlomo Yehezkeli, one of the "Framework" commanders. He treated her with sweet, old-fashioned manners, clicked his heels, and gave her a war name: "Juliette".

That same year, 1956, Morocco became independent, and her

king prohibited all Zionist activities. "The Framework" and "Gonen" continued their activity under deep cover.

Yehudit stayed in Morocco two and a half years. Every Friday "Tata Juliette" as the children called her, would come to the Levi family house for a Shabbat dinner. [Tata meant "Auntie"] But the children were instructed to keep her visits secret and were forbidden to greet her if they met her in the street. She liked little Yitzhak, a future member of the Knesset and minister in the Israeli cabinet; when they met years later, he reminded her that she often held meetings "with unknown people" in their house. When that happened, Yitzhak's father would announce: "We are going to grandma today" and the entire family would hurriedly evacuate the house and leave it to Tata Juliette and her guests.

During those years Yehudit organized the illegal emigration of thousands. She was a treasury of knowledge and culture. She spoke many languages – Dutch, Hebrew, English, French and German; she knew well the ways of the world, the local customs, and kept conceiving original methods for smuggling Jews out of the country, via Europe or neighboring Algeria. For the missions in which she took part, she had to appear with different identities, and her colleagues started calling her "the woman with a thousand faces". A Mossad secret envoy told her once: "You can wake up in the morning as an Englishwoman, end the day as Dutch, and go to bed at midnight as a German." Other activists admired her acting talents; she had decided in an early stage to behave as a slightly deranged woman, so she wouldn't be taken seriously. The police called her "the nutty lady."

Yet, she succeeded to establish close relations with some senior police officers and they supplied her with secret documents, that she photographed at home and brought back in her shopping bag under a load of fruits and vegetables. At home she kept 3,000 fake passports that she received from Israel. She created a special relationship with the French consul in Oujda, in Morocco, a city close to the Algerian border. At that time, Algeria was still a part of France, and every Jew who succeeded to get into Algeria, could easily continue his journey to Israel.

The French consul was a cultured man; during his previous tour of duty in Indochina he had studied the South-East Asian civilizations. His main interest was social philosophy, and he was a staunch admirer of the Israeli world-famous philosopher, Martin Buber. Buber, a professor at Hebrew University, had many thousands of disciples throughout the world. When the consul heard that Yehudit had studied philosophy with Buber, "he almost fainted". He told her that his great dream was to meet Martin Buber or at least somebody who knew the famous philosopher. He spent long hours with Yehudit in his office, discussing Buber – and at the same time the two stamped hundreds of passports with entry visas to Algeria. During Yehudit's stay in Morocco, she and her comrades smuggled 25,000 Jews to Israel by the various stratagems that she invented.

Finally, the entire operation in Morocco was taken over by the Mossad, and Yehudit came back to Israel. Her new assignment was at the "Bitzur" [fortification] department, that was in charge of protecting and rescuing Jewish communities throughout the world. She became passionately devoted to her new job and chose a codename for herself, that could express her fervor: "Flamenco" – dance of fire...

And on this May 9 1960, she was on her way to Argentina. She did not know why she had been chosen by the Ramsad for this mysterious mission, thousands of miles away from home.

*

The trip did not turn well. The flights were delayed, the connections changed; she spent many hours waiting at the airports on her way. She was 24 hours late in arriving in Buenos Aires. It was May 11, 1960, late at night, and she checked in a hotel. The following morning, a man she did not know met her and gave her a sheet of paper, which was covered with names and addresses of cafés in the city center. Beside the name of each café a time period was marked in tiny numerals: 09.00–09.30, 10:00–10:30, and so on, all along the day. The stranger told her: "Your meeting is at eleven o'clock." She checked her wristwatch: it was 10:30. She left her suitcase at the hotel, took a taxi and asked the driver to take her to café "Las Violetas." The times marked on the sheet she had received, beside the address of Las Violetas, were 11:00 -11:30. She entered.

A short, bald man in a gray suit was sitting beside a small table, with his back to the wall. This was the Ramsad, Isser Harel. A tiny cup of coffee was placed before him. He had conceived the café system himself. Every morning his assistants noted on sheets of paper the cafes and the time he would spend in each, so that his men, who got this itinerary, could find him at any moment, without using telephones.

Yehudit had heard the stories about Harel that drifted in the Mossad hallways. She had met him a few years ago, when the Mossad had replaced the other organizations and taken over the secret immigration from Morocco. She had been impressed by his creative mind and his efficacy. He was said to have extraordinary instincts too; once he had unmasked a major KGB agent, Ze'ev Avni (nicknamed "Pygmalion") just by questioning a negligible detail in his cover story.

Isser had arrived in Palestine at the age of seventeen from his native Russia (now Belarus) aboard a cargo ship. The British police officers in the port of Jaffa did not even check the meager provisions the teenager was carrying in his backpack. Had they done so; they might have found the revolver concealed in a round loaf of bread. Isser had joined a kibbutz, then served in the British coast guard. before the Haganah had recruited him to its nascent secret service, the "Shai". He had rapidly risen in the hierarchy of the shadow world. After the creation of Israel, he had been appointed head of the Shabak. When Shiloach, seriously wounded in a car accident, had resigned from the Mossad, Ben-Gurion had appointed Harel as Ramsad as well. In these new functions, as "the man in charge of the security services" Harel had amassed tremendous power, both in the internal and external domains.

In the spring of 1960, he was contacted by Fritz Bauer, the Attorney General of the State of Hesse, in Germany. Bauer revealed to the Israelis that he had obtained the false name and the address of Adolf Eichmann, the Nazi colonel who had been in charge of "the Final Solution", the massacre of six million Jews. After the war Eichmann had escaped to Argentina, where he lived under the false identity of Ricardo Klement.

Bauer, a staunch Nazi hunter, feared that if he gave the information to the German services, some former Nazis would certainly warn Eichmann and help him escape; therefore, he had decided to alert the Israelis. Harel had driven his car to the desert kibbutz where Prime Minister Ben-Gurion was living and told him about the astounding message from Bauer. Ben-Gurion had said: "Bring him, dead or alive," and after a short silence he had added: "It would be better to bring him alive, this will be very important for our youth."

Harel had flown to Argentina at the head of the Mossad operational unit, with the mission to abduct the Nazi criminal and bring him to Israel. That was the most important and complicated mission the Mossad had undertaken ever. Last night, the operation had been carried out. The operational unit, led by Rafi Eitan and Peter Malkin, had captured Eichmann and brought him to a safehouse, in the outskirts of Buenos Aires.

A few days before Eichmann's capture, Isser had decided to include Yehudit in the mission. Rafi Eitan believed that Isser had done so because of the aryan looks of Yehudit and her phenomenal command of foreign languages. But Isser's decision stemmed from a more profound reason. He strongly believed that women should operate as Mossad officers. That was a major change in the Mossad policy, and for good reasons. For a while Isser had directed Shula Cohen and Waltraud Lotz, and admired their capacities. He also appreciated the work of slight, elegant and energetic Yael Posner, a doctor of physics from Berlin University. Recruited by Shiloach, she did not work in a laboratory but had become the "legend inventor" of the Mossad. She prepared the cover stories and the false documents of every Mossad warrior sent abroad; the crowning of her career had been "operation Finale" (Eichmann's capture).

But Friedman's mission was the first case when a Mossad amazon was employed in a team, with equal rank and responsibility as the men. That was how a new chapter in Mossad history started, as women became front line warriors in the Mossad operations.

*

Isser greeted Yehudit, skipping the usual niceties, and told her, trium-phant: "We got him!"

"We got whom?" she asked, confused.

He raised his head in surprise. "Don't you know why you're here?"

"No. They said that I'll be told when I arrive."

Isser laughed. "So I'll tell you."

*

Yehudit was stunned when she heard, from the Ramsad himself, in what mission she was participating. So far, she hadn't guessed that she would be part of an operation that would amaze the world. When she left Israel, she did not know what her trip's goal was.. "They told me", she wrote later, "that Isser Harel had required that I be sent to South America, to an operation that he himself was commanding. In the Mossad one did not ask questions, and when I was told that Isser wanted me to come, I only asked when I should leave." Now, in Las Violetas café, she realized that because of the delays in her flights, she had missed the excitement of the previous night, when Eichmann had been captured and brought to the Mossad safehouse. She should have been there, she thought.

Isser told her what her functions would be. The safehouse was a big villa on the way to the airport. Eichmann was held in one of the rooms, transformed into a cell. Initially, the safehouse had to serve for a night or two until an Israeli plane arrived and took the prisoner to Israel. But for technical reasons the plane arrival had been delayed by ten days. During that time the Mossad operatives had to stay with the prisoner in the villa. To avoid suspicions by neighbors and passersby, Isser had decided to stage a show: the villa allegedly had been hired by a couple of vacationers, a man and his wife, who spent a large part of the day on the lawn, having drinks and reading newspapers and magazines. The "husband" was going to be a veteran agent, Mio Meidad, the "wife" – Yehudit Friedman. She was also to take daily care of the prisoner, shave him and cook his meals.

After the briefing, Isser told Yehudit to get into a waiting car, that would take her to the villa.

She got there after a half-hour trip. The driver did not speak to her. The villa was pleasant, new, surrounded by a manicured garden. Beside the wall stood two chairs and a low table. The Israeli guard was waiting for her, and let her in. She walked in, quite nervous. In the living room she saw about ten men. At first, she did not recognize anybody, then she noticed a friend, Peter Malkin. She did not know that he was the man, who last night had jumped Adolf Eichmann, outside his house, and neutralized him before dragging him to the escape car with Rafi Eitan.

"Peter," she exclaimed, dashing toward him, "I know everything. It's so wonderful. I'm so grateful for the chance to help."

She read surprise and disappointment in the men's looks. they were stressed and upset. They had to stay put for ten days and wait for the plane, like sitting ducks, while knowing only too well that the police and the Nazi organizations in Buenos Aires would be searching for the disappeared Eichmann all over the place. Their morale was rather low, but the news that a woman was arriving had cheered them up. "Spirits rose with word of the impending arrival of the female agent", Peter Malkin wrote, "We all knew how dramatically the right woman could alter the chemistry on a team and make even the most tedious operation suddenly more livable." They heard that the woman was a bold and smart warrior. Some expected to see a Mata Hari, beguiling and mysterious, walk into the villa. One of them, Uzi, had put on a jacket and a tie for the first time in his life.

Then the door opened and Yehudit stepped in.

"This must be the Old Man's idea of a joke", muttered Uzi, pulling off his tie.

"It was not merely that Yehudit was hardly the most attractive of Israel's agents", Malkin wrote, cruelly describing her brown eyes "made enormous by thick lenses", and her "awkward physical manner".

"We expected a stunning woman, like a Mata Hari" said another warrior, Reuven. "And here she was, a chubby woman, not tall, not pretty, with glasses in a gold frame … we wouldn't have looked at her in the street."

That was Mata Hari?

*

Alluring or not, Yehudit quickly integrated in the team. They had to spend ten days together, in seclusion, before flying to Israel. As instructed by Isser, she kept getting to the garden every day, lounging, drinking and reading beside her "husband". She also cooked Eichmann's meals, tasted them before serving him and gave him pills, that the team doctor had prescribed. But she categorically refused to wash his plates. The first morning, she brought Eichmann his breakfast on a tray – a hardboiled egg with crackers. Malkin fed him. "She stood there, deeply unsettled," Malkin wrote," watching as Eichmann was fed the way one feeds a little child" [Eichmann was cuffed and could not use his hands]. Watching him, she thought of the millions who had been gassed, shot, tortured, burned alive on that man's orders. She could not understand how a Jew could feed such a creature. When the meal was over, she said: "I won't touch these plates, I'm unable to wash them, I feel dread and disgust." Isser had asked her to shave the prisoner as well, and she did it a few times, relieving Malkin from his daily duties. But when she ran the sharp blade on his face, she felt more than once the urge to thrust the razor in his throat and liquidate that "monstrous" creature. "Every day," she said later, "I held the blade against his throat. I had to use all my willpower to hold back my hand."

She regarded Eichmann as a monster that should be killed, without mercy. But when she faced him, hearing his voice, she discovered a despicable, submissive man; she felt revulsion, but not a yearn for revenge. "What bothered us most," she felt, "was his being such nothing. This man who had murdered millions of Jews, we wanted him to be Genghis Khan, Attila the Hun, we wanted him to be a monster, but he was nothing, zero." She wrote later: "All the people who were involved in the operation expected, somehow, to meet Satan himself. We had the feeling that only a satanic and horrifying creature could have been able, just by signing his name, to send scores of thousands of Jews to their death…After all, one doesn't easily meet Satan's emissary on earth. We expected something terrible, formidable in its wickedness – and what we found was a dismal, groveling clerk, who even did not understand the historic meaning of his actions, and kept repeating "I only followed orders" and "I was just a small cog" or "I did not touch anybody myself…"

That was how Yehudit lived through what seemed a never-ending nightmare. She carried out her functions well, but had one problem. She was religious, and could not touch the team's food. She lived on hard-boiled eggs and stale bread, and drank Coca Cola. One of the men pitied her, He feared that if she did not get kosher food she might die…He drove to downtown, found a Jewish kosher food store, and brought her kosher meat. But his efforts were in vain, because the plates and the kitchen appliances were not kosher…

After ten days the Israeli El Al liner arrived. Isser and his team smuggled the drugged Eichmann aboard the plane, dressed in a flight officer's uniform, and brought him to Israel. Yehudit stayed behind with another warrior, to clean and erase any trace of the abduction. She returned to Israel with a regular commercial flight, the first woman to serve as an equal to the male warriors.

*

Shortly before Eichmann's trial started, she crossed a very young redheaded woman in Malka Braverman's office. The redhead came out of the Ramsad's office and nonchalantly waved to Malka. Isser's secretary noticed the frown on Yehudit's face. "Oh, this is the little girl," she said with a smile.

"Little girl?"

Malka told her the story.

Since Eichmann had been brought to Israel, he was under intense interrogation at the jail. The daily reports about his depositions were taped and typed, then translated into Hebrew and sent to Isser.

The Ramsad received a report every morning and noticed some handwritten remarks and comments in the margins. The conversations of Eichmann with his newly arrived lawyer from Germany, Dr. Robert Servatius, were also translated and the mysterious handwriting appeared on these reports as well. Isser was very impressed by the notes, and the shrewd mind that had produced them.

"Who wrote that?" he asked Malka.

"Oh, that's a little girl. She knows German."

"Bring over the little girl," he said.

They brought her. She was 22 years old, tall and slim, with short-cut red hair and blue eyes. She really looked like a teenager. Her name was Aliza Magen.

"You know German?" he asked.

She told him her story. She was the daughter of a Jewish family from Berlin. In 1933, soon after the Nazis seized power in Germany, her father, a lawyer, was informed that he would not be allowed to plead in a German court anymore. That was enough. The family immigrated to Palestine and settled in Jerusalem. Aliza was born there, and German was her mother's language. She joined the Mossad after her military service. She easily integrated in the organization. One of her jobs was to translate the Eichmann interrogation reports, and she added her comments.

"Why?" Isser asked.

She coolly answered: "While translating I wrote some insights."

When Eichmann's trial started, Isser demanded that she came daily to his office. She kept expressing her opinions and analyzing the statements of Dr. Robert Servatius at the trial. "Isser was very interested in the trial," she recalled years later. "He understood that I perceived not only what was on the surface, but also what was beneath."

Yehudit and Aliza met; they were to see each other quite a lot in the following years. Yehudit was present at the Eichmann trial, but not in any official capacity; she sat in the audience like hundreds of other Israelis. Eichmann was sentenced to death and executed; but Isser did not forget the two women, Yehudit and Aliza, and used them in some of the Mossad most complicated missions. Like "Tiger Cub" in 1962.

*

One question resonated in the Israeli social life in 1962: "Where is Yossele?"

Yossele, the eight-year-old child of the secular Ida and Alter Schuchmacher, had been abducted by his own grandfather, Nachman Shtarkes, a religious fanatic. The old Hassid feared that the child's parents would cut off the child from the religion and raise him as a secular boy. He therefore kidnapped the child and apparently smuggled him out of the country, to some ultra-Orthodox community abroad.

Yossele's parents turned to the police, the Knesset, the Supreme Court. Nothing helped. Even the arrest and the jailing of the tough grandfather did not yield any results. Yossele's abduction shook the secular community in Israel and triggered an increasingly violent confrontation between secular and ultra-Orthodox Jews. Many feared that the explosive situation could ignite a civil war. Ben-Gurion called Isser and asked: "Can you find the child?"

Isser agreed, and launched "Tiger Cub", an unusual, unprecedented operation. The Mossad, built and trained to fight Israel enemies, had now to penetrate into the closed world of Hassidic Jews in Europe, and find a child... Isser established his advanced headquarters in Paris and dispatched his officers to Hassidic Yeshivas and synagogues all over Europe. Mossad warriors, so far used to participate in bold, risky operations, now donned Hassidic clothes and behavior, and spread out in the fanatic ultra-religious world, trying to find where is Yossele. They failed. In many cases they were unmasked, ridiculed, attacked by the Hassidim; even the most elaborate plans failed miserably.

An officer who was not unmasked was Yehudit Friedman. This "woman of the world" who so far had played the roles of modern and liberal European women, again changed identities. Now she played the part of an ultra-Orthodox woman, lonely and miserable, trying to find a match in one of the Hassidic communities in Europe. Being Orthodox herself, she was familiar with the rules and the way of life of the Hassidim, and could easily blend in their communities. Isser wanted to gain access to the locked and suspicious "Satmar" community in Antwerp, in Belgium, and entrusted the mission to Yehudit.

She had two very important advantages – her being religious, and her perfect knowledge of the Flemish – Dutch language.

Yehudit knocked on the door of a Satmar community leader, a rabbi. She was wearing a wig and a long, shapeless dress. She introduced herself as a single woman, hoping to find a husband. He invited her to stay in his home. She agreed even though that was a risky situation: a part of her family came from Antwerp, and somebody could identify her.

She stayed with the rabbi's family for a few months, speaking broken Yiddish with her hosts, concealing her knowledge of the Dutch language. She was sure that the family knew the whereabouts of Yossele, and insisted to stay with them as long as needed. She would sit in the kitchen and pretend to study the Torah, but actually listened to the conversation of the rabbi with his family. Quite often she heard them talking about her. How would she find a match, they said, she is not a spring chicken, and how she looks, the poor woman. But in their conversations, she discerned some veiled hints about the missing child; and finally overheard some fragmented phrases that held the key to the mystery: a story about a woman who had taken the child, disguised as a little girl, to America. She hurriedly flashed a message to Isser.

The child is in America.

*

Yehudit did not know that at these very days Aliza Magen shared the mysterious woman's room in Chantilly, France!

It was a strange journey. One evening in June 1962 Malka had called Aliza and told her:" You're going to France." At first, Aliza had no idea what her mission was. "In Tel Aviv, they stuck a passport in my hand," she recalled later, "and told me: go! So I went." It was an emergency, Aliza's Mossad commander said. She was not even told what she was supposed to do. She flew to France and was driven to a secluded house at Chantilly, near Paris. There she met some senior Mossad officers, and Isser himself. They took her to a room, guarded by Mossad warriors. Inside she met a Jewish pious woman, who introduced herself as Ruth Ben-David. "She is ultra-Orthodox", Isser explained to Aliza, "and she cannot be left alone in the presence of a man. She is going to be interrogated now, by some men, and you must be with her all the time."

It turned out that while Yehudit was eavesdropping in an Antwerp kitchen, Isser's people had found the mysterious woman who had smuggled the child. Mossad officers had discovered a beautiful Frenchwoman, bold, blond and blue eyed, who had been active in the anti-Nazi Resistance during the world war. Her name was Madeleine Feraille. She was Christian but had established close relations with the ultra-Orthodox communities in France and Belgium and served as a courier between the Hassidic centers. After the war she converted to Judaism and as Ruth Ben-David, she continued working with the ultra-Orthodox, carrying documents, money and commercial samples between France and Belgium. Like Flamenco, she was expert in changing identities. One day, she was dressed in a modest long garb, with a turban covering her hair, as the devout Ruth Ben-David; the next she was Madeleine Feraille again, perfumed, charming, irresistible in her elegant outfits, a real refined Parisian. The Mossad officers quickly realized that it was very difficult to shadow the elusive woman. She acted as a consummate secret agent; she did not have a permanent address, no office and no archives; she carried all her documents in her handbag. But there was a chink in her armor: she had a post office box. Mossad operatives succeeded to open the box and found out newspaper ads: Madeleine Feraille was selling her house! They established contact with her, as German businessmen, and on June 21 lured her to a house in Chantilly, "their attorney's home", to sign the sale contract. There she discovered she had been tricked and captured by the Mossad; she resumed her Jewish identity, and as a fervid ultra-Orthodox woman was served kosher food, supplied with religious books, and was assigned a roommate, Aliza Magen.

Isser's men who interrogated her and her son who lived in Israel, discovered that she had sailed to Haifa, on her Hassidic rabbi's orders. There she had falsified her passport, and entered Yossele's age and a girl's name: Claudine. The child, dressed as a girl, was taken to Europe, and kept in a Yeshiva as a boy. But when Mossad agents started closing on the Hassidic centers, Ruth dressed Yossele again in girl's clothes and flew with him to America. In a dramatic confrontation Isser succeeded to break Ruth Ben-David who finally disclosed the child's address. "The boy is with the Gertner family," she said, "one twenty-six, Pen Street, Brooklyn, New York. They call him Yankele."

With the FBI help, Israeli diplomats in New York rushed to Brooklyn, found the child and brought him back to Israel, to a delighted family and a festive secular population. That was a great victory for Isser. He also had been deeply impressed by Ruth Ben-David's faculties and tried to recruit her to the Mossad. But he was too late. Ruth returned to Jerusalem, and married the seventy-two-year old Amram Blau, the head of the fanatical sect of "Neturei Karta."

*

Yehudit returned to Israel. And despite the whispers behind her back in Antwerp, she married that same year, 1962, her boyfriend of twenty years, Mordechai Nissiyahu. One could not imagine a stranger union: Mordechai was a huge, sturdy man, secular, a sworn left-wing activist, one of the ideologues of the Labor movement. Yehudit seemed tiny when standing by him. She was Orthodox, quiet, of right-wing opinions, the opposite of her simmering husband. Mordechai was a close friend of Michael Bar Zohar, who met Yehudit many times, and never could suspect that the silent, reclusive woman was one of the greatest Israeli amazons.

Two years after their marriage Yehudit gave birth to their son, Haim. She pursued her career at the Mossad, and carried out many missions abroad, in Europe and the Middle East. In one of her missions to Egypt, she had to cope with an experience which was the nightmare of every secret agent. At Alexandria airport she was recognized by a European, who had known her years before. He cried happily: "Yehudit! What are you doing here? How are you?" This was one of the very rare times when she felt in danger. She knew that if her identity was exposed, in an enemy country, she was doomed. At first, she ignored the man's shouts, but as he kept calling her she turned to him, feigning total bafflement and said in English: "You must be taking me for somebody else!" Before he could answer, she scurried in the opposite direction.

*

Yehudit Friedman, now Yehudit Nissiyahu, traveled the Middle East and the world, operating as a Dutch, a German and a Belgian, recruiting and handling agents, penetrating major circles of government. Her plain appearance did not hinder her activity, on the contrary. For many, she was just an ordinary woman. Eliezer Palmor, (an Israeli diplomat), met her for the first time in Oslo. She had come to visit some Mossad warriors, incarcerated in a Norwegian jail, after a Mossad failure in Lillehammer (see Chapter 11). Palmor expected to see a glamorous, alluring master spy, and was there for a surprise. He knocked on the door of her hotel room. " Before me stood a fatty, short woman, redheaded and freckled, who had lost long ago the graciousness of her youth. She was wearing a kind of shapeless gray dress and looked like a housewife who had wandered to a place where she did not belong… If I had seen her in the street I never would have thought that she was in that business." Palmor, however, like many others, soon was to discover Yehudit's unique intelligence and ingenuity.

She raised to the position of Manpower Department head. During her trips abroad, she often would cloister in her hotel room, and read loads of books she carried with her; or visit the city museums and assist at an opera performance. When the Mossad decided to execute a war criminal, Herberts Cukurs, in Montevideo, Yehudit prepared the files and the plans of the mission to the most minute detail. The major Mossad warrior who was charged with the operation was Mio Meidad, her "husband" from "Operation Finale" …

Her commanders sang her praise. "In every organization like the Mossad," future Ramsad Ephraim Halevy said, "there may be people who are not excellent, even mediocre. But one also needs "islands of excellence" that would inspire the others. Yehudit undoubtedly was at the very core of the excellence island."

She resigned from the Mossad in 1976, at the age of fifty-one. She went back to school and graduated in law studies. Even though she was now retired, she eluded cameras as if they were Satan himself. "If only one photo of me popped up at the wrong place," she told her niece Ruthy Ben-Haim, "somebody might die." She also rejected the repeated proposals of a famous Israeli writer, Shulamit Lapid, to write her biography.

Yehudit got several jobs and was also active in right wing organizations. But what mattered for her most of all, the apple of her eye, was her son, Haim. Born in 1964, Haim emerged as a mathematics genius, and after receiving his Ph.D. degree was on his way to post-doctorate studies in the United States. Mordechai and Yehudit were enormously proud of their son.

But fate ruled otherwise, and horrible blows befell Yehudit Nissiyahu. In 1994 her husband contracted cancer and was rushed to the hospital. While she stood by her husband's bed, Yehudit was urgently called out by a nurse who delivered a dreadful message: "Your son, Haim, is dead."

Haim was on a trek in the Annapurna Mountain in Nepal with his girlfriend and another couple. After a day of climbing, he went to sleep with his girl; in the morning he woke up and asked her: "What time is it?"

"You have another half hour, go back to sleep", she said. He turned to the other side and suddenly started gurgling. A few minutes later he was dead.

Cardiac arrest, the doctors said. That was an awful blow for Yehudit and Mordechai. She tried, in vain, to find consolation in nostalgia. "Thank You God," she said at Haim's funeral, "that You gave him to me for thirty years." But to his friends who tried to console her she said:" You are very precious and I am grateful, but nothing can fill that void in me."

Mordechai died three years later and she remained all alone. She built a library in Katmandu, Nepal's capital, in memory of her beloved son. Every year, at the same date, she would fly to Nepal, rent a helicopter with a pilot, and overfly the area where Haim lost his life.

The tragedy cast a dark shadow on her last years. She became gravely ill and died in 2003. "Every year she prayed that it would be her last", her niece Mira Davis told the reporter Uri Blau. "She actually gave up. She kept close contact with Haim's girlfriend, studied languages and kept herself busy. But she was broken inside, and just waited…"

CHAPTER 8

Isabel Pedro

High heels in Cairo

AFTER THE RETURN OF YOSSELE ON JULY 4 1962, ISSER Harel and the Mossad enjoyed a marvelous acclaim. Isser was feted and congratulated from all over, but that did not last. Barely a few weeks later, on July 21st, Nasser displayed his rockets in Cairo, the danger of the German scientists exploded in the headlines of the newspapers, and many reacted with fury against the Mossad. It had neglected its essential mission. The Germans were developing doomsday weapons in Egypt, but the Mossad best agents, disguised as rabbis, were looking for a child in Europe. That was the Mossad? This was its task? And where was Isser Harel?

Isser immediately sent his best officers to his advanced headquarters in Paris, and alerted his secret warriors in Egypt. [A detailed account about the German scientists in Egypt appears at Chapter 4, The Mysterious Mrs. Lotz] Yet, the Mossad was operating in total darkness. The Ramsad had to find, at all costs, a German scientist who was involved in the Egyptian project and interrogate him. Indeed, after a few weeks, Aliza Magen heard that the Mossad had succeeded to recruit a German scientist. The man worked in Egypt but was in Europe on a related mission; but when approached by the Mossad officers he got scared and refused to talk. The Mossad senior officers decided to call Aliza.

"He was so frightened," Aliza recalled. "The Mossad warrior who was with him failed to calm him down. They called me to Paris. I came. They told me: "You've got to meet him. Perhaps, if he sees a young woman – I was twenty-four – he would calm down." Besides, German was her mother's language. She flew to Salzburg, in Austria, and met the scientist, Otto Joklik. The meeting took place in an isolated house. "Indeed, I succeeded to establish good contact with him." She then told her colleagues: "Listen guys, I can persuade him to come to Israel for debriefing. 'What?' they said." They did not believe that this girl that they called "Lizchen", could do it.

"I told them: 'I'll bring him to Israel.' Then I got in touch with him again."

She told Joklik: "Come on, come to Israel for a visit." He got terrified by the very idea."

But she kept talking to him. "I'll fly with you, and I'll be with you all the time. I guarantee your safety. Trust me, you'll have nothing to worry about."

"Lizchen" gained his trust.

"So, I brought to Israel the first German scientist. That was a total success. He was great." The scientist, an engineer, indeed told the Israelis everything he knew. "Suddenly we got an opening to this group that operated in Egypt and was an enigma for us. This was my first achievement. Later I brought another one."

Isser then launched his violent campaign against the German scientists. (See Chapter 4) But he needed more intelligence, which meant – more warriors on the ground, in Cairo.

*

Ten months before, October 1961.

Pretty as a picture, slim and elegant, Isabel Pedro disembarked in Haifa port from the Israeli passenger ship "Theodore Herzl". Isabel was twenty-seven. "My father drove to the port," her niece Ruthy Aner recalled, "to take her to our home, in Haifa's suburb Kiryat Haim. I was a little girl then and I saw a young woman like I never had seen before. She was different. Amazing, sexy, beautiful, shapely legs, wearing a ring with a purple stone on her finger, gold bracelets on her wrists. I'll never forget how she was dressed: a brown pleated skirt adorned with gold thread, a soft silk blouse, high heel shoes. She was rather petite, but the high heels made her look tall. And her languages! She spoke English, French, Portuguese, Yiddish and all the dialects of German. Beside her native Spanish, of course. She was born in Montevideo, Uruguay. To those languages she soon added Hebrew, which she studied in a specialized school, in kibbutz Usha. She would come to visit us at weekends, and after finishing her Hebrew course she moved to (the town of) Givataim, in the outskirts of Tel Aviv."

Ruthy was impressed by Isabel's vast knowledge and her ability to connect with people. "In life you have two little bottles", Isabel once told her wide-eyed little niece. "One of them is full of perfume, the other with poison. You decide which one you choose."

Isabel, the daughter of a flax oil manufacturer in Uruguay, had studied architecture and art at the Montevideo University. Since her childhood she had been active in the Zionist youth movement "Hebraica". As the daughter of a respected, well to do family, she had studied ballet and played the piano. In 1953, at the age of nineteen, she had married a local Jew but the marriage had been a failure; they separated after a year and a half. Isabel had to wait seven years for the divorce papers, and after getting them she right away had set out for Israel in a group of 35 young people. They embarked on a Spanish ship that was to take them to Genoa in Italy where they would board an Israeli vessel.

Isabel had the knack of easily making friends and her beauty did the rest. During the sailing, she met a Spanish naval officer, Juan Antonio, who succumbed to her charm. They had long, pleasant conversations on board. Antonio made some romantic advances, but she kept her distance, and settled for no more than a casual friendship.

"Our group disembarked in Genoa," she told reporter Shlomo

Nakdimon, "and Antonio gave me his family address in the Castile district in Spain. He invited me to visit. How could I imagine that one day this casual meeting on a ship's deck would serve Israel's security?"

*

In Israel, she studied interior architecture in the Technion Tel Aviv branch. Her parents who had stayed in Uruguay supported her financially. She had graduated in architecture in Montevideo, but needed a Technion diploma in order to practice in Israel. A flock of suitors quickly formed around her, but she did not care about them.

A year later Isabel walked into the district police station in Jaffa and met a female lieutenant. She told her that two young strangers had knocked at her apartment door in Givataim. After some hesitation she had opened the door. "You have nothing to fear", one of them had said, "we want to offer you a job overseas. It has to do with Israel's security."

She let them in, but spoke with them, standing, in the hallway. To her surprise, those two knew perfectly well who she was, and could tell her the story of her life in minute detail. That was, in the least, suspicious.

"Who sent you?" she asked, but they ignored the question. They just kept repeating that their superiors were sure that she could "play an important role abroad for the security of the nation."

She was not convinced, and they did not ask for a response. "Think about it," one of them said before leaving. "We'll come back for your answer. Everything we told you is true."

That night she could not sleep. She was in Israel barely a year, a new immigrant, divorced and childless. "I was only twenty-eight", she recounted later. "I suspected that these people were engaged in women trade, for prostitution. They probably focused mostly on young and innocent new immigrants." Pedro asked the officer to find out if her visitors were genuine messengers of the state authorities.

Two days later, the policewoman appeared at Isabel's apartment. "You have nothing to fear", she said. "These people are what they said they are. Their offer is serious, they want you to work for Israel."

The two men knocked on her door again, the following morning.

"I want to meet your superiors," she said. "The people who sent you over. I need to know more facts and understand why they need me of all people."

The visitors invited her to a meeting, two days later in the afternoon, at café "Vered", in Tel Aviv. The café was located on the bustling Dizengoff Street.

Isabel got to "Vered" earlier. She wanted to check up the place and choose a quiet corner. She settled down by a side table on the upper floor. A few minutes later an older man, wiry and balding, sat down in front of her. She ordered orange juice, he asked for a cup of tea. He did not tell her his name. She did not know until later that this was the Ramsad, Isser Harel.

He went straight to the point and asked her to join Israel's secret service.

"Why me?" she asked bluntly.

He smiled and said: "What we know about you justifies our offer. You can make a significant contribution to Israel's security."

Isabel weighed the pros and the cons. She had a great profession with the prospect of a successful career in architecture; she also wished to correct the Montevideo mistake – get married again, this time with the right guy, and start a family. On the other hand, she was tempted by the chance to play a part in Israel's struggle for survival. She hadn't served in the IDF, perhaps she still could do something for the country. That was an impressive personal challenge.

"Give me a few days", she said, after a long silence.

*

Two days later, she agreed to the Ramsad's offer and officially joined the Mossad.

Her life changed dramatically. She was utterly different from other women who were recruited to the Mossad those days. The Israeli society was quite egalitarian, rich people were very few. And that fashionable, elegant young woman, used to high living standards and refined ways and mores, did not belong there. Yet, she was treated and trained exactly as the other amazons.

After a short basic training she was sent to some test missions; and the first was to stealthily approach the Dora military base, south of the city of Netanya, and photograph its buildings and installations. But she barely had started to click out her Zeiss camera, when the heavy hand of an army officer landed on her shoulder. "What are you doing?" he yelled. "Do you have a permission?"

She answered in French, pretending she did not speak Hebrew. She pointed at a sketching pad she carried in her bag, and tried to explain by hand gestures that she was drawing landscapes on the base of photographs.

The officer did not let go and alerted the police. A couple of officers took her to the Netanya police station, but there too, they could not make her speak. She did not show her fear, and stuck to the role of an innocent artist. A police van arrived and took her to Jaffa headquarters. In the interrogation room she was assailed with questions by two angry police officers. They threatened her with trial and prison and expulsion from the country. She answered in French and after hours of questioning was finally thrown in a cell.

An hour later she was released without any explanation. She walked down Bustros Street, that was close to the police station and suddenly bumped into one of her Mossad instructors. "They caught you," he said, "that was very bad". She suddenly realized that the entire event – the military base, her arrest, her grilling in the interrogation rooms – was staged. It was a Mossad exercise, intended to test her ability to withstand pressure and threats. "If they had captured you in a similar assignment in an enemy country," her tutor went on, "that might have ended in jail or even something worse." Pedro shrugged. "The final result is the only thing that counts. I'm out and that's what really matters."

Her next assignment was to penetrate the Reading power plant in north Tel Aviv, and memorize the machines and instruments she'd see there. The power plant, dating from the mid-fifties, had been built mostly underground, for fear of aerial bombardments. Late at night, Isabel sneaked into the plant. She got into the shallow part of the Yarkon river and entered a large pipeline discharging a bubbling flow of hot water, used for cooling the plant systems. The pipeline led into a large underground hall. Isabel examined the two giant turbines, the control panels and the intricate pipes and tubes installation. She then got out, wading in hot water up to her thighs. Isabel thought that the task she was undertaking, at night, in a murky river by the sea, was very far from her parties in high heels and expensive dresses... Afterwards, she wrote a detailed report on what she saw; her instructor complimented her on her ability to remember details.

The initiation course continued as a private seminar, held in a Tel Aviv apartment at Bugrashov Street, discreetly rented by the Mossad in Tel Aviv. Mossad officers came over and taught her to analyze air photographs, read topographic maps, discover and shake tails, identify various kinds of weapons, use a Morse transmitter and write with invisible ink. She learned methods of "recruiting sources", intelligence gathering, and memorizing documents and maps. She spent four months in the apartment, often treated by the elderly owner to "Gefilte Fish" – stuffed fish, which was the lady's culinary pride.

At the end of the course, she was told that she would be sent to an enemy country. The country chosen was Egypt, where French was still spoken by a large part of the elite and the government. She liked the choice of Egypt, because of its wonderful antiquities.

Before setting out on her mission, she was invited to a meeting with the Ramsad in a Tel Aviv restaurant specialized in Jewish home cooking. She had met Little Isser there a few times already, but when she sat at their usual table, the man who joined her was not Isser Harel anymore.

She had heard rumors about a grave crisis that had poisoned the relations between the Ramsad and the Prime Minister. A heated dispute had opposed, for the first time, Little Isser and Ben-Gurion. Ben-Gurion angrily objected to the assassination attempts by Mossad officers on the German scientists; he also disputed Isser's views that the German government secretly supported the scientists' activity against Israel. Many of the Mossad senior officers had noticed that after the Eichmann trial Isser Harel had changed, and seemed obsessed by suspicions and hostility against the new Germany. After a stormy confrontation in Ben-Gurion's office, Isser had resigned.

A new Ramsad had been appointed: General Meir Amit, the Head of the Intelligence Department [AMAN] of the IDF. A lean, swarthy veteran of the Independence War, Amit was born in Tiberias to a couple of Ukrainian Jews, immigrated to Israel in 1920. A career soldier, he was younger than Isser and not his greatest fan; as commander of AMAN he did not believe that the German scientists in Egypt were a mortal threat to the existence of Israel. His assessment of the situation was more sober, and he claimed that the rockets they were building were antiquated and inaccurate. He also rejected Isser's report maintaining that the German scientists were developing death rays capable to destroy all living things. Foreign Minister Golda Meir had even mentioned that weapon in an emergency meeting with President Kennedy. But Kennedy did not take the allegation seriously; it seemed borrowed from the Flash Gordon comics. The future was going to prove Amit (and Kennedy) right.

A few days after his appointment, Amit met with Isabel on the eve of her departure. Before he met her, he read the reports of her instructors: "She possesses a quick mind, an ability to find her way in unfamiliar places, a capacity to interpret air photographs." He came to brief her about her assignment, but their conversation started otherwise. Isabel said to him, with disarming candor: "I'll be proud to bear the title of a Mossad warrior. But I do not know to use a weapon, I do not want to know to use a weapon, I shall not be a part of any killings. My weapons are my eyes, my ears, my memory and of course my camera."

Amit listened to her in silence. None of Mossad or AMAN officers had ever spoken to him so frankly. And yet, he had to steer the conversation to practical matters. He raised the subject of her mission in Egypt. "We shall need intelligence about infrastructure sites," he said, "army movements, army bases."

"I know. I've been through quite a few briefings and I have read a lot about Egypt. I'm also excited about visiting the ancient Egyptian sites that I like so much . . ."

He smiled. When they parted, he cast a look on the tight tricot outfit she was wearing, that enhanced her voluptuous figure. "Don't leave this at home," he advised her. "You look good in it."

On her way home she felt like in seventh heaven. Her dream was coming true. In a few days she would depart on a Mossad mission in an enemy country She was determined to succeed, and had no doubt that she wouldn't disappoint her superiors. She believed in her ability and her good fortune.

At the end of April 1963, she was driven to Lydda airport by a Mossad officer, who escorted her to the gangway of the El Al flight to Paris. As the plane soared she thought that this was the beginning of a new chapter of her life; from now on she'd be on her own, with a new cover and a new identity; dreadful danger would follow her wherever she went. Still, she did not feel fear, only exciting anticipation.

She landed in Paris and the following morning entered the café of "George v" luxury hotel. She chose a small table and after a few minutes she was joined by a middle-aged man in a gray suit. He was short, sturdy, his wrinkled face dominated by bushy eyebrows and a trimmed mustache.

"My name is Michael", he said. He was the commander of the Mossad operational unit "Hamifratz", charged with infiltrating warriors and agents in enemy countries. She later learned that he had been in charge of the attempted assassinations of German scientists, on Little Isser's orders.

They met several times, in various Paris cafes. "Michael" asked questions, inquired about her personal situation, persistently questioned her about her willingness to risk her life, and her capacity to penetrate the Egyptian governing elite. "He apparently liked my answers very much", she said later to "Maariv" reporter Dalia Mazori. "When my departure for Egypt was approaching, he told me: 'Go, do what you feel like, where you feel like and when you feel like.' I think there could not be a better compliment. It was an expression of total trust in my judgement and my power to fulfill my task."

Michael did not hold long meetings. For security reasons he preferred short meetings, in cafes and restaurants, and after hours even in bars and night clubs. "These are the best places for discreet meetings." Michael explained, using the method developed by Little Isser.

But in the present case, Michael deviated from his habit, and spent more time with Isabel. He attached great importance to a mission in Egypt, carried out by a woman ready to risk her life. He was a former underground fighter, a leader of the extreme right-wing group Stern. He had spent a great part of his life in mandatory Palestine, hiding from the British police, disguising himself and changing identities. When finally apprehended by the British he had been exiled to Eritrea for a few years. He wanted Isabel to do better than him, and toiled hard in building her an ironclad cover.

The "legend" he conceived was of a rich woman, an amateur painter, who had connections with people at the fringe of the glamourous Paris society. He focused on Russian exiles, who had escaped to France from the Soviet Union after the October revolution, and were known as "White Russians." Many of them used to meet at the famous "Café de la Paix", on the Paris Opera Square. Isabel started spending time with the Russians, and soon was integrated in their society. When Isabel would enter the café, wearing a magnificent fur coat she had brought from Montevideo, all eyes would lock on the beautiful, elegant lady. That was exactly what Michael wanted. If anybody came later, checking her story, many Café de la Paix patrons would remember the gorgeous lady in the white fur coat…

In his meetings with Isabel, Michael spoke at length about the conflict between Israel and Egypt, and described Gamal Abd el Nasser as the worst enemy Israel ever had. He spoke of his efforts to equip his army with modern weapons and his goal, to annihilate the Jewish State, "Egypt is very important to Israel ", he concluded. "Your mission would be to travel throughout the country, focus on military targets, explore unusual events, mix with the elite, and use your senses as you deem right."

Michael also revealed to Isabel the decision to let her keep her real name and passport, as they added to the credibility of her cover. But shortly before her departure it turned out that her passport could become a mortal trap for her – it contained Israeli visas and immigration stamps. Traveling with such a passport to Egypt was out of the question. Michael found the solution: Isabel spilled on the passport red nail polish that stained most of its pages. She boarded the train to Amsterdam, and handed the damaged passport to the Uruguayan consul, while apologizing profusely. The consul issued her a new passport, and she took a flight to Milan. There she walked in the Egyptian consulate and applied for a long-term tourist visa to Egypt. The consul asked for the purpose of her trip, and her projected extended stay, and she explained that she wanted to study Egyptian archeology. "The consul," she told later, "was more interested in my bare legs than in my reasons, and no more questions were asked."

And a last trip, before setting out for Egypt. She traveled to Spain, and visited the home of the naval officer Jose Antonio, who had courted her so assiduously on her voyage from Montevideo to Genoa. Jose was away, but his parents welcomed her warmly in their Castile home. She asked them if she could use their address, so that they would forward her mail to Israel. "I explained that I was on a trip around the world, and I did not want my family in Israel to know where I was at every stage of my journey. Therefore, I will send them letters and postcards via their address in Spain. Is that okay?"

Her hosts readily agreed. Isabel suspected that they were descendants of the Marranos [Spanish Jews who converted to Christianity centuries ago, fearing the Inquisition]. She also guessed that they saw her as a potential bride for their son. They parted on the best of terms, and she flew to Cairo.

She landed in Cairo with her Uruguayan passport. She told the immigration officer she was an architect and a painter who came to study the Egyptian antiques. She then boarded a train to the city center. An American tourist, who sat beside her in the train, advised her to check in the Hilton or Semiramis hotels, where single women could be safe. She chose the Semiramis, because the American told her it was popular with upper class Egyptians.

At the reception she picked various tourist guides, and immediately centered on the Zamalek Sporting Club, a favorite spot of the Cairo elite. On her first visit to the club she saw that many of the clients were foreigners, mostly Germans. One of them drew her attention and she suspected he was an Israeli spy; his efforts to obtain information from the Germans were too obvious and quite risky. Isabel was certain that beside her, there were other Israeli spies operating in Egypt; perhaps he was one of them. She rushed a message to the Mossad, describing the man's behavior, and urging for his immediate recall – if, indeed, he was an Israeli spy. She was right. His name was Wolfgang Lotz... He was not recalled, but arrested with his wife two years later.

But her most urgent task was to establish connections in Egypt's capital. At the Zamalek club Isabel met a few high society women and was invited to their homes; she met an Italian girl who introduced her to the Italian consul, and he on his turn, introduced her to several senior officials and army officers. In the antique shop "Ali Baba" at the Semiramis, Isabel met a young archeologist, Murad Ghali (a fictional name) who invited her to join him in his travels throughout the country. She offered him a book by an Argentinian archeologist, that described ancient Egypt and the pyramids. The first trip with Ghali was to the south of Egypt. But beside the antiquities, Isabel watched important military movements of army and heavy weapons heading south, toward Soudan. The Egyptian army used trains for this purpose, and also was in the process of developing the railroad system in the country for similar purposes.

Her next trip with Ghali was a shorter one, to the Giza pyramids. She climbed the "great pyramid", and was awed by its intricate design. "Is this what the Israelites built in Egypt," she thought, "when they were Pharaoh's slaves more than 4000 thousand years ago?" After the tour she joined her friend at the Mina House hotel for a drink. In the lobby she saw a famous television reporter, known for his close connections in government circles. She approached him and introduced herself; she showed him a few of her drawings and spoke of her interest in Egyptian archeology. They met again, several times. In one of their meetings he introduced her to an armored corps colonel, and he became her unwitting source on the Egyptian tank units.

She bought a car, and in one of her trips from Cairo to Alexandria saw a large airbase, populated with scores of Tupolev 16, Soviet-made heavy bombers. She stopped the car, counted the aircraft and memorized their make and descriptions and continued her trip. In Alexandria port she recorded numbers and makes of Egyptian Navy ships. "I sent to Israel intelligence reports on a variety of subjects," she told Dalia Mazori, "mostly about the Air Force. I watched movements of weapons and infantry, and did not like them, but could not stop them...

In Aswan, in the deep south, a huge dam on the Nile was being built, financed by the Soviet Union. Isabel knew that the dam was a major target for the Israeli armed forces. "I had to get the dam construction blueprints. It seemed to me my most important mission. Instead of attacking with tanks, and planes and artillery, one bomb would be enough to bring the dam down." And she got the blueprints while sailing on a ship close to the dam site. "During the sailing I became friendly with the first officer who narrated to me, in detail, the story of the dam construction. They had to save the temples of Abu Simbel that had been hewn in the rock under the reign of Pharaoh Ramses the Second." The dam waters were going to cover the archeological treasure; therefore, an ambitious, unprecedented project was conceived, to move the huge Abu Simbel statues to a new, much higher location. "I introduced myself as an architect interested in archeology. The officer brought me a file with detailed blueprints of the new dam, including its foundations in the depths of the Nile."

Isabel photographed the maps and the plans, and sent all the materials in a large envelope to the family of Jose Antonio, in Spain. From there the envelope traveled, as agreed, to a post office box in Tel Aviv. Isabel regarded that mission as the most important in her career. She kept sending her reports in innocent letters via Spain. She had a radio transmitter that she had smuggled into Egypt, but kept her messages to a minimum; she knew that electronic transmissions could be intercepted by the Egyptian *Mukhabarat*.

In the meantime, the tension between Egypt and Israel kept growing and Pedro could feel that a major conflict was brewing, Yet, she succeeded to conceal her feelings from her Egyptian friends.

Pedro operated in Egypt for three long years. During that period, she visited Israel three times, flying via Paris. She stayed with her relatives in Israel but did not even hint what she was doing "in Europe". Only one morning, while applying her makeup, she took some mascara from a tiny bottle, and told her niece Ruthy: "This comes from Cairo market." Ruthy inwardly chuckled. Yeah, she thought, one of Isabel's stories, pure fantasy. During another visit Isabel accompanied Ruthy to a conference of the technical school in Atlit. "I learned Morse once", she said. Ruthy again was amused. Sure, she thought, Isabel knows Morse…

Isabel's mission in Egypt became more dangerous when Mossad's greatest spy Eli Cohen was apprehended and hanged in Damascus, and the Lotz couple were arrested in Cairo. "I knew I was in danger every moment", she later said, "but I was not afraid. Fear did not exist in me." She integrated in Cairo's social life, visited the Casino and myriad nightclubs and restaurants, and gently put an end to the courtship of a local journalist. In early 1965 she agreed to participate, in a small role, in an Italian-Egyptian film about the quest for an ancient treasury. During the shooting she met an Egyptian producer who offered her to host, in French, a weekly TV program on art, centered around her experience, as a foreign visitor to Egypt. She was very flattered, but she rejected the offer. "I could have been recognized", she said.

After three years in Egypt she asked to return to Israel. She underwent a long, detailed and exhausting briefing in Mossad headquarters. Her superiors offered her a job as an air traffic controller at Lydda airport, but she refused. She returned to her original profession, Interior architecture, and did well.

One day the circle was closed. She was invited to plan the house interior of no other but Little Isser, the Ramsad who had recruited her ages before. "His wife hosted me warmly and I turned their home upside down. Isser would come, throw a look, say that it was okay, and go away. He was so discreet; he did not even ask me about Egypt. Of course, he recognized me."

Finally, she married a former member of the Irgun underground and had two sons. "This marriage was because of his mother," she said. "She fell in love with me, caught me and said 'You're mine.' My future husband hadn't even met me yet. His mother decided for him. At the wedding Isabel discovered that quite a few of the groom's relatives and friends were former Mossad officers." Many veterans of the Irgun and Stern right-wing groups were guests at her marriage. One of them was future Prime Minister Menahem Begin. Another one was her Paris handler, "Michael", who also bought one of her paintings. His real name was Yitzhak Shamir, another future Prime Minister.

And the resplendent fur coat still hangs in Isabel's closet, in Tel Aviv.

CHAPTER 9
Nadine Frej

A tragic love story

The following chapter is an interruption in our narrative, but its unique story justifies its inclusion.

IN 1963 THE NEW RAMSAD, MEIR AMIT, SENT SAMI MORIAH to Paris, as head of the Mossad advanced center of operations. Sami was one of the Mossad best warriors since its creation. He had participated in countless bold missions in enemy countries; one of them had been establishing contact with Shula Cohen in Beirut, in the early fifties.

But now, beside directing Mossad operations in enemy countries, Sami was charged with another, painful mission.

*

Nadine Frej (fictitious name) was born and raised in Jaffa. She was the youngest child of a rich Arab family, that did not escape from Israel during the Independence War. The family was Christian, but completely identified with the national Palestinian aspirations to get rid of the hated Zionist occupation. Nadine studied in a catholic school for girls and impressed her teachers by her intelligence. She was a beauty, tall, slender, her heavy black braid resting on her shoulder, her face flawless, dominated by a pair of magnetic black eyes.

She was sixteen that day when she met a young man, slim and handsome, in her home. Her father introduced him. "This is Fouad," he said, "he is a new teacher in our school, and he will live with us for a while."

Nadine and Fouad exchanged some niceties but could not avert their eyes from each other. In the following days, Nadine was deeply impressed by Fouad's manners, his command of the Arab language and the vast knowledge he displayed in his conversations with the family. She talked with him for hours, first when surrounded by the family, later when they secretly started meeting alone. A great love sprouted between them, and they decided to marry. To Nadine's delight, her father gave them his blessing. But there was a problem: he was Muslim and she – Christian; how would they marry? Finally, after failing to get help from his spiritual leaders, her father decided on a civil marriage.

In 1957 the Frej family, including the young couple, emigrated to France. At first, the father faced grave economic difficulties, but Fouad was of great help. He told Nadine that he had saved a substantial sum of money while dealing with real estate in Israel, and now he could contribute to the family. In France, too, he successfully closed a few business deals. A while later, Fouad and Nadine decided to spread their wings, return to the Middle East, and settle in an Arab country; but they failed in their efforts to get long-term visas to Syria and Egypt, and had to stay in Paris. Nadine gave birth to a baby girl, but the child died a few months later, and Nadine was devastated. They had a second child, a healthy little boy. Fouad flew often to Syria on short business trips; after a while, though, he told Nadine that he had to spend a few months in Lebanon. "It's better that you and the child stay in Paris", he said.

Nadine was lonely and unhappy in Paris, a bustling city she did not like, and found solace in the arms of Nabil (fictitious name), a young Palestinian student. Nabil had become a friend of the family after meeting Nadine and Fouad at a gathering of Arab emigres in France. Nabil had radical views on the Israeli-Arab conflict and believed in all out armed struggle. Nadine shared his views and kept her love affair in deep secret; but after a while her lover decided to break up with her, mostly because of his respect for Fouad, whom he admired as a true Palestinian patriot.

Fouad lived alone in Beirut for two years, and finally brought over Nadine and the little boy. The family was reunited. Their life returned to normal, and Nadine got pregnant again.

And then, one sleepless night Nadine surprised her husband in his study, bent over a radio set, in the middle of a wireless transmission.

She froze on the threshold.

Fouad looked at her. His look betrayed confusion, distress, despair. He finally blurted: "I am a Jew, not a Muslim! I am here on a mission for Israeli Intelligence."

*

Back at the end of 1954, a top-secret course had been held by the Israeli Shabak, the Internal Security Service. It was a course for "Mistaarvim", meaning "Those posing as Arabs". At that time the Israeli Arabs lived in villages and towns under tough military regime. Every village was controlled by an IDF military governor, and severe limitations were imposed on the Arabs' travel in the country. Yet, Isser Harel felt that he needed vital information about the feelings and plans ripening in the closed Arab society. He was expecting a new war, a new attempt by the Arab nations to destroy Israel. The Arab peasants – so he thought – would become a 'fifth column' that would assist the Arab armies. He therefore decided to plant secret agents in a few Arab villages and neighborhoods throughout Israel. Those agents would be Jews who would pose as Arabs, behave and speak like them, and would integrate in the Arab society for many years. That way they would obtain first-hand intelligence about the Arabs' views and plans.

Isser launched a long and thorough search for likely "Mistaarvim." He appointed the Deputy head of the Mossad Yaakov Caroz, and the master-spy Sami Moriah to head the project. They selected ten young men, most of them Jews born in Iraq. They were trained in a secret site outside Tel Aviv, that used to be a British officers' academy, and later the headquarters of Hassan Salameh, the leader of the Palestinian Arabs during Israel's Independence war. The "Mistaarvim" studied the ways and mores of the Israeli Arabs, learned the local slang, that was different from the one they had brought from Iraq; they underwent a thorough study of the Islamic faith, memorized Koran verses, and dressed like local villagers. Some of them were sent, dirty and ragged, to the streets of the Jewish cities, were arrested by the police and jailed as "infiltrators" from the neighboring Arab countries. Only after a while they were released and sent to their assigned villages. That was how Avner Porat (fictitious name) was trained, became Fouad Ayad, and was sent to Jaffa. But in spite of the strict orders, he fell in love with Nadine and married her.

*

When he confessed, that terrible night in Beirut, Nadine was petrified. The shock was dreadful. In one moment, her world crumbled to pieces. At first, she could not believe a word she heard; but there stood her husband, broken and desperate. He kept repeating – I am a Jew; I was sent by the Israeli intelligence.

She stood in front of him, shivering, unable to say a word.

Later that night, after the crushing shock, a terrible fury surged in Nadine. Her husband, her lover, had betrayed her not once or twice but at every moment since their eyes met in her parents' house, in Jaffa. She burst in tears and sobs; and when she became coherent again, she accused him of maliciously using her love for him. "You married me not out of love but because you wanted to use me for your spying!" she shouted.

Her intense nationalist feelings added to her wrath. She supported the Palestinian struggle against the Zionists, and suddenly had found herself married to one of the most dangerous enemy agents. A terrible inner storm raged inside her, she felt she was losing her mind.

Fouad tried to deny her accusations, and convince her that his love for her and their son was sincere. It had nothing to do with his mission.

On the contrary, his handlers did not initiate and did not approve of their relationship. He married her only out of love, he said, she was the love of his life.

Nadine finally calmed down. And then, in what turned to be a moment of common confession, she revealed to him her Paris affair with Nabil. Now it was Fouad's turn to listen, stunned, to her words. They kept fighting and hurling accusations at each other till dawn.

After that awful night Nadine collapsed and miscarried. When she recovered she said to Fouad: "I want us to leave and go back to Paris."

He refused. "I am not here of my own will", he said. "I have been sent here and cannot just get up and leave. I have a handler and I can't move without his authorization."

Nadine was torn by a terrible dilemma – leave him or stay with him, knowing that he was an enemy spy. She stayed. She did not forgive her husband's betrayal for a single moment. Nevertheless, after that night she protected him and even helped him. She did not spy for him in Beirut, but did not reveal to the authorities that her husband was a spy – a revelation that could lead him straight to the gallows. When he carried out his wireless transmissions, she would lock the entrance door and not allow anybody to get into their home.

This strange situation lasted for six more months, until they returned to Paris. Fouad was not a Shabak officer anymore; now he operated for the Mossad. In Paris, Nadine's former lover Nabil surfaced again in their lives. It turned out that he was active in a budding terrorist organization. Nadine's loyalty again was being tested. She had to choose between her support for the Palestinian cause and her ties with Nabil – and her fidelity to the husband who had betrayed her. Once again, she chose Fouad, and did not divulge his true identity and occupation to Nabil and his friends.

A close relationship developed between Fouad and the Palestinian extremist group. With the help of his Mossad handlers, Fouad rented an apartment in Brussels, that allegedly was to serve as his secondary office. The Mossad officers prepared the apartment for operational use, Microphones and other instruments were planted in its walls, and Fouad put it at the disposal of his "Palestinian friends." Their meetings, deliberations and decisions were duly recorded and relayed to the Mossad station. Fouad was warmly congratulated for his success.

But precisely this success triggered a new soul-searching for Nadine. She was a nationalist Arab, but felt she was harming her people's combat. She told Fouad she wanted a divorce. He refused. Sami Moriah, who had been appointed head of the Paris station, tried to help him. He brought over from Israel the Chief IDF rabbi, Shlomo Goren, to calm down Nadine. Rabbi Goren succeeded; not only did he convince Nadine to stay with Fouad, but also talked her into converting to Judaism. When she completed the conversion process, he married her and Fouad again, this time in a traditional Jewish wedding...

Yet, at the same time, Sami Moriah started receiving alarming reports. It turned out – by the recordings of the Palestinians' discussions – that they had started suspecting Fouad. Some of them claimed that he was an Israeli spy. Sami and his superiors decided to cut short Fouad's stay in Europe and send him, with his family, back to Israel. In the summer of 1966, they sailed to Haifa.

Nadine and her son received Hebrew names and Israeli identities. They did not know that two years before, the Ramsad and the head of Shabak had decided to put an end to the "Mistaarvim" operation. It turned out, that except for Fouad's missions, their work for more than ten years had been insignificant. They had been sacrificed for nothing and the entire operation had been a mistake. The Mistaarvim had lived a life of lies in order to obtain totally useless intelligence. Some of them, like Fouad, also had married Arab women. Sami Moriah was charged with the hardest task – to summon the families to Paris and reveal the truth to the Arab wives.

Those were excruciating meetings. The reaction of the poor women was heartrending. One fainted when hearing Moriah's words, others burst in screams or tears and escaped back to their native villages. A secret Rabbinical Court headed by rabbi Shlomo Goren converted two of the women. The rabbis also ruled that even though their children had been born to non-Jewish mothers, they would be recognized as Jews, because their fathers had been engaged on a secret mission. Some of the families returned to Israel under Jewish identities; but their sons were not drafted to the IDF. One of them had cynically asked his mother: "If there is a war, whom should I shoot – my Israeli or my Arab relatives?" These families suffered from severe identity crises and almost in all the cases the future of the wives and their children was troublesome and miserable.

The Mistaarvim themselves felt cheated and frustrated; they grieved over their lost youth, that had been taken away for a nonsensical project. That was one of the distressing results on the Mistaarvim project, that finally harmed both Jews and Arabs. The years that the Mistaarvim lived a mendacious life in the Arab society, and often in a mixed family – caused irreparable psychological harm to the Jewish men, their Arab wives and children.

That painful blow also struck the Fouad and Nadine family. Even after the conversion and the return to Israel, the anger and the guilt feeling of Nadine did not fade away. She kept demanding a divorce, Fouad kept refusing, but finally they decided to separate. Nadine enrolled in The Hebrew University and successfully completed her studies in sociology. She finally got her divorce and returned to Paris with her son. The boy wanted to stay in Israel, but had to settle for his father's visits to Paris, that became more scarces as time went by.

Fouad married again, but in 1971 he got a heart attack and was rushed to the hospital, for open heart surgery.

The Mossad officers, charged with delivering to Nadine her monthly pension, informed her of her ex-husband's malady. She immediately flew to Israel, settled in his hospital room and sat beside his bed, day and night, for long weeks; she took care of him with love, washed and shaved him. His second wife understood and accepted that strange situation.

Fouad recovered this time, but in 1974 died of cancer.

Nadine stayed in Paris and married a Palestinian activist.

AUTHORS' NOTE: *This book deals with Mossad female warriors. Nadine was not a Mossad warrior, perhaps the opposite. But her life with a Mossad officer, her distress and torment, her suffering for her help to Fouad – and to Israel – make her, together with other Mistaarvim wives, worthy of a bow and a recognition in our story.*

Part Three

Mr. Mike Harari and His Ladies

CHAPTER 10

Mike

1968

O N AN APRIL MORNING, SHORTLY AFTER LANDING IN
Israel, Waltraud and Wolfgang Lotz were invited to the residence
of President Zalman Shazar. The President wanted to convey to them
Israel's gratitude for their activity in Egypt. The couple arrived in
Jerusalem with the Ramsad, Meir Amit, who had obtained their release
from Egypt. But the small group that walked into Shazar's office that
morning included another man, whose name and photograph were
top-secret. This was Michael ("Mike") Harari, the deputy commander
of the Mossad Caesarea department.

Mike, born in the Tel Aviv picturesque Neve Tzedek suburb, was
considered by his peers as Israel's ultimate secret warrior. At the age
of thirteen he already was a Haganah messenger; he then falsified
his birth certificate, adding two years to his age, and enlisted in the
Palmach [the Haganah elite "storm companies"]. He participated in
some of the most spectacular coups of the Palmach including the
raid on Atlit Camp, where illegal immigrants were imprisoned by
the British; he also took part in a symbolic mission, the "Night of the
Bridges" when all the bridges connecting Palestine with the neighboring countries were blown up by the Palmach. Mike was arrested
by the British and thrown in jail. After his release he sailed to Italy

and smuggled Holocaust survivors to Palestine, braving the British senseless blockade. After the creation of Israel he served in several secret organizations, joined the Mossad, carried out cloak-and-dagger missions in France and Ethiopia, and finally landed in "Caesarea". There he founded the Kidon (Bayonet) unit, the special commando charged with the most dangerous missions, including assassinations. And in 1970 Mike was appointed commander of Caesarea by the new Ramsad, Zvi Zamir, his comrade from the Palmach days.

Slim, dark-haired, with a large square forehead over shrewd brown eyes. Mike was a dominant figure in the Mossad. He became known in the Mossad for his efforts to recruit and promote foreign-born warriors to Caesarea. Together with Zamir he initiated a far-reaching reform in Mossad personnel. Zamir told me that when handed command of the Mossad by his predecessor, Meir Amit, Caesarea was composed of "great guys, who spoke only Hebrew and Yiddish." So they decided to recruit people who did not look Israeli, who were fluent in foreign languages, and most of whom had been born in Europe or in other, English-speaking countries. Only that way, Zamir believed, could they operate under cover in foreign lands without being exposed.

One of Mike's main achievements was assigning women to risky, front-line missions in enemy countries. Mike perceived, more than any of his predecessors, the tremendous potential and unique abilities of female warriors. He recruited young women to his department, spent hours in long, heart to heart conversations with them, instilled in them the feeling that somebody cares for them and protects them; he used to tell his ladies, that he would cancel any mission, be it the most important, if he only suspected that it could endanger their life or freedom. Mike became a kind of father figure for a whole generation of amazons, and they felt attached to him for the rest of their lives. They spoke of Mike with deep affection and respect. That's how he transformed all these young women, born in Israel or – mostly – in foreign lands, into brilliant Mossad warriors.

One of them, who was to become the most famous Mossad amazon, was Sylvia Rafael.

CHAPTER 11

Sylvia Rafael (1)

The most notorious of them all

ONE MORNING IN JANUARY 1974 KING HUSSEIN OF JORDAN entered the dining room of his Amman palace, and settled by the breakfast table. His servants poured him strong black coffee and served him his favorite food. He unfolded the morning paper and perused the front page. And then he froze.

A photograph showed the face of a woman he knew well. She had visited his palace many times and taken photos of his family and himself. One of the children she had photographed over and over was little Abdullah, the future king of Jordan. She was a press photographer, and the palace staff had nicknamed her the unofficial court photographer, because of her many visits to the Royal residence. King Hussein knew her as Patricia Roxburgh, a Canadian based in Paris. But in the newspaper before him she was referred to as Sylvia Rafael, an Israeli Mossad agent. How could that be? Charming Patricia – an enemy agent? Her first visit to Jordan had been as an official guest of Hussein's own government! Patricia, the warm, friendly Patricia – an Israeli spy?

[Another version of this story is that the king received the news from his secret services and not from the media, but that seems hardly credible].

*

Smart, pretty, very tall, her bright eyes betraying a mischievous character and a sharp sense of humor, Sylvia had been born in 1937 in Graaff Reinet, a small town near Capetown, South Africa. She had two brothers; her father was Jewish, her mother – a Calvinist Christian. According to the Jewish religious rules, she was not Jewish, as she had been born to a non-Jewish mother. To complicate the matter, her father was an atheist. Yet, she got a painful reminder of anti-Semitism the day she saw a band of children, pushing a Jewish girl in tears in a barrow. and yelling: "We'll take you to Hitler!"

The parents decided to send the appalled Sylvia out of town, to a prestigious boarding school for girls in Port Elizabeth, where she spent several years. She emerged from her teens as a vivacious girl, merry, curious and witty – and a staunch Zionist. She was eleven years old when Israel was created, and developed a deep, naïve concept of the Jewish State, the answer to the Anti-Semitic event that had shocked her so. At sixteen she already organized the Port Elizabeth celebration of Israel's fifth anniversary; she organized a big rally of the youth Zionist movements, and recited, with a choked voice, "the Silver Platter" a famous poem about the self-sacrifice of Israel's youth in the battle for Independence. She also hoisted the Israeli flag over her parents' house and spoke to them about immigrating to Israel.

Still, she had other dreams for her future. She wanted to become an actress, and her schoolmates often met her in the school hallways, passionately declaiming Shakespeare's plays. Afterwards, she studied arts in the South African and Rhodesian universities. She liked sketching and painting with watercolors. When she graduated, independent and curious, she traveled to Europe, crisscrossed the continent, but settled in England. She stayed there for long months, tried working at any possible job, but could not get employed at the only job that interested her – a bartender... During those years a new dream sprouted in her heart – travel to Israel and contribute to the nation's defense. She had just read Leon Uris's new book, "Exodus", that moved her deeply.

On her return to South Africa she met a young, successful lawyer, Avri Simon, the son of a prominent Jewish family in Port Elizabeth. He proposed to her, and his father, an entrepreneur, even built a dream house for the young couple. But Sylvia backed out. "Not now," she said to Avri, "first I want to go to Israel for a year or two. Come with me!" He refused. Finally, she flew to Israel alone, armed with a present from her father – a camera.

She had dreamed to take part in Israel's struggle for existence, but on arriving to Israel, at the age of twenty-two, she had to face a different reality. First she settled in kibbutz Gan-Shmuel as a volunteer, and there she was sent to work at the canning factory. David and Dorit, the young couple that hosted the fiery volunteer, quickly agreed that she could contribute better to the Zionist dream by doing something else than filling cans with marmalade. She moved to Holon, a town adjacent to Tel Aviv, and was hired as an English teacher in a secondary school. This job, too, was a disappointment. That was the Land of Israel that she wanted to defend?

Yet, she did not let go. She decided to stay in Israel, perhaps she would find a way to fulfill her dream. She sent a letter to Avri, in South Africa, breaking off their engagement.

The breakthrough came from an unexpected direction. She had rented an apartment in Tel Aviv with Hanna, a girl she hadn't met before. Hanna was a student at Bar Ilan University. Hanna's boyfriend, Zvi'ka, visited the apartment a few times and occasionally chatted with Sylvia. He did not tell her that he was a member of the secret services, an instructor at the Special Missions school of IDF unit 188. That unit was in charge of warriors in enemy countries, like Dafna and Shlomo Gal, Waltraud and Wolfgang Lotz and Elie Cohen. The unit was soon to merge with Caesarea. The "school" was nothing but an unkempt apartment in an old house on Allenby Street in Tel Aviv. After meeting Sylvia a few times Zvi'ka went to his commander, Motti Kfir, the head of the school. "Perhaps it's worthwhile that you meet that Sylvia Rafael," he said to Motti, "I think she may be suitable."

And so, one night in October 1962 Sylvia got a phone call from a man she did not know, who invited her to a meeting, "to offer her a job." The following day Sylvia met Motti Kfir in Café Herly. Motti was very pleasant and courteous; he introduced himself as "Gadi", an employee of a government company that operated in conjunction with the Defense Ministry. She poured her heart out – she wants to contribute to the state, but the IDF won't take her because she is too old – twenty-five! True, she is not Jewish according to religion, but she feels Jewish and looks for a challenge in Israel. Kfir assailed her with questions – on her parents' family, the reasons for her coming to Israel, her present job, her habits, her friends... He was impressed by her sincerity and the humor in her answers. When she asked repeatedly what kind of work he had in mind, he answered that it was an employment with many challenges and many trips abroad.

He watched her when she got up and left. Many of the café customers stared at her as she walked. Perhaps she was a bit too pretty, he thought; the success of the Mossad warriors abroad partly depended on not stirring up too much interest; on the other hand, perhaps she would learn to use her alluring looks to achieve her goals.

At their following meeting, Kfir was more focused. He spoke to her about a job in the IDF intelligence department, and admitted it was a fascinating job, but "sometimes dangerous." He also gave her a code name. "Ilana" but warned her that she had to pass several tests, a psychological examination, a security checkup, and a training that would last a few months.

"Suits me," she said.

Kfir reported to his superiors, and "Ilana" came to a session with the psychologist. She described to him her dreams and fears since her early childhood. When he asked if she had other fears when growing up, she laughed: "I was afraid that I would remain an old spinster. I did not have a boyfriend until I was sixteen."

The psychologist submitted a detailed report to the Mossad. "Responsibility and problem solving are central elements in her life. Resourcefulness inspires her not to shrink from unknown situations; unexpected change, risks, or breaking new ground, but rather to welcome them unto her life."

Sylvia went through some more tests, and the Mossad people still remember a phrase she said in one of the meetings: "The word impossible does not exist in my lexicon." She also passed the security checkup with flying colors; and the final assessment report placed in her personal file stated: "The Special Operations unit is a uniquely suitable place for her. She has a marked inclination toward independence, steady resourcefulness, a talent for bonding with others and quickness of movement . . . She is proud to have found a framework that she can rely on, something that she can truly belong to with pride."

Kfir invited her to his office and shook her hand. "You're in," he said.

*

She was speechless. She felt that was the greatest day in her life, and decided to celebrate. But not by drinking at parties and restaurants. In the early hours of the following day she ascended to the top of Mount Masada by the Dead Sea. Masada was the last bastion of the Jewish rebels against the Romans in Palestine in 70 A.D. When the mount was surrounded by Roman legions, the defenders committed suicide. The Roman soldiers who stormed Masada, found hundreds of bodies, of the fighters, their wives and children. Sylvia felt an emotional bond with the handful of warriors who had set out to fight the mighty Roman Empire. The popular Israeli slogan "Masada will not fall again" suited her passionate character and her innocent dream to join the men and women who defended Israel's existence.

The Mossad training course, held in an apartment on Dizengoff Street, in Tel Aviv, was directed by a veteran Mossad warrior, named "Oded", His real name was Avraham Gehmer. His father had been murdered by Arab terrorists before the creation of Israel. Avraham grew up in kibbutz Shiller, fought in the paratroopers' commando, served in the Shabak and finally joined the Mossad. Handsome, slim and silent, Gehmer led Sylvia in the tortuous pathways of the shadow world: reading air photos and maps, rules of behavior in dubious surroundings, concealing explosives in anodyne-looking objects, radio transmissions, undercover missions in foreign countries.

Gehmer also was beside her when she set out to execute her outdoors exercises. These were exercises in tailing suspects, noticing and evading surveillance, handling weapons, preparing explosive charges. Gehmer sent Sylvia, playing the role of a reporter for the

London "Daily Mirror", to interview a women activist, Beba Idelson. Beba was delighted.

The following exercises were more challenging. One was the traditional penetration in the Redding electrical plant, that had been performed by Isabel Pedro and other amazons. Another routine exercise was the penetration into a military base, the phony arrest, the night interrogation and the jailing in a dark cell. This time Sylvia was sent to the Allenby camp in Jerusalem, and after the arrest and interrogation by brutal "police officers", spent a tough night, tied, lying on the floor in a stinking cell. She did not break and stuck to her cover – a *bona fide* tourist who had lost her way. In the morning, after failing again to break her with threats and accusations, the police officers gave up and took her to another room where Avraham Gehmer was waiting. He hugged her and said: "I am proud of you." Only now she realized that her arrest and harsh interrogation had been an exercise, intended to test her behavior in a desperate situation.

The most exacting exercise, however, was the one Kfir and Gehmer had conceived especially for her. One night, they sent Sylvia to a Jordanian village across the border in order to find ways for a warrior to reach, undetected, the well in the village center. Sylvia did not know that the "Jordanian village" actually was Kafr Kassem, an Arab village in Israeli territory. In the map that Kfir and Gehmer gave Sylvia, they had erased the real border line, and moved it to the west, to make her believe that she was operating in enemy territory. Sylvia crossed the bogus border, entered the village stealthily, carried out her assignment, and "returned to Israel". In her debriefing she admitted that she had been frightened, a little bit.

Her training was over. Her instructors and Sylvia exchanged parting presents – Sylvia gave Kfir and Gehmer their portraits she had sketched; they gave her a set of watercolors and a copy of the famous Rudyard Kipling poem "If", then took her to a graduation dinner in a Yemenite restaurant. Gehmer sent an official report to his superiors:

"The candidate was discovered to possess outstanding character traits. She is very thorough, extremely intelligent and has the capacity of learning and absorbing large amounts of information...she exhibits high motivation and absolute identification with the Jewish people.... All her instructors sing her praises. She received excellent grades throughout the training period. She exhibited initiative and ingenuity in infiltrating highly guarded areas and successfully completed investigative missions... She has a unique ability to adjust to difficult situations... and carry out what is required of her in the best possible way."

*

Mike Harari watched from afar his new Caesarea warrior build her cover. Together with the Mossad experts he created for her a "legend" of a foreign professional photographer. Sylvia was sent to an intensive course with Paul Goldman, one of the most famous press photographers in Israel. Goldman had documented the last years of the British Mandate and the first years of Israel in 40,000 negatives; he had gained world fame when he photographed Prime Minister Ben-Gurion standing on his head at Tel Aviv beach... Goldman initiated Sylvia in the art of photographing, and took her with him to some of his assignments, including a visit to Ben-Gurion's home. She assisted Goldman while he was taking photos of "the Old Man". Ben-Gurion himself spoke with her and was interested in her experience as "a volunteer" in Israel. If he only knew, she thought...

At the end of this stage. Sylvia had to go abroad in order to establish her cover story. She received a Canadian passport on the name of Patricia Roxburgh. She did not know that Patricia Roxburgh was not an invention! Patricia really existed. She was a Canadian, a chubby and bored young woman, employed in the Wills and Legacies department of a Montreal lawyers' firm. One day, during a trip to Niagara Falls, her Jewish boyfriend hugged her warmly. "Do me a favor", he said.

"Anything", she managed.

"Lend me your passport for a year or two. Israel needs it."

How could she refuse?

The Mossad experts cooked the passport, and replaced Patricia's photograph with Sylvia's picture. Sylvia became Miss Roxburgh, a press photographer and an aspiring painter. She flew to Canada and rented an apartment on Vancouver Island. Victoria, the major city on the island and the capital of British Columbia, was a charming town, proud of its large artists' colony and its old neighborhoods, whose streets and buildings seemed transported from the nineteenth century.

Sylvia quickly adapted to her life in picturesque Victoria. As a savvy young woman, cheerful and easygoing, she made quite a few friends, started photographing and published some photos in the local press. After six months, when her cover seemed solid, she flew to Paris and rented a studio in the city center. In the meantime, a Mossad collaborator, an Englishman, with connections all over Europe, activated his contacts in Paris. A famous Parisian lawyer joined the operation and called Louis Delmas, a famous writer, journalist, radio anchorman and the owner of a photographic agency. On his recommendation, Delmas invited Patricia to his office. He had no idea who she really was, and never suspected her of being a Mossad amazon. But when he saw her photographs, he was very impressed, and offered her a job.

A few weeks later he gave Patricia her first assignment. Djibouti.

*

The Air France plane landed in Djibouti, a French colony on the Horn of Africa, to the sound of gunfire and the ominous glow of fires that raged in the small city. The few passengers gathered their belongings and hurried to two ramshackle buses that headed to the city, escorted by French paratroopers in armored cars. From the bus window Sylvia watched the dead bodies lying by the road, beside houses in ruins and burnt-out cars. She started clicking her camera. The gunshots grew louder as they approached the city. Gangs of Afars and Issas, the main tribes in the minuscule Djibouti, wandered in the streets and exchanged automatic fire, while the paratroopers and Foreign Legion fighters kept trying, in vain, to stop them. A few bands were busy looting stores or firing at the white settlers' homes. These were the worst riots in years.

Patricia checked in the Miramar hotel. Armed guards stood at the entrance. She sent her luggage to her room and hurried out, despite the anxious warnings of the hotel staff. They tried to explain that the situation in the streets was out of control and the wild riots might degenerate into a massive massacre. She did not listen. Armed with her cameras, she walked the city streets during the following days, and reached devastated neighborhoods, miserable shantytowns and scenes of fighting. She photographed militants of both sides, gutted out houses, families mourning their dead, wounded children and women. She sent her photos to Paris with the planes of the French Air Force. She was the only photographer at the Djibouti riots, and her photos were printed in newspapers and magazines all over the world. This first mission on behalf of the Delmas agency was crowned with great success.

Shortly after her return to France, Sylvia got a call from Louis Delmas. He said he wanted to set up an exhibition of her Djibouti photos in Paris. The French Ministry of Culture also was interested to sponsor the event. "We'll call it 'Living proof from Djibouti – the photography of Patricia Roxburgh." She hesitated at first – she was not interested in personal exposure – but finally agreed. And so, the Djibouti exhibition was inaugurated at a lavish reception in the halls of the famous Ritz hotel, at Place Vendome. Sylvia's photographs from Djibouti, in color and black and white, hung on the walls. A select crowd of businessmen, media moguls, government officials and foreign diplomats assisted at the party. Expensive suits brushed against fashionable gowns, waiters in white jackets served champagne and snacks. And the belle of the ball, in a black evening gown, lovely, tall and slender, was of course Patricia Roxburgh.

While she chatted and joked with the guests, Sylvia noticed an elegant gentleman who followed her and seemed very interested to talk to her. Finally, he approached and introduced himself. He was the ambassador of Jordan in France. They chatted a while and she told him how interested she was to photograph people and landscapes in the exotic Arab lands.

"Would you have lunch with me?" he asked. A few days later, when they met in a Parisian restaurant, she was in for a surprise. The ambassador, speaking on behalf of his government, invited her to visit Jordan as an official guest of the Crown.

She loved the idea, Louis Delmas was excited, and the Mossad gave the green light. Her trip to Jordan lasted a week. She got a warm welcome, toured the country and took her pictures. Everything was perfect except for an incident during her visit to Al-Wehdat refugee camp. While she stood there, taking photographs, she was assailed by several young men, armed with submachine guns, who shouted that she was a Zionist spy. They were Palestinian terrorists; they snatched her camera, took the film out of it, and one of them was sent to develop it. She faced them with firmness and poise. Finally, the guy returned with the negatives that showed nothing but landscapes and portraits. The Palestinians calmed down, returned the camera to Sylvia, and apologized.

Before she left, she was invited to the Royal palace, where she photographed King Hussein and his family. This was her first – but by far not the last – of her visits to the palace. During her following trips to Jordan she kept photographing the Royal family and became friendly with Hussein and his queen.

Shortly after returning to Paris, Sylvia heard two short knocks on her apartment door; they were followed by a moment of silence, then two more knocks. That was the Mossad code, and she opened the door. Avraham Gehmer walked in; he had been assigned as her handler in Paris. Some moments later, more knocks. This time it was Motti Kfir. Lately he had been appointed head of the Caesarea operational headquarters in Europe. "You're leaving tomorrow," Avraham said. "We've got to hit someone."

She took the night train to Rome, where she met with Mike Harari. He introduced her to another Caesarea warrior, Shlomo Gal. Belgian born, tall, bespectacled, his forehead crowned by an unruly forelock, Shlomo was a gifted painter. He had spent a few years in the IDF before joining the Mossad, had been wounded in several battles and decorated for courage in the battlefield.

Mike briefed the two of them. They were to play the role of a newly married couple of artists, traveling to Libya on their honeymoon. They would get a car, drive to Naples and reach Libya by ferryboat. Explosive charges would be planted in the car by a Mossad team. Sylvia and her "husband" had to reach Tripoli and park the car in a square, close to the home of "the target", a major leader in Muammar Gaddafi's administration. The target was a staunch ally of Palestinian terrorists, financed their operations and supplied them with weapons and intelligence. He was dangerous and had to be killed.

In a few days a national holiday would be celebrated in Tripoli, and the target was supposed to leave his home in the square. Mike instructed Sylvia and Shlomo to watch the house from a nearby position and activate the explosives by remote control the moment the target came out of home. Attentive to every detail, Mike also gave wedding rings to the newlyweds.

The following morning Sylvia and Shlomo put on their rings, received their car and drove to Naples. An unexpected hitch, however, almost aborted the mission. The couple was already in the port, when it turned out that all the ferryboat tickets had been sold out; the Mossad officer who was supposed to buy their tickets had failed to do so. They had to get on the ferryboat, come what may, because the mission depended on their arrival in Tripoli a few days before the hit. At this moment, Shlomo and Sylvia got a glimpse of Mike's ingenuity. He darted to the loading area of the ferryboat, deftly slipped a wad of bills in the hands of Giovanni, the official in charge of boarding cars and passengers – and the explosive car with the two Mossad warriors smoothly rolled into the boat's belly.

They arrived in Tripoli, checked in a hotel and parked the car at the designed spot in the square. They also found a position, near a bustling café, that offered an unobstructed view of the target's house. Now all they needed was the final order from headquarters, to activate the explosives. Till then, they had to wait at the hotel. They sat in their room and waited. Sylvia, however, was restive. She feared that the hotel staff might get suspicious of these two foreigners who were spending the days sitting in their room and doing nothing. She rushed to the hotel reception, and sent one of the employees to buy painting utensils – tripods, canvases, colors, brushes... The moment the Libyan brought them the materials, she and Shlomo placed the tripods in their room and started painting the mosque and the buildings they could see from their windows.

The cleaning women and the other service employees saw the paintings; very soon everybody in the hotel knew that the honeymooners were a couple of dedicated artists, who could not resist the opportunity to paint the exotic views of Tripoli.

Finally, the authorization code arrived from Paris. The holiday was tomorrow; Shlomo and Sylvia passed a tense, stressful night, waiting for the sunrise. But when morning came and they rushed to the square, they found out that the place was full of festive crowds, families with children, merry groups of teenagers. Close to the target's house, street vendors had established their stalls, selling fast food, souvenirs and flags. Shlomo flashed a message to headquarters, saying the mission can be carried out, but many civilians may be killed. The answer arrived at once: "Mother is ill. Return home immediately!"

The mission was aborted. The two warriors got in the car, and a few hours later were in the ferryboat again, sailing back to Italy. They got on the upper deck, removed their wedding rings and threw them in the ocean. The honeymoon was over. They returned to Paris in the same train, but in different cars.

Despite the cancellation of their assignment, Sylvia was delighted. "I'll never forget," she told her superiors, "that you canceled an operation so as not to harm innocent bystanders. I'm so impressed by your moral standards."

*

In the early sixties, the Mossad gradually changed its major functions from being an intelligence gathering organization into a shock unit fighting terrorism. On January 1, 1965, the Palestine Liberation Organization, created by Yasser Arafat and his cronies, carried out the first coup of its military wing, the Fatah, in Israel. A commando coming from Jordan tried to bomb some targets in Israel and failed; but in the following months and years the Fatah activity increased, resulting in bombings and murders.

In one of the early operations against the terrorists, Sylvia Rafael was sent to Beirut. According to Dr. Ronen Bergman's account, the Ramsad had convinced Prime Minister Levi Eshkol of the necessity to assassinate Yasser Arafat and several Fatah leaders. That was to be accomplished by sending them letters containing, each, 20 grams of explosives, a lethal dose. The letters had to be sent and postmarked from Beirut in order to look authentic. Sylvia flew to Beirut, purchased stamps and dropped the letters in the Lebanese mailboxes. The letters reached their destination, but the results were disappointing – some of the letters did not explode, some were defused by their suspicious targets; a few Arabs were lightly wounded. The operation was called off.

Sylvia was already back in Paris, but soon plunged again into a hectic succession of missions. She was often sent to professional assignments by Louis Delmas, but in most cases she traveled on Mossad missions. From Paris she flew to Damascus, Baghdad, Amman and Cairo, and even to North Africa. Protected by the Patricia Roxburgh identity, she collected intelligence and even participated in violent coups against terrorist groups. Using her photographer cover, she visited the camps of Palestinian terrorists in Jordan and Lebanon. She was never suspected, even when red alert was proclaimed in some Arab countries. According to one version, she stood on her Cairo hotel balcony on June 5 1967 and watched the Israeli Air Force jets, as they dived over the International airport, triggering the Six Day War.

In 1968, on her thirty-first birthday, Sylvia was sent by Delmas to photograph the launching of a new river boat in the Seine River. The launching ended, as usual, with a party on deck. Mingling with the merry crowd, Sylvia discovered that she was not the only photographer covering the event. On the deck she met a handsome young man, light-haired and blue-eyed, armed with a professional camera. He introduced himself as Eric Strauss (a fictitious name), a photographer with the famous Magnum agency. She noticed that he was quite interested in her and not only as a competitor . . . When food was served, they sat together. He was smart, witty, amusing with his stories about his travels and his hobby – mountain climbing. He was younger, less than thirty, and she liked him. A lot.

The sad part in her life was the loneliness. She needed human warmth and love, perhaps even more than other amazons. Her letters to her family in South Africa, bare of any hint about her real work, were full of longing and love. But letters to her parents could not dissipate her feeling of solitude. Between the missions she lived all alone, without friends and family, without the possibility to share with someone even an innocent experience. She strolled alone in the city, went alone to the movies, to concerts, to museums... And suddenly, here was this young man.

When the party was over, Eric invited her to dinner, but she refused, fearing that he could be a foe in disguise, an enemy agent who was trying to approach her. She took his phone number and promised to call; but her first call was to Gehmer, her Mossad handler. She told him that she liked Eric Strauss, and wanted to see him again.

"Let me check that," Gehmer said.

The Mossad did not approve of intimate relationships between its warriors and strangers; on the other hand, it did not want to deprive them of the last remnant of normal life. Sylvia was a young, hot blooded and romantic woman. If the man was clean, her handlers thought, they should not object to their relations. The Mossad experts immediately got into the matter. A request from the German intelligence service produced a detailed file on Eric Strauss; another file was supplied by Interpol. Reports also arrived from colleagues in the French services. The investigation result was clear: Eric Strauss was indeed Eric Strauss, with no suspicious activities or connections.

Sylvia got the green light, and the same evening she called Eric. They went out for drinks and dinner, and the dessert was a visit to Eric's bachelor flat, that ended in the morning. Sylvia left Eric's abode as a woman in love. She remembered her connection with Avri in Port Elizabeth, and only now realized that it had been nothing more than friendship. But for Eric she had fallen head over heels, and the same happened to him. Their affair turned into a passionate love story.

They spent a lot of time together. Occasionally she would inform him that she must travel on an assignment for Delmas, but never revealed the where, why and the probable length of her absence. He had no choice but get used to her mysterious voyages. She suffered from having to conceal her real occupation from her boyfriend, and after a few months came to her superiors with an original idea.

Eric, she said, lately had resigned from Magnum. He was looking for a different job, challenging and exciting. Why not recruit him to the Mossad? That way, she thought, the last barrier between the two of them would be removed.

Mike Harari hesitated, but finally agreed. "I know a company that collects intelligence," she said to Eric. "They are looking for agents who could work for them in Europe and perhaps elsewhere. They are connected to Israel. Could that interest you?" He asked for more details, but she insisted that this was all she knew. Eric finally agreed to meet the "intelligence collectors". Several Mossad officers met him in Paris and interviewed him; then they flew him to Israel and lodged him in a Mossad apartment on Bloch Street, in Tel Aviv. The preliminary talks continued in a Mossad safehouse, where he met more Mossad experts and a psychologist. The Mossad also organized sightseeing tours throughout Israel for the prospective recruit.

Eric quickly realized that he was being screened in order to join the Mossad. He also learned that his girlfriend, Patricia, was a Mossad warrior. That revelation dissipated his doubts about her mysterious trips. He agreed to the Mossad offer, and after long months of training returned to Paris as a Caesarea warrior. His relationship with Sylvia became even closer once they could talk openly about their work.

But their elation evaporated very soon. Eric's commanders decided to infiltrate him into an Arab capital as a resident agent, for the next few years. At first he and Sylvia believed that they could maintain their relationship during his visits to Paris; but soon it became clear that this was impossible. They were not allowed to exchange letters or messages, and phone each other; the dates of their vacations did not match; gradually they grew apart and their mutual feelings faded away. Ironically, it was his joining the Mossad that caused the collapse of their love. The disappointed Sylvia never forgave herself for her initiative. She was in her thirties and her dream to start a family one day, and to have children, seemed now to be a mission impossible.

Perhaps because of that failure, she acted differently the second time she fell in love. Two years later, in Paris, she met a young reporter of the London Times. His name was Jon Swain and he was only 21. He felt that she was "pursuing" him and "made sure she was the subject of his desire." Her beauty, her sagacity and her charm conquered him and he fell in love. They spent impassioned nights in her little apartment on the right bank of Paris. With one difference from Patricia's affair with Eric Strauss: this time she did not inform her superiors.

The affair developed without nobody at the Mossad having an inkling about it. According to Jon Swain, Patricia was extremely interested in Libya and Gaddafi, and suggested that the two of them travel to Tripoli; he would interview Gaddafi and she would take his photographs. He agreed but failed to obtain an entry visa to Libya and that was the end of the project.

Their affair lasted long months and peacefully died as time went by. And only in 1973, when the real identity of Patricia was exposed, (See Chapter 12) Swain experienced the shock of his life. Years later, he candidly revealed his affair with Sylvia Rafael, "a trained assassin" in an article in the Sunday Times: "Fresh-faced, I fell into the honey trap laid by Israel's Mata Hari." Jon Swain described his affair with Sylvia Rafael – now he knew her real name – and concluded his article: "I will always look back with amazement at my brush with the world of international espionage and the fact that the lovely girl I had known was a spy who killed in cold blood".

*

On September 5, 1972, Sylvia was alone at her Paris apartment, when "Breaking News" flashes on the television reported a bloody terrorist attack in Munich, where the Olympic Games were in full swing. The reports mentioned the Palestinian terrorist organization "Black September". The terrorists, the first reports said, broke into the Olympic village, killed and sequestered Israeli athletes.

Black September was a new terrorist group, created only lately and in deep secrecy by Yasser Arafat.

Those days, the Fatah organization was in deep crisis. The Fatah terrorists had been expelled from Jordan in September 1970, when King Hussein felt that he was losing control over his kingdom. Since the 1967 Six Day War and the debacle of the Arab armies, the terrorists had become the only force that continued fighting against Israel; their popularity and appeal had greatly increased and many young Palestinians had joined their organizations. The Fatah members had turned Jordan into their main base. They moved through the country with their weapons in total impunity; they gained control over the refugee camps, many neighborhoods in Amman, towns and villages along the Jordan River, which had become the border between Israel and Jordan. For them, King Hussein's authority did not exist anymore. They had become Jordan's real masters. The king hesitated for a long time about the measures to take. His army, as well, was becoming frustrated and restive. When King Hussein visited the armored corps, he saw a brassiere flying like a flag from a tank antenna. "What's this?" he angrily growled.

"This means that we are women," the tank commander answered. "You do not let us fight."

Finally, Hussein decided to get his country back, and unleashed his army against the terrorist bases and the refugee camps. It was a terrible massacre, with thousands killed. Terrorists were shot in the streets, hunted and executed without trial, while the Jordanian artillery mercilessly shelled the refugee camps. During the massacre, most of the terrorists escaped to Syria and Lebanon. The Palestinians would remember the month September 1970 as "Black September."

Yasser Arafat became obsessed with revenge. He was trying, however, to project an image of a peaceful man, determined to find a solution to the Palestinian problem without bloodshed. He could not send the Fatah, that was identified with him, to violent revenge operations. Therefore, he decided to create, inside the Fatah, a new, ultra-secret, terrorist organization, that would carry out bloody coups against his enemies. That organization would deny any connection with Arafat's Fatah, and be free to bomb and massacre, while Arafat entered the UN Assembly Hall, with an olive branch in his hand. He named the new organization "Black September". Black September's chief was Abu Yussef, one of the major Fatah leaders, but its real commander was a young, handsome and charismatic man, Ali Hassan Salameh, nicknamed by his comrades "the Red Prince."

The first operations of Black September were directed against Jordan – sabotage, assassinations of secret agents, murder of a former Jordanian Prime Minister as a vengeance for September 1970. But after the attacks on Jordan – came a bloody attack on Israel.

*

Sylvia, in tears, helplessly watched the unfolding story of Black September's attack in Munich. Eight armed terrorists, wearing ski masks, had broken into the Israeli apartment at the Olympic Village. They killed two team members and took nine hostages. The German police arrived but seemed at a loss facing the terrorists. Reporters, photographers and television crews from all over the world clustered around the Olympic Village, and for the first time in history the public could watch an ongoing terrorist operation. Israel offered to send over the IDF special anti-terrorist commandos, but Germany refused. Thanks but no, thanks, the Germans said, we are in control and we know how to handle the situation. The only concession they made was to allow the Ramsad, Zvi Zamir, to fly to Munich and watch the operation of the Bavarian police to neutralize the terrorists.

The German police tried to trap the terrorists by a ruse: they offered them safe passage to an Arab country of their choice, if they agreed to release the hostages. Black September agreed; the terrorists and their prisoners were driven to the Fürstenfeldbruck airport where an aircraft allegedly was waiting for them. The terrorists immediately saw through the scheme, and a firefight erupted between them and the German police. During the ensuing shootout the terrorists murdered all the hostages. A German police officer was also killed as well as five of the eight terrorists. The other three were captured but released after the hijacking of a Lufthansa aircraft by another Black September commando.

The Ramsad Zvi Zamir returned to Israel after witnessing the appalling incompetence of the German police. Prime Minister Golda Meir was devastated. "Once again," she said, "bound and tied Jews are being murdered on German soil." Golda, traumatized, decided that she would not let the Munich massacre go without punishment.

But how?

A few days after the Munich massacre Zvi Zamir and Aharon Yariv, the Prime Minister's adviser on terrorism, came to Golda's office. They warned her that Black September intended to launch an all-out war against Israel and several Western countries. We must stop them, they said. We cannot kill and capture all the Black September terrorists. The only way to prevent their attacks is to find and kill their leaders. Zamir and Yariv also hinted that the Munich massacre should be avenged. We have the men, they said. Caesarea is ready to undertake the assignment and go after the terrorist chiefs. Crush the snake's head, Golda's visitors said, and Black September will collapse.

Golda hesitated for a long time. It was not easy for her to send out a team of young people on an assassination campaign. She started speaking in a low voice, as if to herself. She spoke about the tragic march of the Jewish people, always persecuted and massacred. She spoke of the Holocaust. Finally, she raised her head. "Send the boys," she said.

Zamir called Mike Harari, the new chief of Caesarea, and appointed him commander of the operation, that he called "Wrath of God."

But Golda believed that she must establish a civilian control of the operation. She could not rely only on Yariv and Zamir's promise that the Caesarea team would hit only terrorist leaders. She had to make sure that innocent people would not be killed. She therefore created a top-secret committee that included, beside her, Defense Minister Moshe Dayan and Deputy Prime Minister Yigal Allon. The three of them became a sort of tribunal that had to review and approve any killing by the "Wrath of God" team. They were called the X committee. Yariv and Zamir were instructed to submit every file and name to the trio for approval. But who was responsible enough, cool headed enough and knowledgeable enough, to prepare the files? Zamir immediately summoned the best person for the job. Aliza Magen.

Aliza Magen had been very active in the Mossad since the campaign against the German scientists. In early 1965 she had prepared, together with Yehudit Nissiyahu the Mossad mission to locate and kill the Nazi criminal Herberts Cukurs in Montevideo,

She later participated and commanded many Mossad missions abroad. During that time, she became a close collaborator of Mike Harari, whom she held in high esteem. And in 1972 she was appointed main referent at the "Wrath of God" operation. Aliza and her team prepared the files of the terrorist chiefs who had to be killed. "At first we collected all the materials about them," she said years later. "We got information from AMAN, from Shabak and other sources, and [we had to answer] what did each of them do, to deserve becoming our client."

The first of them was Wael Adel Zwaiter. Aliza's people had worked for weeks, shadowing and researching him, till they got the proof that he was Black September's commander in Rome.

The "Wrath of God" mission had its first volunteer – Sylvia Rafael.

*

On the very morning after the Munich tragedy, Sylvia rushed to "David", her new handler in Paris. The horrible picture from Munich haunted her; she was distressed and miserable. She demanded to be included in any mission against the massacre perpetrators. David promised to forward her request to his superiors, but warned her that such decisions were taken by pragmatic considerations and not by the warriors' personal demands. She brushed off his warnings; he had never seen her so agitated.

For a month nothing happened. Sylvia ground her teeth and waited. One evening, in early October, she entered the Olympia Hall on Boulevard des Capucines in Paris, went along the back corridor to the stage, and photographed the greatest French singer, Yves Montand, at a live show before an enthusiastic audience. Then she hurried to the Delmas offices and delivered her film for development. She was back home after midnight, and the phone was ringing.

David was on the line. "I am sorry to tell you that your sister has been wounded in a car accident," he said in English. "Her condition is grave...We should go to visit her tomorrow."

She immediately understood the meaning of the code formulas. An urgent mission was to be launched, and she had to participate in it. The following morning, she met with David, and a few hours later she boarded the night train to Rome. She could not sleep during the trip.

At Rome Central Station a Caesarea warrior was waiting for her. She did not know him but she recognized him by his blue necktie, strewn with tiny white stars, that David had described. He introduced himself as "Danny" and handed her a bag in which a hidden camera had been installed. After she left her luggage in the hotel, where a room on the name of Patricia Roxburgh had been reserved, Danny led her to one of the more elegant streets of the Italian capital and pointed at a mid-sized building. "This is the Libyan embassy," he said. "There is a clerk there, Wael Adel Zwaiter."

Danny described Zwaiter to Sylvia and gave her a detailed file about him. Sylvia realized that the man personified the deviousness of Black September. On the face of it. Wael Zwaiter was a bashful Palestinian, skinny, vegetarian, soft-spoken, a sworn opponent of all kinds of violence. Born in Nablus, a graduate of Damascus and Baghdad universities in Philosophy and Classical Arab literature, he was the 30-year-old son of a family of teachers and intellectuals. His father, Muhammad, was a well-known historian and an excellent translator of Rousseau and Voltaire into Arabic. His aunt Faiza was one of the leading intellectuals in Nablus. Wael had been living in Rome for the last fourteen years and worked as an interpreter at the Libyan embassy for the meager monthly salary of 100 Libyan pounds. Like his father, he used to translate books and articles from and to Arabic.

In the Roman Arab community, the gentle Zwaiter was known as a pacifist who rejected terror and violence, and some rumors maintained that in the past he had suggested to the Israelis to establish a Palestinian State in Jordan and the West Bank.

What the public did not know was that this nice Dr. Jekyll kept secretly metamorphosing into a Mr. Hyde, a sworn, cruel terrorist, who headed the Black September secret section in Rome. Lately, acting on Zwaiter's orders, two handsome Palestinians had seduced two English girls on a tourist trip to Rome. They convinced the gullible girls to extend their trip to Israel; the Palestinian Casanovas promised to join them in a few days. In the meantime, they talked the girls into bringing some presents to their relatives living in the West Bank. One of the presents was an expensive record-player. The girls did not know, of course, that their new boyfriends were sending them to their death: the exquisite present was loaded with explosives and equipped with an altimeter; it was going to explode the moment the plane reached a cruising altitude. The two girls checked in their luggage at the airport and took off in an El Al plane to Israel. The charge exploded indeed in the storage compartment of the plane; but following some previous attempts to blow up an El Al plane in flight, the airplanes storage compartments had been covered with thick armor plates, and the explosion did not damage the aircraft. The plane landed at once, the two English girls were located; the Palestinians, of course, had left Italy a few days before, but their traces led to Wael Zwaiter. He was questioned by the police and released. The Italians did not find anything.

But others did.

That day in October, when he walked out of the embassy, Zwaiter did not notice a couple of lovers sitting in a car facing the building. The woman was holding her large bag in a strange manner. Patricia Roxburgh was taking photos again, but this time she did not send them to the Delmas agency. Instead, the film was sent to "Hadar-Dafna", a huge, fortress-like building on King Saul Boulevard in Tel Aviv, that housed the Mossad Headquarters.

During the following days Patricia and Danny followed Zwaiter. They found out the names and addresses of his friends, and his own address, a modest apartment on Piazza Annibaliano. In the meantime, some warriors arrived from Israel, rented a car and apartments that would serve as safehouses. On October 17 Sylvia and Danny followed Zwaiter after he left the embassy, and went to the home of a friend, Janet von Braun. The fifty-years-old lady had prepared a light dinner, and at 22:30 Zwaiter went home after buying rolls, a newspaper and a bottle of fig wine in the neighborhood store. In his pocket Zwaiter was carrying a copy of the book "A thousand and one nights" that he was translating in Italian.

A middle-aged couple passed by him; these were Mossad warriors charged with making sure that he was their man.

In the building, by the elevator, two strangers were waiting for Zwaiter, and shot him with twelve Beretta 0.22 bullets.

That same evening, Sylvia took the night train to Paris.

*

Now that Zwaiter had been killed, his deep cover was no longer necessary. A Beirut paper published his obituary signed by several terrorist organizations that mourned Zwaiter as "one of our best combatants."

But he had not been the only wolf in sheep clothing.

In early December the phone rang in the Paris apartment of Dr. Mahmoud Hamshari, a leftist scholar and historian of Palestinian origin. Hamshari picked up the receiver.

"This is Patricia Roxburgh. Remember me?"

"Of course." Hamshari had met Patricia years before, at the opening of her Djibouti exhibition. "How are you? Preparing a new exhibit?"

"I sure am." She eagerly described the new exhibition she was preparing, consisting mostly of portraits; she also spoke of her trips to Jordan and the great photographs she had taken there. Then she added: "I'd like to interview you."

"About what?"

"Your academic work and your political opinions."

He answered that he already had been interviewed for the Paris weekly "Jeune Afrique" [Young Africa]. He was cautious and wary; he did not want to be interviewed again right now. Lately, after Zwaiter's assassination in Rome, he was taking strict precautions. In the street, he was watching for people who might be following him; he left cafes and restaurants before his food was brought to his table; and often asked his neighbors if any strangers had inquired about him.

"Your interview in "Jeune Afrique" was published a year ago", Patricia said. She kept asking and he finally surrendered. They agreed to meet in a few days, in a café that he had chosen, not far from his home at 175, Alesia Street.

Sylvia put down the phone receiver. She knew that she had to meet and keep Hamshari for at least an hour. She also knew the truth on the suave Palestinian, who had been living in Paris for quite a few years with his French wife, Marie-Claude and their little daughter. He indeed was the official representative of Arafat's PLO (Palestine Liberation Organization) in Paris, but it was common knowledge that he condemned violence and terrorism. Annie Franco, who had interviewed him for "Jeune Afrique" a year before, had written: "He is engaged only in diplomatic and informative activity. He does not need any precautions because he is not dangerous. The Israeli secret services know that well."

Well, the Israeli secret services, and Sylvia Rafael, knew a few more things that Franco did not know. Franco did not know about the young Palestinians who used to visit Hamshari's apartment in the late afternoon, carrying heavy suitcases. Hamshari's Portuguese maid was not allowed to get out of the kitchen during these visits. Franco did not know either, that Hamshari had participated in the plot to assassinate David Ben-Gurion in Denmark in 1969; nor about his involvement in the 1970 explosion of a Swissair liner bound for Israel that took the lives of forty-seven people. Today Hamshari was the second-in command of Black September in Europe, and his home served as a weapons store for the terrorists that operated throughout the continent.

Sylvia's interview with Dr. Hamshari lasted about an hour. She diligently noted his answers and took a few pictures of him. At the same time two Mossad warriors penetrated in Hamshari's empty apartment and went to work on the telephone in his study.

The following day, December 8, at 8:00 in the morning Marie-Claude Hamshari left home with her little girl. Half an hour later, a car arrived and parked by the curb, across the street from the house. Two men sat in the car. A third man walked into the neighboring café and ordered coffee and croissants. He asked permission to use the phone on the counter and dialed a number he knew by heart.

"Hello?" A man's voice.

"May I speak to Dr. Hamshari?"

"Speaking."

The caller raised his left hand. From the car windows, across the street, the two men watched the café. When they saw the prearranged sign, one of them pressed a button in the remote control device he was holding. Hamshari heard a shrill whistle in the receiver, and a thunderous explosion ensued. A large explosive charge had been placed under the desk. Hamshari collapsed, seriously wounded. He died in the hospital a few days later. Before his death, he whispered to his friends: "This is the Mossad. Nobody but them could have done that."

*

These were the first missions of "Wrath of God." After them came several operations, in Cyprus, Athens, Cyprus again, Paris again… Sylvia played a major role in the missions. One after the other, Black September's arch-terrorists in Europe were eliminated.

But the leaders of the organization, and among them the mysterious Red Prince, were not bothered, and for one reason: they stayed safe and protected in Beirut, beyond the Mossad's reach.

Or were they?

CHAPTER 12

Yael

A screenplay about an English adventuress

NOVEMBER 1972, LONDON
"What exactly would you like to see?" asked Emily Jones, (fictitious name) one of the veteran guides of the Victoria and Albert Museum in London. In front of her stood Sharon Harris (fictitious name), a young, pretty and slim woman whom she already had seen several times walking through the exhibit halls of the museum, as if looking for something specific.

"I'm looking for a story about some woman, perhaps British", Sharon answered with an American accent, "who might have traveled to some faraway country and was active there... Some story which is not widely known."

"For what purpose, if I may?"

"I am a writer, I want to write a screenplay about a strong, bold woman in the past who had sailed to some exotic country, perhaps in the Middle East..."

The Middle East? Perhaps Gertrude Bell, Emily Jones thought, but then dismissed the idea. Gertrude Bell, who had journeyed to the Middle East in the early twentieth century, was considered one of the founders of modern Iraq and had wielded a strong political influence. But she was already the subject of many books, articles, research papers and documentary films. Lately Jones had heard rumors about a feature film on Bell's life that was said to be in the making.

Then Jones had an idea. "Come," she said, and led Sharon to a wing closed to the public. It housed rooms where artifacts, manuscripts, documents, and memorabilia of historical figures were stored. The two entered a small room. Along the wall, Sharon saw cupboards containing scores of drawers, labeled by subjects, dates and names.

Jones opened several drawers, one after the other. They held boxes with writings of people from the past – diaries, letters, official documents and books. She gave several boxes to Sharon Harris, but after a brief glance the young woman returned them.

"Perhaps this may interest you," Jones said after a while, taking another box from a drawer. It bore the name "Lady Hester Stanhope". And from another drawer, much larger, she took out a few old books, and a stack of yellowing papers, covered with handwriting.

Sharon picked up the books, the three volumes of "Memories of Lady Hester Stanhope as told to her personal physician Dr. Charles Louis Marion." They had been published in 1845. Sharon started leafing through them and the handwritten letters. Jones then was struck by Marilyn's sudden burst of excitement. These books and letters told the amazing story of a British noblewoman, the niece of Britain's Prime Minister William Pitt the Younger. She had run away from her despotic father at the end of the seventeenth century and was appointed secretary to the Prime Minister. After Pitt's death she became notorious in London, mostly due to a few sensational love affairs. She then left England, sailed to the Middle East and had many adventures and new lovers, then landed in Lebanon, where she lived for the rest of her life with a guard of faithful Druze and Bedouin warriors.

Sharon's eyes were shining. Here was the kind of story she was looking for – a noblewoman's life, intrigues in London, scandalous love affairs, reckless journeys in foreign lands, death in a dark castle in the mountains…

She asked Jones if she could come back the following day to

continue her reading. Jones agreed, and Sharon started visiting the Victoria and Albert daily to research the fascinating story of Lady Hester.

Jones gladly helped, but could not guess that Sharon Harris was not Sharon Harris, and not a screen writer – but a Mossad agent named Yael (born Elaine), preparing for a secret mission that would amaze the world.

*

Elaine had not been a Zionist, neither were her parents, who also had no interest in their Jewish religion. Born in Canada, she grew up in Princeton, New Jersey, where her physicist father was engaged in research. Science was all that mattered to him. In their neighborhood there were only three Jewish families. Every December Elaine's family had a Christmas tree. And the only time Elaine encountered anti-Semitism was when a kid, walking behind her in the street, shouted at her "Move, dirty Jew." The little girl turned back and responded: "I am a Jew but I am not dirty."

Little Elaine was amused by the frequent mistakes of the mailman who confused her father's name with Albert Einstein's, and kept delivering their mail – and vice versa – to the world-famous physicist who also lived and worked in Princeton.

Elaine was the third daughter in her family, "the prettiest but not the smartest" as she would admit. Her family was warm and loving, and she grew up as a "soft and innocent" child. But behind her softness, she developed a strong sense of justice and always took the side of the underdog, be it people or animals. She wrote a verse to the color purple which she considered undervalued.

"Purple became my favorite color,
It did not seem to fit into the everyday palette of life,
and seemed too obtrusive and forlorn,
I saw it as a kind of "underdog" and "dishonored" color
that deserved more attention, care and respect..."

Her first revolt against her family came when she brought home a black kid, braving America's informal apartheid. She on purpose started walking on the sidewalks reserved for blacks. Still, her friends and family remembered her as a quiet, introverted girl, who loved animals and wanted to become a veterinarian.

At her father's insistence, she enrolled in a prestigious nursing school, but then dropped out and took a new direction – computers. After graduating she got a good job in Manhattan – high salary, company car, great apartment. And after a stormy love affair she married Wayne, the son of a fiercely Zionist family, whose Zionism did not go as far, though, as immigrating to Israel.

Her marriage collapsed after five years, and she felt ashamed for what she regarded as her failure. Then she started looking for a different direction for her life. Her father had an Israeli cousin, Zevulun, who had been sent to the US as a representative of the Israeli aircraft industry. Elaine had long, fascinating conversations with him, and started thinking of going to Israel for a while, getting a job and learning Hebrew. She had started to feel a deep attachment to Israel. It was the world's underdog, she thought, a small nation surrounded by vile enemies sworn to annihilate it. Could she help? Then the 1967 Six Day War erupted, and she started packing. Her father was against it, but her mother kept quiet. Elaine left her apartment, sold her furniture, and as she put it, "stuffed her life in a small suitcase". When she landed in Israel she was 32, ready for her new life.

She got a job in a computer company and rented a small apartment in a high rise in Herzliya, an affluent suburb of Tel Aviv. She also bought a secondhand sports car; and that beautiful young woman in a shiny, roaring automobile in the Tel Aviv streets, was quite a sight.

But she made few friends and before long felt she did not really belong in Israeli society. She was lonely, melancholy, and found no interest in her way of life. She wanted only some peace and quiet, but Israel was not the serene land of her dreams. She thought of returning to the US, but then, during the 1968 War of Attrition and the bloody terrorist attacks she became overcome by a deep patriotic emotion, something she had never felt. So she decided to give Israel one more try.

She did not know Hebrew and that was a serious obstacle in her efforts to integrate. She enrolled in a night Ulpan – a Hebrew school. She did not learn much Hebrew there, but did meet one of the Ulpan employees, Ian, and they became close. He told her that he had a part time job at a branch of the Secret Service, in charge of the security of political leaders. And he also was connected to the Mossad, he said.

At first, she did not believe him and thought he was only trying to impress her. Until then she had had no interest in the shadow world of espionage and its cloak-and-dagger operations. But Ian's stories fascinated her, and she got hooked. She realized that if she were in the Mossad, she could devote her life to the defense of Israel. As she later said, she felt "an urge, that I could not otherwise describe, but as an overwhelming desire to join the Mossad....I was obsessive, I wanted to work there though I really did not know why. I felt that all my life I had been waiting for this moment." She had never liked the espionage movies; and she always felt it would be too scary to be a spy.

But she nonetheless asked Ian to introduce her to his Mossad friends. A few weeks later, in early 1971, she got a phone call. A voice asked her a question: "Elaine? Do you want to do something for Israel?"

"Yes", she said.

And that single word was to change her life.

*

A few days later, another phone call. "Can you come to Café Stern in Tel Aviv?" The voice gave her a date, an hour, and directions.

At Café Stern she was met by two young Mossad members, "Shlomo" and "Eitan". She did her best to impress them by wearing a new, elegant suit and arriving in her sports car. But this did not work very well, or so she thought, especially when she forgot where she had parked her car and had to ask the Mossad officers to help her find it. Only years later would she read the report that Shlomo had submitted to Mike Harari, the commander of "Caesarea": "A woman, very fashionable and elegant, not outstandingly beautiful but feminine and gracious, well-to-do (driving a Volvo sports car). And I hesitate.

On one hand, she is exactly what we are looking for; but something in her naivete, in her total motivation, makes me uncertain. Something like 'it's too good to be true.' Please meet her."

Elaine met Mike at the old Mossad Headquarters, "Hadar Dafna House", an ugly, fortress-like building at King Saul Street in Tel Aviv. It was a Sabbath afternoon, and the labyrinthine corridors were deserted. Mike was waiting for her in a small, gray room. She did not know anything about him but felt impressed by his warmth, his pertinent questions and his deep voice. Somewhat embarrassed, she answered his questions, told him about her happy childhood in a secular Jewish family, her marriage that misfired, her reasons for coming to Israel. But Mike kept on being inquisitive. "Why did you come to Israel and not to France, for instance? How did your parents take it? What did your friends say? What happened to your dream when you had to adjust to life in Israel?"

"The dream almost fell apart", she admitted, and confessed that she had considered going back to America, but the struggle of the Israelis against all their foes made her feel that she, too, might now join the "togetherness" that characterized the Israeli society. She felt a deep desire to help Israel and went as far as saying that Israel was today in dire straits, like a child who needs her, Eileen, as a parent. Yet she could not pinpoint the event or the process that had ignited in her this overwhelming urge to join the Mossad.

For a long moment Mike did not speak. He felt that Elaine was an innocent and naïve woman; he doubted her ability to withstand the pressure of covert work. "I realized that you were kind of an outsider," he told her years later, "used to live alone, but in need of a warm and caring environment, and I asked myself – would she truly be able to operate, alone, in a hostile environment?" He wondered if her femininity, her poise, and her beauty – Elaine's great assets – were not also her weaknesses. And her sudden urge to join the Mossad aroused his suspicion. "People who want too much", he often said, "always make me suspicious." As the meeting progressed, he remained still undecided. And yet, what tipped the scales for Mike, was the poignant moment when she looked him straight in the eyes and said: "I want to be worth something. I want to do something worthwhile. If I am to have any value in your eyes, I want to help Israel."

That heartfelt plea shook Mike. Elaine left with an awkward feeling, thinking that "it would never happen." But a month later, she was invited to the Ramsad himself. After meeting her, Zamir also hesitated. Could this young woman withstand the stress of covert operations in a cruel enemy country? But finally he accepted Mike's advice – and agreed to recruit her. Elaine was no more. "Yael" was born.

*

Four months later Yael was summoned to a Mossad course. "They called it "course", she recalled, "but I was the only student..." She spent days and many nights in a hotel room. Various Mossad officers came to this room where the "course" was conducted, lectured and briefed her on the different aspects of secret warfare. "I learned to identify tanks of different makes, to read a map, etc." They took her to a shooting range where she learned to shoot a gun. She also was sent out to field exercises. In one such exercise she was charged to convince a businessman that she was a welfare worker and make him donate samples of his products. She carried out exercises in the Tel Aviv streets, like spotting agents who were tailing her, shaking off the tails or finding ways to change her outward appearance in seconds. Sometimes she was given unexpected assignments by her instructor, Avraham, like: "See the apartment house across the street? In five minutes, I want to see you up on the third-floor balcony with a glass of water in your hand. Go!"

In retrospect, the course was the hardest period in her life. But she was determined to succeed and feared she would fail. All the time she was stressed and under pressure. One of her assignments was the classical Caesarea test that many other amazons had been subjected to: approaching a highly classified military compound and photographing it. She was sent to a military installation in Jerusalem, arrested by police, taken to a police station, and interrogated.

As in all the previous cases, teams of officers and detectives relayed each other through the long night, showing her the photos she had taken, shouting at her, hurling questions, blinding her with powerful lights. Under their pressure she gave confused answers but did not break down; nonetheless she felt that she had failed. Why was she arrested? What was her mistake that had attracted their attention?

At dawn, finally, they let her go, and, to her amazement, she met her instructors outside the police station. They told her it all had been an exercise, so as to check her capacity to withstand pressure. She had passed the exam, they said. But she realized that the night in the police station had shown her a new truth. She suddenly realized that things often are not what they seem to be, and behind every reality there well might be another, hidden truth. "My naivete and my direct and simple way of looking at people and events changed forever."

She gave her all to succeed in the course. And occasionally one of the Mossad people would throw at her: "Why do you make all these efforts for us?" She felt deeply hurt by this question. They still saw her as an outsider, somebody who does not belong, while she wanted them to feel that she was a part of this "us". One of her instructors told her once, rather surprised, that she seemed not to fear at all to go on a mission in an enemy country. But she felt a different fear, deep inside: a fear to fail in such a mission. She remained convinced that she must become a Caesarea warrior, and if she did – she would achieve great success. She also wanted to prove that a woman can be as able as a man, and her instructors promised her that if she succeeded in the course, she would get the same training and assignments as a man. At that time, Yael did not know of any other female warriors in Caesarea, but suspected she was not the only one.

During this course that lasted for months, she had no private life. Occasionally, she was able to go to her apartment for a few hours of sleep. She would cross her neighbors in the building lobby and muse about the difference between her and them. They had no idea, she thought. Once, in the underground parking, she saw a young, handsome man in a paratrooper's uniform, officer epaulets and a red beret. They exchanged long looks. She liked him. Then they crossed each other the following morning and exchanged a smile and a "Good morning" greeting. Wow, she thought, he lives in my building? And

The Syrian reactor. The secret photos, obtained by the "trio" warriors, saved Israel from a grave danger (US Government)

"Bomb the Syrian reactor!" asked Prime minister Olmert, but President Bush refused (Eli Ohayon, Israel's Government Press Office)

Sarah Aaronson – the first
female warrior in Palestine
(Courtesy of Aaronson House)

Yolande Harmor – the
enemy's war plans were sewn
in her shoulder pads
(Courtesy of the family)

Shula Cohen − "Monsieur Shula" −
sentenced to death by hanging
(Courtesy of the family)

Waltraud with Wolfgang Lotz in a Cairo night-club
(Egyptian Press, Yedioth Ahronoth Archive)

Marcell Ninio − the terrible tortures made her try to kill herself
(Egyptian Press, Yedioth Ahronoth Archive)

Yehudit Nissiyahu − Tata Juliette in Morocco, Flamenco in Buenos Ayres, and a wretched Orthodox woman in Antwerpen (Shaul Golan)

Isabel Pedro − In silk blouse and high heels, straight into the lion's mouth (Courtesy of the family)

Patricia Roxburgh in Jordan with the Queen and the children. Her real name – Sylvia Rafael, a Mossad warrior (Courtesy of the Royal Palace of Jordan)

Sylvia at Kibbutz Ramat Hakovesh
(Courtesy of the family)

Sylvia and her Norwegian husband.
(Courtesy of the family)

Yael. Golda kissed her and said: "This little girl did all that?"
(Courtesy of the family)

Mike Harari – The ultimate Israeli secret
warrior (Courtesy of the family)

Aliza Magen − She broke all the glass ceilings, and nobody was surprised
(Yuval Chen)

Cindy − a honey trap with no honey
(Yedioth Ahronoth Archives)

Yola − "Mudira Kabira", the desert queen, in Soudan (Courtesy of the family)

The Ramsad Yossi
Cohen hopes to see,
one day, a woman as
Head of Mossad
(Shaul Golan)

Israel's Security
Prize was awarded
to the team that stole
the Iranian Nuclear
Archive
(Chaim Tzach, Israel's
Government Press Office)

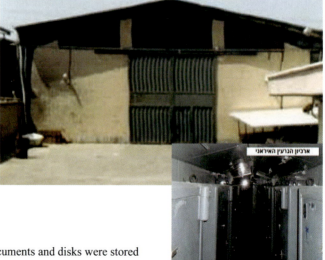

Only five Iranians
knew the whereabouts
of the Nuclear Archive.
Five Iranians – and the
Mossad
(US Government)

The safes where the documents and disks were stored
(US Government)

then, for a second, came a whiff from far away and she felt the desire to live a different life, one like any young woman her age. Just for a second – and then she pulled back.

She completed the course. Only years after retiring would she read her instructors' assessment: "... [She has a] serious attitude, very sincere and direct in her reports, including [reporting] her failures. She is very brave and daring, with an extraordinarily strong motivation, considering her mission as a service to the nation..." But, they added, "she still lacks self-confidence. Her persistence to execute her orders is extreme, and she might carry out her mission despite the risks involved." Their conclusion: "She would be best as number two to another warrior." They did not think she could carry out an assignment by herself and recommended she'd be employed at a secondary role.

Mike Harari, though, discarded the report. "There is in her," he said, "much more than you have seen. My decision is that she'll now start her service as a Caesarea warrior."

*

In May 1972, when she was 36, Yael landed in Brussels. This city had become the Mossad secret advance headquarters; after President de Gaulle's new hostile policy had forced the organization to abandon its Paris base. Now, Yael had to establish her European cover. She rented an apartment, applied for a postal address, opened a bank account, and got a job in a computer company. And though her course was over, now she still had to carry out several training missions, first in Europe, then in "target countries" meaning hostile Arab states. One of her first trips was in Egypt, where she happily rode a gray horse to the pyramids. Her cover was that of a scholar, researching inscriptions and documents about women in ancient Egypt.

She moved about under different covers. "I had many passports with different names from different countries. I was someone but I was no one." In Brussels she met her handler, Shaul, who knew everything about her. After several of her missions he reported to Mike Harari that Yael is "very cool, calm, understands the goal of each mission, uses her experience to achieve her task, displays a quiet and radiating confidence... Her femininity, her grace, good manners and very modest behavior, her discipline and refraining from argument, may be wrongly taken for frailty and dependence on strict orders. But she uses these qualities so as to chart her way and accomplish her mission." Shaul discerned in her an "unswerving determination to carry out any mission." Yael, indeed, learned to use her frailty and her apparent naivete as a tool, a means to gain the trust of strangers and make them want to help and protect this sweet woman.

In Brussels, Yael kept implementing her decision of focusing entirely on her operations and avoiding any outside distractions or commitments. Her neighbor was an old blind woman whom she spontaneously helped. They became close, but Yael put an end to that relationship. She had a short love affair with the manager of her computer company, Mark – but once again she retreated, despite the pain. She was determined to avoid intimacy which might lead to personal questions about her past, her friends and family. On a visit to Israel, she found a note in her mailbox, from a neighbor who had seen people entering her apartment in her absence and wanted to warn her. The note was signed by "Michael (the guy with the uniform)." She remembered him, the handsome paratrooper she had met in the parking area. Once again, she thought about him, but then just left a note on his windshield: "Everything is o.k., thank you, Yael." Again, she had turned the page. During her first assignment in Lebanon, she deftly eluded the courtship of a young French businessman, to concentrate on her reconnaissance mission.

In September 1972, after she returned from Beirut, she was shaken by news of the massacre of 11 Israeli athletes at the Munich Olympics. The Mossad then started planning "Wrath of God". Yael, though, did not know about it and was not part of the Kidon team that launched "Wrath of God" against Black September.

Later she was informed by Shaul, that her new mission was taking shape. She would have to go to Beirut again, but not for a few days as before. This time she was to stay in Beirut for several months. The question was – what would be her cover? After several days of heated discussions, Shaul and Yael agreed that her best cover would be of a writer preparing a screenplay for a film or a TV series based on a real story from Lebanon's past.

The idea appeared perfect, but at first, she was wary. She loved reading, but she was not a great writer. Well, perhaps not a writer at all, but she could learn how to behave like one. She flew to Israel and was introduced by Mike to his friend, Shabtai Tevet, a writer. Tevet invited her to his study, and showed her his desk – covered with books, papers, pencils, all in delightful disorder. Blank pages in one drawer, drafts in another. And of course, a sturdy typewriter, stuffed with partly printed sheets and carbon paper. When she returned to Brussels, she knew exactly how her desk in Beirut should look like.

Now, the new "screenwriter" had to find a subject for her script. Her research brought her to London, to the Victoria and Albert museum. and to the adventurous life of Lady Hester Stanhope.

*

"Lady Hester and the story of her life fascinated me," Yael later recalled, "and I easily could identify with her times ... I was thrilled by her personality and its inner contrasts. She was feminine, passionate and tempting, a trailblazer, an adventuress, fanatically devoted to achieving her aspirations, but also aggressive and weak, egocentric and generous, a woman who lived a lonely life in a foreign land, far from her family and her homeland." Some of Yael's friends believe that her identification and admiration for Lady Hester actually revealed a lot about Yael's own longings.

After reading letters, documents, and books on Lady Hester. Yael produced an outline for a 13-episode television series. With the help of Shaul she obtained an appointment (or perhaps somebody else pulled strings?) with a noted British producer. He was impressed by her story and her enthusiasm. And when she left his office, she carried in her bag a signed contract for writing a full screenplay, based on her outline, for a television series named "Queen of the Desert." She became so excited by this idea and by the compliments she had got for her outline, that she began regretting that the screenplay writing was no more than a cover story.

But her cover now was foolproof; she could reserve a seat on a flight to Beirut. Landing there for the second time, she had an awkward feeling about the bustling city. She had been told it was "Paris of the Middle East". Well, it was not West Beirut had become the bastion of Palestinian terrorists who controlled large parts of the city, carried weapons, invaded civilian neighborhoods where they established headquarters, weapons stores, and training facilities. Their armed militias set up roadblocks and checked passersby 's identities. The PLO leader, Yasser Arafat had set up his command post in Beirut. Black September, too, had set up its secret headquarters in Beirut, like several smaller but no less fanatic terrorist groups.

That was where Yael was to carry out her mission. And yet, she also found out that East Beirut, which was mostly Christian, was a thriving international city, with banks, business offices, luxurious stores, night clubs and discotheques. But what most impressed Yael, was the warmth and the generosity of the people she met there, who were to become her close friends and even protectors.

*

Before leaving for Beirut she was told that her code name for this assignment was "Nilsen". Romi Ben-Porat, the Caesarea Intelligence officer, instructed her to gather information about three men who were said to be "the brains behind Palestinian terrorism": Kamal Adwan, responsible for terror operations in Israel and the West Bank; Kamal Nasser, head of the political department of the Fatah and its spokesman; and Muhammad Yussuf al Najjar, (Abu Yussuf) the commander of Black September. All three lived in a two-building apartment compound on Rue Verdun Street. Yael was sent to rent an apartment close to their compound, and to watch and report the movements of the three Palestinians.

Before her flight Mike Harari came to Brussels to see her. "He told me to collect real time intelligence on the targets during the day and night...We talked about means of communication, and reactions to possible scenarios." Mike said: "Yael, at the very end you will be there alone. With your knowledge and experience, and with who you are, you can bring it all together and do it your way. I trust you."

In Beirut, Yael first spent a few nights in the Bristol hotel, and then toured the Rue Verdun on foot. She had a stroke of luck. She discovered an apartment house, just across the street from the twin high rises. She met Fouad, the owner, a nice middle-aged man, speaking adequate English, who lived in the building with his sisters. Yes, he said, he had an apartment for rent on the fourth floor. Yael visited it. It was perfect. From the living room window, she had an excellent view of the windows and balconies of the three Fatah leaders: Kamal Adwan's on the second floor and Kamal Nasser's on the third floor of one building and Abu Yussuf's, on the sixth floor of its twin. She rented the apartment.

Now she had to establish a fully normal residence in Beirut. She bought a car and reconnoitered her neighborhood. A convenient grocery store was down the street, and she started visiting it. She adopted a routine – writing most of the day, modest shopping, mostly for food, writing letters to a "friend named Emil" in Belgium. And in her innocent-sounding letters she reported, with coded phrases, what she did and saw.

When the Fatah guards outside the twin houses stopped her and asked questions, she casually answered: "I live here." Then they did not bother her again. She found a beauty salon where she became a frequent customer and strolled all over Beirut, which she got to know well.

Yael also took out a card at the American University Library, where documents about Lady Hester and her times in Lebanon were kept. Actually, it was Lady Hester, emerging from the nineteenth century's stormy past, who gave Yael her best introduction to Beirut society. When her landlord heard that she was writing a screenplay about "the Queen of the Desert", he was overcome with enthusiasm. He immediately threw a welcome party for his new tenant, and invited several intellectual figures, including a Lebanese writer who had published a book about Lady Hester! Yael now had a common topic with him and the two embarked on long discussions about this woman they admired, her refusal to wear the hijab, her impudent trip to Palmyra with her Bedouin bodyguards, her initiating the first archeological digs in Ashkelon, Palestine, searching for a trove of gold – and instead discovering amazing sculptures. Back in her flat, Yael placed her desk exactly under her window overlooking Verdun street and opposite the twin high rises. So she could observe the two buildings anytime in day and night.

*

On April 7, 1973, a couple of months after she had settled down, she went for a drink in the opulent bar of the Intercontinental Hotel. There she saw a young man sitting in a corner. She looked at him, frowning, as if he seemed vaguely familiar. "Didn't I meet you at the Louvre, in Paris?" she asked.

He shrugged. "I have never been in Paris."

That was the prearranged exchange of code phrases. He was Eviatar, a Caesarea warrior who had accompanied her during her prior visit to Lebanon.

She was most pleased to find another Caesarea warrior beside her in Beirut. They went to a restaurant where she reported on the information she had so far gathered – when the lights in the three men's apartments were on, and when they were turned off, who was looking out the windows and at what time, the approximate times when the three used to leave their apartments and when they were coming back, the cars they were driving, the drivers or bodyguards who escorted them, the visitors who came ... She added general information as well, about the nearby Bristol hotel, the parking lots in the neighborhood, the police presence, and other details.

And besides this oral report to Eviatar she sent others by mail to "her sweetheart Emil" in Brussels, and slipped messages in code between the lines.

She met Eviatar again two days later on April 9, 1973. They had a great time. She was wearing an elegant sports jacket and had tied a green silk scarf around her neck. They went for drinks and dinner at the roof restaurant of the Phoenician hotel. It was a beautiful, balmy evening. "Tell me about Lady Esther", Eviatar asked, and Yael plunged into her dramatic story. At a certain moment he asked, casually, "What about your neighbors from the house across the street?"

"They are home today, all three of them."

"Good"' he said. "Go straight home and stay away from the windows."

When alone, he flashed an urgent message to his Mossad contact.

And Yael did not know, that by her words, she had just triggered operation "Spring of Youth."

*

At that very moment, missile boats of the Israeli Navy were approaching the Lebanese coast; scores of paratroopers from elite units and the *Sayeret Matkal*, the fabled commando unit of the IDF, dressed in civilian clothes, stood on the decks, waiting for the fast Zodiac dinghies that would take them ashore; the first to step in the rubber dinghies would be Ehud Barak, commander of the *Sayeret*, his deputy Amiram Levin and Sergeant Loni Rafaeli, all three of them wearing women dresses and wigs, their faces made up. Barak was wearing a form-fitting black dress, and his breast cups actually were filled with hand grenades and old socks. All waited for a message from the beach, that would give or not the green light for the entire operation. It would be aborted if all of the three leaders of the Fatah and Black September were not at their homes in Verdun Street.

And Eviatar's message arrived. "The birds are in their nest."

So, the Zodiacs, laden with soldiers, sped toward a deserted beach, on the outskirts of Beirut.

This all had started a few months before. While the Kidon team was on the war path in Europe, assassinating Black September terrorist chiefs in Rome, Paris, Athens and other cities, Beirut had become a sanctuary for the topmost terrorists in the world. At barely 130 miles from Tel Aviv, the terrorists walked free, planned their coups, were equipped with weapons and explosives and set out on their bloody missions. Israel could not keep tolerating their immunity. "We have to go to Beirut and kill their leaders in their beds," a senior officer had said. "They have to learn that the long arm of Israel will reach them wherever they hide."

The IDF Chief of Staff, General David (Dado) Elazar, toyed with the idea of landing 300 elite soldiers in Beirut, taking over a central neighborhood, and killing the Black September chiefs who lived there. But Barak, commander of the *sayeret*, (and a future Prime Minister) talked him out of it. "With three hundred soldiers you'll start a war", he said. "Leave it to me. I'll do it with thirteen men."

Elazar accepted his proposal and decided even to enlarge the raid. While Barak and his men would attack the homes of the Black September chiefs, another commando would blow up the Headquarters of "The Popular front for the Liberation of Palestine". Other units would attack secondary targets or carry out diversionary tasks. Scores of paratroopers in civilian clothes would land in Beirut, drive and walk in its crowded streets in a most ambitious, daring operation. But it all depended on first-hand intelligence.

In a meeting with Mike Harari, Elazar insisted on real-time reports. The mission will take place, he said, only if we are certain that the three terrorist leaders are at home." I cannot risk the lives of scores of soldiers if I am not sure that the "targets" are there."

"Count on me", Mike said. The accuracy of Yael's report was crucial.

That evening, after parting from Yael, Eviatar knew that in minutes the Israeli soldiers would land. Then on Verdun Street all hell would break loose. That was why, dinner over, he insisted she go straight home and keep away from her windows.

But Yael did not go straight home..."It was a great time for me", she reminisced to journalist Amira Lam. "I was relaxed, in a good mood. I was so happy to have met someone from the 'office' and feel at home. A great evening, and I did not feel responsible for anything at that moment." She strolled in the Beirut streets and finally drove home. First she carried out her security check, to make sure nobody had entered the apartment during her absence, then she looked out at the twin buildings across the street. Lights were on in the three apartments. Her report had been accurate. "I snuggled up on the couch in my room, and suddenly I began thinking about my parents, about my path from the US to Beirut. I thought to myself that if my parents knew where I was now, they would have been shocked, and wouldn't have understood what happened to their soft and innocent daughter."

Meanwhile, at these very moments the Zodiacs were emerging from the dark, hitting the sands of Beirut beach. And in front of them six cars were waiting, with drivers behind the wheels, all Mossad warriors, who had arrived in Beirut a few days ago with false passports and rented the cars. Eviatar was one of the drivers. Barak's fighters jumped in three of the cars, which took off for Rue Verdun. The paratroopers, under colonel Amnon Lipkin, squeezed into the remaining vehicles that headed off toward the Popular Front headquarters.

Yael went to sleep, but suddenly woke up to the sound of gunfire. She crawled to the window and peeped out. "I saw three large vehicles parked on the street. The shots got louder, there were screams, and the lights in the three apartments were turned on." At first, she thought the Palestinians were shooting at each other but then she heard "Come here, come here!" in Hebrew. She realized that right here an Israeli operation was underway. She then connected the scene she saw from her window with her report to Eviatar earlier that evening, though she had not been informed about this raid.

And they now might shoot her by mistake, as only a narrow street separated her flat from the terrorists' windows. Everything was happening fast, a gunfight raging in front of her house and shots were also heard from the three apartments. But the fighting was quickly over, and the attackers boarded their cars and escaped before the local police or army could intervene. And at the same time, she later learned, the Israeli paratroopers had blown up the Popular Front building, killing the terrorists inside and had then vanished.

Suddenly – silence in the street, but it lasted only minutes, and then police officers and soldiers started arriving.

Years later, she became friends with general Amiram Levin, one of the "women" in the operation. He told her that they knew there was somebody in that neighborhood who had supplied his unit with the necessary intelligence, but they did not know who.

When things calmed down, Yael sat at her desk and wrote a letter to her "lover" Emil. She was certain that it would be opened and read by the Lebanese censors.

"My dear Emil," she wrote, "I am still shaking from last night's events. I woke up suddenly in the middle of the night from the sound of explosions. I ran to the window and saw a battle taking place in the street. It was awful. I ran back to the other window, where I thought I would be protected from any stray bullet. After a few hours the quiet returned, and to my surprise I fell asleep. When I woke up I thought it was all just a bad dream. But no, it was real. Those awful Israelis were here. I think I might take a vacation and visit you during the Easter holiday.

"Lovingly yours, Reeba, your nun in Lebanon."

She slipped a coded sentence in the letter: "It was a great show last night. Well done!"

"Without her," Mike Harari said, "it could not have happened."

*

The following day, Operation "Spring of Youth" made banner headlines all over the world. The media described in detail the daring Israeli commandos' attack in the heart of Beirut. The headquarters of the Popular front had been destroyed, with many of the terrorists that had been trapped inside; the three Fatah and Black September leaders had been killed. The Israelis had come and vanished and all they had left behind, were the six cars, neatly parked on Beirut beach, keys in the ignition.

All the Mossad warriors in Beirut had been ordered to leave immediately. All except one – Yael. She was instructed to leave her apartment at once, and check into a hotel for a few days, then fly back to Europe. She started her preparations to leave when her landlord intervened. He seemed worried by her decision. "Don't go to a hotel," he warned her. "It is too dangerous. Foreigners are closely watched now, and there is a manhunt going on for people who might have helped the Israelis. Your hurried moving will arouse suspicions. Stay in our house, and we'll protect you." He offered Yael to stay in his apartment with his sisters.

She hesitated. Her orders were clear; but on the other hand, Fouad's warning made sense. She decided to follow her instincts, and stayed, gradually returning to her routine. She was not scared, but the atmosphere in Beirut was tense and people were very suspicious. "Most of the stores in the area were closed. I remember getting dressed and going downstairs to send the letter I had written. From there I went to the library and the beauty salon. I tried to keep to my normal routine.... It scares me that I was not afraid. Maybe the fact that I was American, that I did not grow up like the Israelis – fearing the Arab street; it made me feel immune."

After five days she said to Fouad that she was afraid of staying in Beirut, and she wanted to leave. He drove her to the airport and parted from her with a peck on the cheek. She went through immigration smoothly and boarded a plane for Brussels.

Meantime, Mike Harari was under terrible stress, expecting her to return. He and the Ramsad had decided to delay her departure for a reason. She had not been "burned", nobody suspected her, and so she could carry out more missions in enemy countries in the future. But wouldn't that be too risky a gamble? Alisa Magen, who had participated in the Spring of Youth planning, was also very worried about the amazon left behind.

But on April 15, Yael finally landed in Brussels. A jubilant Mike Harari forwarded to the Ramsad a "Most Immediate" telegram announcing that "Nilsen" had just landed, and that she was okay. "Congratulations!" he scribbled on the telegram and signed it.

Harari and Zamir took Yael to Prime Minister Golda Meir, to show her what a Mossad amazon looked like. "She was stunned when I entered the room," Yael recalled, "and said: 'This little girl did all of that?' She sat me down next to her on the sofa and when we left, she hugged and kissed me."

*

196 · PART THREE

To protect her cover, but also out of friendship and gratitude, Yael bought some prints in London that Fouad, her landlord had asked for – he had even given her 8 pounds in advance – and sent them to him. Neither he, nor the other people she had met in Beirut, ever suspected her role in "Spring of Youth". And when her story would be partly made public, in 2015, she regretted that they would be shocked and pained by it.

Shortly after Spring of Youth, Yael's father arrived for a short visit to Israel. She did not breathe a word about her real work to him – and he left, still convinced that she was working in a computer company doing classified research for the Ministry of Defense. Neither of Yael's parents ever learned the truth about their daughter's life; she loved them but seldom wrote home, perhaps because she had found her real family in the Mossad.

During a small gathering of Spring of Youth veterans, she met a tall guy, Michael, who had taken part in the operation as an officer at the *sayeret*. He had been one of those who broke into the twin buildings and killed the terrorist leaders. As he was leaving, at the meeting's end, he turned to Yael: "I think we've met somewhere, but I do not remember where."

"In the parking of the house where I used to live then," she said, "in Herzliya Heights."

He was stunned. "You kept quiet the entire evening, you did not tell me a word, as if you did not know me."

"We did not know each other," she said, "perhaps we wanted to. Perhaps I could have devoted myself to the bond between us, but I chose a different path."

After Michael left, she wrote: "If I had written the story of my life I could have imagined Michael as the man I fell in love with, and a passionate affair between us would have produced a relationship that I needed so much...."

But then, she did fall in love with a man, much older, whom she met in Brussels. Peter was his name. She spoke about him to Mike who was not only her commander but also a father figure. She even asked Mike to have dinner with the two of them, and he agreed. Afterward, when she asked him about his thoughts, he told her: "Follow your heart." But this relationship also faded away. "After a short while I put an end to it. Like always – getting near somebody and then moving away, burying the separation pain deep in my heart and returning to my position in the unit."

A short book about Yael's mission in Lebanon by Efrat Mass, was published in Israel. But beside its revelations, it also hid a much bigger truth. During the fourteen years that followed, Yael's mission in Beirut would turn to be the least amazing of her career. She stayed in the Mossad and carried out dangerous missions in the Arab countries surrounding Israel. She served in Syria, in Egypt, back in Lebanon under a new cover; and also in Baghdad, gathering the intelligence that helped Israel in 1981 when it bombed and destroyed Saddam Hussein's nuclear reactor. In one instance she spent four years in an Arab country, achieving incredible tasks. She was promoted and put in command of many missions, in which IDF soldiers or Mossad warriors had to obey her orders. She was tough and exacting, and her accomplishments kept increasing. But…"After fifteen years, I got tired. During one of the missions in an Arab town I wanted to shout in the middle of the street: "I am a Jew! A Jew!" She became one of the greatest Mossad amazons ever, but most of her missions are still kept top-secret.

Yael got a citation from the IDF commander in chief, General Rafael Eitan, after the destruction of the Iraqi reactor. All the other commendations and medals are still secret.

"If we decorated Yael with all her medals and awards and citations," former Ramsad Tamir Pardo told me, "there would have been no place on her chest."

*

Yael left the Mossad at fifty. Once again, she went to an Ulpan, to learn Hebrew. Once again, she did not learn much Hebrew there. Once again, she met a teacher, Johnny, a warm South African architect, and married him. This time she did not have to choose between her love and her calling.

A few years later she became seriously ill, but Johnny took care of her with devotion and love. And still, he admits, Yael jealously keeps her secrets. "After many years of marriage, I know that I do not know..."

Yael lives with Johnny outside Tel Aviv. "My screenplay on Lady Hester was never made into a film," she told me. "Such a pity, it was a good one."

CHAPTER 13

Sylvia Rafael (2)

Fiasco

SYLVIA DID NOT KNOW YAEL AND HAD NOT PARTICIPATED in "Spring of Youth". But after a while she found out that while the *sayeret* fighters were breaking into the three Fatah leaders' homes, the worst, most dangerous and fanatic enemy – Ali Hassan Salameh – was sleeping peacefully only a few hundred yards down the street, in a Fatah safehouse. The Israeli soldiers missed him and even did not look for him, unaware that he was in Beirut. Salameh, wily and clever, knew how to cover his tracks, and the Mossad had no idea where he was hiding.

Salameh, young, handsome and devious, was the son of Sheik Hassan Salameh, the leader of the local Palestinian militias during Israel's Independence War of 1948. An admirer of Hitler, Hassan Salameh had escaped to Germany during World War II. Later, he had been parachuted over Palestine on a secret mission – to instigate a revolt of the Palestinian Arabs against the British, and poison the wells of Tel Aviv. The mission had collapsed, with Salameh's companions killed or captured. He escaped but was killed in the 1948 Independence War. In his lifetime he had amassed a large fortune, and his son, Ali, had grown in Lebanon and Europe as a rich, hedonist playboy. But after the Arab armies' defeat in 1967 he had become a

199

Palestinian patriot and joined the Fatah. In 1970 Arafat appointed him Chief of Operations of Black September. Ali's friends named him "the Red Prince" – Prince, for being the great Salameh's son, and Red – for his obsession for blood and killing. Arafat publicly designed him as his successor. The Red Prince was the man who had conceived and planned the mission against the Israeli athletes in Munich.

One after the other, in Paris, Rome, Athens, Cyprus and Beirut, the Black September leaders were liquidated. Only one remained, the Red Prince, still on his bloody trail. In Khartoum his men had stormed a diplomatic reception, captured the American ambassador and his deputy, as well as the Belgian acting ambassador and savagely murdered them. That could not be tolerated. Golda's X committee gave Caesarea the green light. Salameh had to be found and killed at all costs.

The quest for the Red Prince became an obsession for Mike Harari. He spread his men throughout Europe, alerted the espionage networks and the signal intelligence experts, called on his contacts in other secret services. For three months the search for Salameh brought no results, except for a vague rumor that he was in Germany or in one of the Scandinavian countries, preparing a major attack against Israel. According to that rumor, Salameh wanted to avenge "Spring of Youth" and the recent assassination of Mohamed Boudia, the Black September head in France. But this piece of information was not confirmed by any reliable source.

And then, in mid-July – a glimmer of hope!

In Geneva, Switzerland, lived a young Algerian, Kamal Benaman, a known Black September courier. On July 14, 1973, he suddenly flew to Copenhagen, boarded a connection to Oslo, and after a night in hotel Panorama, took a train to the Norwegian winter resort of Lillehammer, nestled amidst majestic snowbound mountains. Lillehammer, located at a hundred miles away from Oslo, was to host the forthcoming winter Olympics. Three Mossad warriors, the "Austrian" Gustave Pistauer, the "French" Jean-Luc Savanier, and the "Swede" Dan Art (by his real name Dan Arbel), followed him to Lillehammer,

As soon as the report of the three warriors reached the Mossad headquarters, Mike Harari immersed himself in hectic activity. Aware of the rumors about Salameh staying in Scandinavia, Mike was convinced that Benaman had traveled to Lillehammer to meet him. He hastily composed an operational team, that included both experienced warriors and some green newcomers. The Copenhagen-born Dan Arbel was not a seasoned warrior, but was added to the team because he knew Danish and other Scandinavian languages. So was a young woman, Marianne Gladnikoff, who had recently immigrated to Israel from Sweden. She was a software engineer, who had come to Israel out of Zionism. Marianne had just started the Mossad beginners' course. She was pulled out of there and urgently sent to Norway via Zurich, because the Swedish language she spoke was very close to Norwegian. The blond, plump young woman flew over using her real name and her Swedish passport. Her companion on the flights from Tel Aviv was a black-haired Canadian photographer who introduced herself as Patricia.

Among the veterans who joined the small task force were some of the major members of the Wrath of God team that already operated in Europe. Sylvia Rafael and Avraham Gehmer were among them. Gehmer carried a British passport on the name of Leslie Orbaum, a teacher from Leeds, in England. Mike Harari arrived in Norway, carrying a French passport on the name of Edouard Stanislas Lasker. He was followed by the Ramsad Zvi Zamir who carried an Israeli passport on the name of Tal Sarig. The team settled in several hotel rooms and apartments that had been rented by Dan Arbel. Arbel and his comrades also rented some cars at Oslo airport. Sylvia knew Dan Arbel; they had traveled together in 1970, on a reconnaissance mission to several ports in Arab countries.

From the start, Sylvia felt something was not right. In the last few months, she had become experienced in similar missions; therefore, she asked the mission chiefs what the contingency plans in case of a mishap were and what were the escape routes. She was surprised to find out that nothing had been planned. She complained to Avraham Gehmer, who confirmed her worries.

She was also quite upset by the behavior of the team that had landed in Lillehammer. In winter, Lillehammer attracted huge throngs of tourists, while in these days of summer it was just a somnolent provincial town. But on July 19 fifteen Mossad warriors arrived in town, riding their rented cars in the streets, communicating by almost visible walkie talkies. The team attracted needless attention.

And finally, Sylvia thought, what about the target's identification? Is the Red Prince really hiding in this small town? And if he is – where?

The Mossad warriors succeeded to track down Kamal Benaman, who had checked in Hotel Regina using fake papers. The following day they followed him when he left the hotel. He strolled down some side alleys, then walked back, entered cafés and left by the rear door, executed quite a few maneuvers that convinced the Israelis that he was a seasoned secret operative, trying to shake off a likely tail. The logical conclusion was that he was trying to elude a possible surveillance before meeting Salameh.

In midday Benaman was spotted on the veranda of café Caroline, as he sat down under a colorful parasol. Gustave Pistauer, Marianne Gladnikoff and another warrior watched him from a bench across the street. Suddenly two strangers approached Benaman. One of them turned back. Pistauer stirred. The man was Arab! Pistauer compared the stranger's face with Salameh's fuzzy photograph that he subtly took out of his pocket. Now, in the photograph Salameh was shaven, while the Arab who approached Benaman had a mustache. But a mustache could be grown or glued. For a long moment Pistauer examined the stranger's face and scrutinized the photograph. It was not a good photo, rather vague and grainy. But that was all they had. Finally, Pistauer nodded.

Mike Harari received the message, sitting in a car nearby. He immediately reported to Zvi Zamir that his warriors had identified Salameh.

From this moment on, the warriors abandoned Benaman and focused all their efforts to the mustachioed man. They followed him when he left the café and rode a bicycle in the town's streets for a long time, then reached a cheap and neglected suburb. He spent the night in one of the run-down buildings. The following morning the man rode his bicycle to the municipal swimming pool. The Israelis saw him a few minutes later, sitting on the pool edge, and speaking to another man.

What were they talking about? The squad commander ordered Marianne to rent a swimsuit, enter the pool and approach the mustachioed man and his interlocutor. She hurried, rented a bikini, dived in the pool and swam to the far side where the two targets were sitting. She did not understand their conversation because they were speaking French, a language she did not know. She swam a few laps, back and forth, to their location, but that did not help. On the other hand, she had examined Salameh's photograph before entering the pool, and later had scrutinized the face of the suspect. She came out of the pool. "I do not think that this is the same man," she said to her commander. "The eyebrows of the man in the photograph are different, they are somewhat pointed. I am sure, this is not Salameh."

"You do not know," was the answer, "you do not understand."

Sylvia reached the same conclusion. As a professional photographer she could not accept the identification according to a blurred, unclear photograph. Avraham Gehmer agreed with her, but the mission commanders dismissed their reservations. The majority of those who had seen the man, believes he was Salameh, they said. Mike Harari had no doubts either.

Sylvia was uneasy for another reason. In all the reports prepared by Romi, Caesarea's intelligence wizard, there was no mention of Salameh's knowing French, while the man at the pool was fluent in that language. And another point – did it make sense that Salameh, the Black September leader, certainly aware that the Mossad was after him, would ride his bicycle all over Lillehammer without protection and without any effort to shake off possible surveillance? And did it seem likely that he would be staying in a poor suburb of Lillehammer? And go to swim in the city pool, where he is utterly vulnerable? Sylvia shared these questions with her commanders – and was dismissed again. Harari and Zamir were determined to carry out the mission. It seemed that the success of the previous Wrath of God missions had dulled their thoroughness in checking and planning their assignments. The commanders also decided that D-Day would be the same day, July 21.

That evening, in a light drizzle, Salameh and a blond, pregnant woman, entered a cinema in the town center, where they watched "Where Eagles Dare" with Clint Eastwood and Richard Burton. During the film projection a Kidon warrior sat close to the couple, and watched them share a pack of sweets. When the movie ended, at 22:15, they took a bus, that Marianne Gladnikoff followed in one of the rented cars. Three men followed her in a white car – Jonathan Ingleby, Rolf Baehr (the driver) and Gerard-Emile Lafond. They were the hit team. When Salameh and the woman alighted from the bus, on the quiet and deserted Storgten Street, several cars stopped beside them. Ingleby and Lafond jumped from the white car. They drew Beretta guns and fired 14 bullets at Ali Salameh. The woman beside him was not touched. It was a matter of seconds. The two killers jumped in the white car that darted forward and disappeared down the street. In the follow-up car Marianne heard the laconic message, "They took him!"

Zvi Zamir and Mike Harari were delighted. The greatest terrorist was dead. "You did a great job," Mike exulted in the walkie-talkie, "now everybody goes home!"

Police cars and an ambulance arrived at the scene immediately, but Salameh's killers were not there anymore. They were the first to leave the area. The three warriors who had used the white car, left it in the outskirts, and transferred to another car. That same night they left Lillehammer in two escape cars with four other warriors and the following morning departed Norway out of Oslo airport. Zvi Zamir and Mike Harari also left Norway by air and by ferryboat. They left behind a few warriors who had to take care of the rented apartments and cars; they also had to wipe out any proof of the Mossad activity in Oslo and Lillehammer.

They did not know, that last night the Kidon members had not been alone at Storgten Street. Close to the killing scene, in the dense vegetation of the municipal park, a young couple was engaged in tender lovemaking. All of a sudden, they had heard the shots and noticed one of the shooters' cars that had picked up speed and left the premises. The couple even succeeded to note down the car color, make and registration number; they handed over all that to the police. According to one team member, Dan Arbel returned to the abandoned white car, a Peugeot, where he had left a parcel the day before, and drove it to Oslo. He actually had strayed from his original orders to take the train with Gladnikoff to Oslo and then leave the country.

The following day Arbel entered the "Hertz-rent a car" office at Oslo airport and asked to return the white Peugeot. Marianne Gladnikoff was sitting in the car and waiting for Arbel to complete the paperwork. That was first rate negligence, because at the escape stage it was strictly forbidden to return cars that had been used in the operation to the rental companies. These cars had to be abandoned.

That was a fatal mistake. At that time, precisely, the Norwegian radio broadcast a police bulletin describing the getaway car. A Norwegian, sitting in his car behind Marianne and listening to the radio, happened to raise his eyes and then saw the wanted car before him! Excited, he alerted the police. Arbel and Gladnikoff were arrested on the spot. They were interrogated by the team of Steiner Ravlo, an investigation officer at the Oslo police, and broke down right away. It turned out that Arbel was claustrophobic; he told the police that as a child, during World War II, he had to hide in a cellar for many months. When brought to a small interrogation room, he agreed to fully cooperate with the police officers if the room door was left open...

The police officers were amazed. So far, they had been certain that the Lillehammer murder had been connected to drug traffic. Now they suddenly found out that they had uncovered an international espionage affair. "In 1973," Steiner Ravlo said later, "we did not believe that something of this kind could happen in Norway."

Gladnikoff and Arbel led the police to the safehouse where Sylvia Rafael and Avraham Gehmer were hiding, awaiting their departure from Norway. Two other Israelis, Michael Dorff, and Zvi Steinberg, also stayed in the apartment. Sylvia was very nervous; she could not sit idle in a locked apartment and wait. She asked her friends to leave the apartment. But the moment they left the house, they were surrounded by armed police officers. In Dan Arbel's papers the police found the phone number of Yigal Eyal, the security officer at the Israeli embassy. In his home they arrested two more Mossad warriors. Yigal Eyal was declared *persona non grata* and was expelled from Norway with his family.

Sylvia stuck to her Canadian identity of Patricia Roxburgh, and told a convoluted cover story to the police. She allegedly had met Leslie Orbaum (Avraham Gehmer) whom she knew beforehand in a Zurich street, agreed to fly with him to a vacation in Oslo, met there Dan Arbel and Marianne Gladnikoff, quarreled with Leslie, who left her.... The police interrogator, Herald Romingen, did not believe a word. But Arbel and Gladnikoff filled the blanks. They admitted that they were Mossad officers, and revealed details, real names, addresses in Oslo, Paris and other countries, secret rules and operational methods. Arbel even disclosed Mike Harari's classified phone number in Tel Aviv.

Their depositions were utterly harmful and embarrassing to the Mossad. They also revealed the real name of Patricia Roxburgh, and henceforth the police officers addressed her as Sylvia Rafael.

But only after their arrest did the warriors find out the worst mishap of all.

They had killed the wrong man.

*

The young man they killed that night in Lillehammer was not the Red Prince. He was Ahmed Bouchiki, a Moroccan, who worked as a waiter in one of the town's restaurants. He had no connection whatever with Black September. The woman who went to cinema with him, that fateful night, was his pregnant wife, Torril. The Mossad warriors had made a tragic mistake and had killed an innocent man. Years after, in 1996, despite its refusal to admit any guilt, Israel paid 400,000 dollars in indemnities to the Bouchiki family.

Nobody of the Mossad senior officers, even not Harari and Zamir, was blamed or reprimanded, nor asked to resign from office. No board of inquiry was set up, to investigate the worst mishap in Mossad history. One could expect that Zamir and Harari would submit their resignations but it did not happen. Zamir admitted, years later, that the Lillehammer mission failed because of "the sin of hubris", after the successful operations against Black September. Still, after the Lillehammer fiasco Golda Meir ordered to stop all 'Wrath of God' operations throughout the world.

Only months later did the Mossad commanders realize how close they had been to find Salameh. It turned out, that during the Lillehammer operation, the Red Prince was relatively close, in Sweden's capital, Stockholm. "When they killed Bouchiki I was in Europe". Salameh told the "A-Sayad" Lebanese newspaper. "His face and body differed from my description.... I was saved not because of my talents, but because of the weakness of Israeli intelligence."

*

Banner headlines in the world press described the murder in Lillehammer and the capture of the Mossad hit team. The Mossad efforts to release the prisoners failed. Sylvia, Avraham Gehmer, Marianne Gladnikoff, Dan Arbel and another warrior were indicted and had to stand trial.

Before Sylvia's real identity was revealed, the French police asked the Norwegians to let them interrogate Patricia Roxburgh. She was suspected to have participated in the assassination of Muhamed Boudia and Basil al Kubaissi, two terrorist leaders, in Paris in April and June 1973. The Norwegians refused, but sent two officers to Paris, and they visited Patricia's apartment on the Seine embankment. The apartment was empty except for a bottle of Calvados liquor and a copy of "Le Figaro" newspaper dated June 27, 1973, the day before Boudia's assassination. They reached the conclusion that Patricia possibly had participated in the mission, then fled to Tel Aviv for a few weeks, before flying to Norway. But they did not find any proof confirming that theory.

In Oslo prison, Sylvia was deeply disappointed with her Mossad comrades, for several reasons: the faulty planning and execution; the integration of the unexperienced Gladnikoff and Arbel into the team; and the slapdash Salameh's identification. She also was hurt by being left alone at the early stages of her incarceration, as nobody came to visit her and she felt that Israel had abandoned her. A few months later she would describe her distress in a letter to Avraham Gehmer.

"I can't stop turning over in my mind what happened", she wrote, "and the more I think about it, the more convinced I am that the unfortunate events in Lillehammer could have been avoided. Something in me broke after Lillehammer . . . It eroded my desire to continue serving with the people I respected so highly. My heroes had appeared to be men of absolute integrity, but suddenly I saw them in a different light. What a pity . . ."

That letter apparently reached King Saul Boulevard (in Tel Aviv), for a few days later she received an unsigned letter from the Mossad. It contained a poem, unsigned as well, dedicated to her. She would never discover who, of the Mossad leaders, had written it:

"Like a huge vacuum cleaner
the Mossad sucks in
A variety of people,
but only the best remain –

An impressive array of women,
an excellent choice of men,
All of them top-grade clandestine combatants,
and above all – loyal to the end.

They're determined to succeed
in reaching every target.
They are skilled in tracking them down,
even on the darkest night.

Among their ranks was a woman,
who was beautiful, clever and wise,
But she had one defect,
that stood out above the rest:

She considered all of us
to be absolutely perfect.
She viewed us as being
God's messengers on earth.

So please inform her loud and clear
that all of us, either on land or on sea,
And as talented as we may be
are only human, after all.

Please explain that we haven't descended from Heaven,
That we all have faults
And not a trace of wings
And that we too can err...

*

Beside the disappointment, Sylvia suffered from her solitude. That same Sylvia who so needed love, friendship, the company of people, was confined now to a silent cell in the Norwegian prison. When the conditions of her detention slightly improved, she suddenly came across Marianne Gladnikoff in the jail courtyard. Marianne was overjoyed to see a familiar face; but Sylvia turned away and refused to talk to her. She could not forgive her for breaking down at the interrogation. Another blow befell Sylvia a few weeks later. Her father died of a heart attack in a South African hospital, and she could not be by his side, or even speak with him in his last days on earth.

Yet, she was in for a surprise. After a while she was called to the warden's office, and there she was amazed to see her mother, and one of her brothers, Jonathan, who had come from South Africa to see her. Only now did they learn what she had been doing all those years, and understood the reason for her silences, her unexplained trips, her refusal to give them a phone number or a home address. The meeting with them was emotional and loving; but when she returned to her grim cell, she felt even more lonely.

Her solitude and her frustration, however, did not transpire when she was taken to the box of the accused in her trial. She did not utter a single word about her connection with the Mossad and the many secrets populating her life story. Before her trial the world newspapers competed in conceiving dramatic definitions for Sylvia, like "Mata Hari" or "the Mossad assassin". But when, proud and erect, she faced the Oslo judges, she made a heartfelt plea that astounded everybody present in the courtroom, public and judges alike. She spoke of the Holocaust horrors that had decimated the Jewish people, the murders of innocent Israelis by the terror organization, like the Munich Olympics massacre; she insisted on the Israelis dearest hope, to live in peace and serenity like any other nation. But as the terror increased and the world nations stayed indifferent and inert, "we, a group of friends, decided that we cannot hold back anymore, and set off to pursue the leaders of the terror campaign against us. We came to Lillehammer on the tracks of the arch-murderer Ali Hassan Salameh. Our goal was to hit him and nobody else. Because of a fatal error, with no intent of malice, an innocent man was killed."

Her words and her proud stance deeply impressed the public; and when she concluded her statement the audience reacted with a loud, spontaneous applause. The judges were moved like the crowd; but the court, of course, could not accept Sylvia's version about "some friends who could not hold back". The judges based their verdict on the solid proof that the Lillehammer mission had been carried out by the Mossad.

Sylvia knew this, but her words about the "friends" were based on the advice of her lawyer, who had been discreetly hired by the Mossad. This was Annaeus Schjodt, one of the foremost lawyers in Norway. He passionately defended Sylvia, became emotionally involved with her, and gradually a romantic bond overwhelmed them both – the 37-year-old Mossad amazon – and the 54-year-old trial attorney, a married man with two children. The burgeoning love affair became a source of strength for Sylvia during the dramatic trial.

The verdict was relatively light: Avraham Gehmer was sentenced to five and a half years in prison, and so was Sylvia. Marianne Gladnikoff and Dan Arbel got shorter sentences.

Despite of her dire situation, Sylvia did not lose her sense of humor.

When she heard that the prosecutor had asked for a sentence of seven years, but she finally got only five and a half, she quipped: "So far I thought I was a 007, but I turn out to be only 005½".

After her sentence, the life of Sylvia improved. She was transferred to a women penitentiary, where she got a little apartment with basic amenities. The Israeli diplomat, Eliezer Palmor, visited her often. From Israel arrived Yehudit Nissiyahu, head of the Mossad manpower department, and established long-term relations with the young amazon. Sylvia's younger brother David, who was in Israel, also flew to Oslo to meet his sister. Sylvia was allowed to visit Oslo several times with a very discreet police escort. On Passover eve, 1974, she was invited, with the other Mossad prisoners, to the home of Palmor for the traditional "Seder"; Anneaus Schjodt and his wife were the guests of honor. During the dinner, Palmor's little daughter, eight-year-old Amy, discovered a great secret. When peeping under the table the little girl saw that Anneaus and Sylvia were holding hands! She told her mother, and very soon Minister Palmor and the Mossad contacts knew about Sylvia and Anneaus secret love affair. In faraway Norway she had lost her freedom but had found love.

And another kind of love soon enveloped Sylvia. As soon as her name became public, and a few details about her missions were disclosed, myriad letters of affection and encouragement from Israel and other countries started flooding Sylvia's jail. The members of kibbutz Ramat Hakovesh, where Sylvia's brother David worked as a volunteer, decided to adopt her and make the kibbutz her home after her release.

The first to be released were Marianne Gladnikoff and Dan Arbel. A reporter called them "the tragic heroes" of the Lillehammer fiasco. Marianne could not return to the Mossad. She resumed her profession of software engineering but remained lonely and morose for the rest of her life.

Another one who was hurt by the fiasco was Avraham Gehmer. After his release he worked for a while in the Mossad headquarters, but was haunted by the memories of Lillehammer. He believed that a board of inquiry had to review the Lillehammer mishap, but nobody listened. He left the Mossad, changed his last name to Eitan and spent the rest of his life cultivating flowers in Bitzaron village.

Sylvia was released in May 1975, after a year and ten months. Annaeus divorced his wife and married her. She was burned, as a secret operative and could not return to the Mossad. The newlywed couple lived more than twenty years in Norway, South Africa, and Israel. For a while they rented an apartment in Tel Aviv, but spent many months at Ramat Hakovesh where they worked the land like all the kibbutz members. Sylvia was very happy but she had to give up her dream of of bearing children. "That's the price I had to pay", she said to her friend Sarah Rosenbaum.

The terrorist organizations decided to revenge and planned to assassinate Sylvia after her release. They conceived a few attack projects in Scandinavia and in the Mediterranean, but failed to carry them out. Sylvia and Annaeus lived a happy life together. She recovered her good spirits; and even in her most painful moments, when she contracted terminal cancer, and her willowy body quickly melted down under the cruel onslaught of the disease, she kept joking: "All my life I dieted, to lose weight, and now, I do not have to make the effort anymore." She died in South Africa in 2005, nine years before her husband. Before her death she asked to be buried at kibbutz Ramat Hakovesh.

"She was not a secret agent," Mike Harari said at her funeral, that was attended by all the Mossad chiefs. "She was an Empress of a noble race, who had been destined to act as a target warrior in many enemy countries…"

On her tombstone her kibbutz friends engraved her words: "I loved my country with all my soul, and when my day comes, return me to its soil."

CHAPTER 14

Danielle

Two Spies in Love

L ESS THAN THREE MONTHS AFTER THE LILLEHAMMER fiasco, Egypt and Syria simultaneously attacked Israel. On October 6, 1973, while Israel was paralyzed by the fast of Yom Kippur, The Day of atonement, the two armies struck. The Egyptians crossed the Suez Canal and established a bridgehead in the Sinai Peninsula, conquering the Israeli fortresses along the canal and killing hundreds of Israeli soldiers. The Syrian army seized large portions of the Golan heights and the commander of its armored column shouted, ecstatic, in his microphone: "I see the lake of Tiberias!"

Some Israeli leaders feared a total destruction of their state. Golda Meir admitted later that she contemplated suicide; the legendary Defense Minister Moshe Dayan expressed his fears that "The Third Temple", as the State of Israel was called by some, was on the verge of annihilation. But the IDF, surprised and confused at first, regrouped and succeeded to repel the joint onslaught and launch lethal offensives. When the war ended Israeli forces had reached positions at 40 kilometers from Damascus, in Syria, and 101 kilometers from Cairo, in Egypt. But the cost was heavy, Israel had lost 2656 lives, and her leaders feared a renewed offensive by her foes.

During the war and its aftermath, Israel desperately needed fresh, credible intelligence. One of the first warriors sent to the lion's den, was a young woman whom we'll call Danielle.

*

October 1973, Paris.

In the late afternoon they heard several knocks on the door, in prearranged order. Mike Harari got up from his seat and opened the door, A sturdy blond man entered the Parisian safehouse. Danielle looked at him. She did not like him. She was attracted to tall, black-haired men, and this one . . .

"This is Julio", Mike said, "meet Tamar." Tamar was her code name at the Mossad.

"Nice to meet you," Julio said. Danielle discerned a slight South American accent,

Mike turned to Danielle. "Julio will be your husband in Egypt."

She was ready for that. When they sent her to Paris, in the first days of the Yom Kippur war, the Caesarea commander briefed her that from France she would be sent to Cairo as the "wife" of a warrior who already operated in Egypt for a long time. Her future husband needed support and reinforcement, and it was vital to bolster his performances by sending over a female warrior that would play the role of his wife.

In Paris Danielle went through intensive preparations and memorized the legend that they had concocted for her. She knew she had to get to Egypt as soon as possible, because Israel feared a renewed attack of the Arabs on Sinai and the Golan.

After the first meeting in the safehouse she met Julio again for lunch and a long conversation. He told her about his life and his beautiful house in the upscale Zamalek neighborhood. He had been sent to Cairo a couple of years ago, he said; he had a solid cover, as the manager of a foreign company.

A few days later, after they got fake marriage certificates, they boarded an airliner bound for Cairo.

*

This was Danielle's first assignment. She was born in a pleasant provincial town in France and went to school with 2000 girls. "I was a happy child", she said later, "the clown of my class." She was talented, sharp, best in her class, a star in the drama ensemble. She called one of her sisters, suffering from brain damage, "the silent angel"; and since her childhood, Danielle knew that she could not invite her friends home, could not speak about her sister's illness, and could not disclose matters that should be kept secret. When her parents divorced, she wanted to immigrate to Israel, but at that time the age of maturity was 21, and she was not allowed by law to make her own decisions.

She moved to Paris, studied at the Sorbonne university, took part in the May 1968 students' revolt, and marched in Paris' streets with hundreds of female students fighting for their independence and freedom. She was twenty-one when the eminent Israeli professor Saul Friedlander (today at UCLA) came to Paris for a lecture. She approached him: "When should I immigrate to Israel?" she asked. "Right now, or after I graduate?"

"Right now," the professor advised.

She did. She settled in Jerusalem and enrolled in the Political Science and International relations faculties in Hebrew University. In the students' dorms she joined a group of Anglo-Saxon and Latin American students. "I kept my distance from the French," she said. "Half of them were pro-Palestinian radicals, the other half fanatical right wingers. I was on the left; I could not fit in those groups."

The pretty, naughty girl was not even aware of the adventurous streak in her character. She got a motorcycle driving license and used to dash from Jerusalem to her relatives in Tel Aviv and Netanya on the saddle of a BMW powerful motorcycle. She always took with her two helmets, the second one for some hitchhiker that she might pick up at Jerusalem's outskirts. Before she let him on her bike, she would warn him: "You're sitting behind me, holding the handles on your sides, and not touching me. I want to reach my destination alive." That way she always stayed out of trouble.

Till the day when she got a letter in the students' dorm. It was sent from "the Bureau for International Cooperation" and requested that she call a certain phone number to fix an appointment in Tel Aviv. At first, she thought that was a prank; but a student she knew checked the letter and told her: "Look, it's embossed with the State official seal, perhaps this is something serious."

In Tel Aviv she met her mother who had just arrived from France, and went with her to buy a modest and respectable dress for the meeting. The man whom she met in a small office at the government compound, assailed her with questions on her life, and after an hour of intensive interrogation asked her: "If I told you that there is a task that our pilots cannot undertake, our paratroopers cannot undertake, our infantry cannot undertake – but you can, what would you say?"

"Yes!", she immediately said. And only later asked: "What do you want of me?"

He answered: "To be our eyes in an enemy country."

"Yes," she repeated. She understood that the "Bureau for international cooperation" was a cover for the Mossad.

The stranger made her sign several forms, coordinated communication ways and means with her, and demanded that she sever all the relations she had with people she knew – her friends, her boyfriend, the students in her class. He also asked her to drop out of school. One of the conditions to her admission was that she would not marry in the next five years,

Why do they recruit me? she asked herself and guessed the answer – because I know languages, because I got a foreign passport, because I am intelligent enough to deal with unexpected situations. She now expected to be summoned to a Mossad warriors' course but that did not happen. Before the course started, she was called to a meeting in Tel Aviv. She was ushered into a room where all "the big chiefs" of the Mossad were sitting. They questioned her repeatedly, and at the end one of them said: "Listen, you are still young. Go back to school, and when you graduate, come to us. After your service with us you can get married and start a family."

"No way", she said, "I am twenty-two years old. The studies will last another three years. Then I'll come to the Mossad. You asked me not to get married for five years. I'll be therefore thirty. One does not marry at the age of thirty."

The meeting ended and she drove her motorcycle back to Jerusalem. She thought that everything was over, but it was not. A few months later she got a telegram, to report at a certain address. That was how she started the Caesarea basic course.

She liked the course and the assignments she got. Her instructors trained her to be a press photographer, and during the course she met Sylvia Rafael who was about to conclude her activity in Paris. She probably was to replace her. The two of them struck a warm friendship and she regarded Sylvia "as an older sister."

One day she was sent to the leader of "WIZO", the Zionist women organization, to interview her "for a Belgian magazine". Not only did she succeed to make the lady talk, but she also made her divulge her recipe for a cheesecake. When she brought the recipe to her instructors, one of them said: "Today you got the recipe from the Zionist organization chairwoman, tomorrow that could be Jehan Sadat [Egypt President's wife]."

She set out to her first mission with Mike Harari. They flew to a francophone European capital, and she was charged to rent an apartment as a student in the local university. It was an easy assignment, but she spent long hours with Harari; he seemed impressed by her knowledge and character. And in 1973, when the Yom Kippur war started, she was urgently dispatched to her first mission in an enemy country. She told her mother that she was being sent to Africa by the Ministry of Foreign affairs. But her secret mission was unusual – to impersonate the fresh wife of Julio, in Cairo.

In the plane that carried them to Egypt, Julio said: "You'll see my superb apartment in Cairo. I prepared a nice separate room for you."

She fired up. "What? What are you, a puritan? And where is the logic? You are bringing a young bride home and you put her in a separate room? You have servants at home, do not you? If they saw the master's wife living in a separate room from the moment she arrived – they will immediately report that to the *Mukhabarat*. I am ready to be arrested and imprisoned for an error I may commit, but not because of such nonsense. Look, I took part in the students' revolt in 1968!" The students' revolt was a permissive event, and the liberated young women chanted slogans about free love and burned their brassieres in the university campuses and the streets of Paris, "I have no problem being with you in the same room and the same bed! "

And so it was decided: The master and his wife will sleep in the same room.

*

She quickly became familiar with Cairo's streets and monuments, the vestiges of its antique splendor, the murky Nile – but also with the military compounds, the roadblocks, the closed areas. One could breathe the hatred to Israel spread by posters, newspapers, broadcasts and songs, all of those hailing Egypt's "decisive victory" in the October War. But she had to live with all that and even join the anti-Israeli chorus.

Julio wanted to show her the Egyptian night life, and in the first evening took her to "Sahara City", a vast tent with a show of music, Arab songs and belly dancing. She saw him slapping his thighs to the music beat, and felt that he was already deep into the Cairo ambience. During the following days he introduced her to his friends – foreign diplomats and businessmen, Egyptian officers and senior officials, famous socialites who loved spending long nights in Cairo's exclusive nightclubs. Julio used to ride horses with some of his friends, and she wanted to join him, as horse-riding had been her favorite hobby in Israel. But that was strictly forbidden, as she had met in Israel many foreign tourists who had gone riding with her, some even on a two-day trip in Galilee. Mike feared that she might be identified by one of those casual acquaintances who happened to visit Cairo – and that could lead her straight to the gallows.

Gradually she also realized why she had been so urgently sent to be at Julio's side.

Julio apparently had been involved in a love affair with the daughter of a European diplomat in Cairo; and the passionate affair had reached a dangerous stage. Julio had been ordered by his case officers to cut off his connection with the girl. He did so, but the imposed separation had broken him, blurring his senses and self-control. Besides, his superiors felt that his reports in the last few months had been unsatisfying and discerned in his activity a fatigue probably caused by his long stay in Egypt and his turbulent lifestyle. Danielle was supposed to operate on his side, undertake complicated missions and steer his life into a secure and regular mode.

But it was not that simple. Julio's friends did not understand how, suddenly, Julio's rapports with his girlfriend had been terminated. And now, he had returned from a vacation in Europe with an unknown woman he just had married! Nobody knew he had an extra girlfriend tucked somewhere in Europe, certainly not a fiancée. Danielle had the impression that they were staring at her belly non-stop, apparently guessing that he had got her pregnant, was forced to marry her, and that was the solution to the enigma. She decided to play the role of the naïve bimbo and told everybody that she used to see Julio during his vacations in Europe, and the moment he mentioned marriage, she immediately said Yes.

A few months later she was summoned to Paris, to report about her activity. While she was speaking of Julio's business, Mike angrily cut her short. "I sent Tamar over there – and I got a Julietta [he meant a female Julio]. I want to hear what Tamar is doing!"

She indeed took matters in hands and soon outshined her spouse. She carried out clever intelligence-gathering missions; she traveled to the city of Suez, visited the War Museum there and surreptitiously examined the Israeli tanks and personnel carriers captured during the Yom Kippur war. Trying to obtain information about the Israeli missing soldiers, she asked one of the guards to take her pictures beside the armored vehicles; she positioned herself for the camera standing close to the tanks' flanks, so that their serial numbers would be included in the photos. She shivered when looking inside the armored vehicles and seeing the stains of dried blood....

In Cairo she repeatedly drove her small car to the military compounds, to find out if Egypt was planning a new war. She looked for roadblocks, troop movements, closed roads and areas; at night, she approached the Army General staff buildings, to find out if the lights were on till a late hour. When driving, she had to beware of the "Bawabs", the Cairo houses' guards, who sat by the building doors all day long, watching the passing cars. If they noticed that the same woman, in the same car, was passing by them day after day, they might become suspicious and report to the authorities.

Still, acting with Julio as a married couple made their work much easier. While a man walking alone at night in sensitive areas might raise suspicions, a couple walking the street or sitting in a car would seem natural. Danielle and Julio were among the first to use the "new desert highway" from Cairo to Alexandria; they sent home a report about the military camps and installations along the road. They also drove at night to a restricted zone and were stopped by the police beside a roadblock. "Where are you going?" an officer asked. She smiled and mentioned a famous nightclub. "And where are you coming from?" She gave the name of another club. He looked at her, frowning. "Why did you leave that club?" She gave him a naïve, innocent look. "It was very boring there," she chirped. He let them go and did not check the car. "If he had," she recalled, years later, "he would have found a lot of things that were not supposed to be there..."

They lived together in Cairo, but when they "went on a vacation in Europe", they split, and each went their own way. She feared to be recognized at an airport and kept wearing a hat and large sunglasses. She also did not react when somebody addressed her in Hebrew. When she arrived in Israel, she preferred staying at home, and went out only once, to have dinner with Zvi Zamir and his wife. She feared a chance encounter with some university friend and having to lie about her life and work. In the Mossad offices a pile of letters from her mother was waiting for her and she had to write answers, that of course would arrive on future dates. Her mother never understood why the answers to her letters arrived much later from various African capitals.

*

When she met Julio again at the airport, Danielle noticed a dramatic change in his behavior. "I missed you", he said gently, and told her that he had been thinking about her, all the time, during their separation. She liked that. She had got used living with Julio, had started liking him, and the common life in an atmosphere of tension, loneliness, fear of dangers, and joint missions had strengthened the bond between them. She did not hesitate, and making the first move turned to him and said frankly: "We live together. Let's take that up to the end. We'll see what will come out of it." That way, sex was added to their life together. Very quickly, passionate love developed between them. They could not stay away from each other. It grew into a deep, fiery love. They started talking about staying together after they returned to Israel, getting married and raising a family. She knew that once he had a girlfriend in Israel, but he had left her long ago. Today, all that she wanted, was to marry him and spend the rest of her life with him.

She returned to Israel after a year and a half, shortly ahead of him. And as she had agreed with Julio, she asked her superiors for an authorization to marry him. That authorization was needed, as both intended to stay in the Mossad. Mike's answer was unequivocal and disappointing. No way, he said. Their fictive marriage was intended to serve their assignment in Cairo but had to be ended here. Angered, she revolted, started fighting the order at all possible levels; she expected that Julio, on his return, would join her combat.

And here came the second disappointment that broke her heart. Julio arrived – and did not fight. He did not stand by her and did not ask for permission to marry her. She was ready to fight "to the very end", but Julio, diffident, backed off. In Egypt they had sworn that in Israel they would live together, but Julio delayed it, arguing that first they had to wait for the arrival of the container with their personal effects; he later found other pretexts for the delay.

She did not understand why. She loved him with all her heart – and he avoided her. Finally, she rented an apartment for herself alone, and he rather abruptly disappeared. He also left the Mossad, while she moved up the ladder. She started as an interpreter from French to Hebrew, then was appointed as a senior instructor at Caesarea, and successfully confronted the male reluctance of being told what to do by a cute young woman. Weren't they tough and hardened, "the best former combatants of the IDF elite commandos"? But she overcame that obstacle as well. For a long time, she was kept in Israel, out of concern that she might be recognized if sent to missions abroad. Finally, that measure was canceled and she was back in operations, as "combat assistant" who puts in place the outer cover of missions throughout the world.

When the Mossad veterans' convention in Caesarea took place, she called Julio. "We'd better be seen there together," she said,

"Of course", he confirmed. "I'll call you before the meeting, I'll come to pick you up, and we'll go there together."

He did not call, and did not come. She went to the convention alone. Julio did not show up.

After a while she fell in love with another man, Rami, (fictitious name) and they got married. On the eve of their wedding, Rami asked her: "Just imagine that today, tomorrow, the doorbell rings, you open the door – and there stands Julio with a bunch of flowers and says "Sorry, I made a mistake. Let's get married." What would you have done?"

Danielle answered: "I would have married him right away!"

That was a hard answer to swallow, but Rami forgave her. They married and have been living happily together for 46 years, raising children and grandchildren.

And Julio? She heard that he had married his former girlfriend and had two daughters. But he failed to cope with life outside the Mossad. Like Wolfgang Lotz before him, he could not live a normal life. He tried a few jobs, one after the other, fell flat, then divorced and returned to South America where he had been born. There too, he came to nothing; he invited his ex-wife and their daughters to a family reunion in Corfu but canceled at the last moment. He had hit rock bottom in loneliness and despair.

Passersby discovered his body on a South American beach, He was shot in the temple. His hand still clutched the revolver.

*

Danielle retired from the Mossad, leaving a wake of praise and gratitude for her lifelong "heroic activity".

She initiated a few meetings of ex-amazons at her home. That was the first time they could reminisce, reveal and share stories that maybe would never be told. She discovered that many Mossad pensioners, like her, were still bound by strict orders to keep their identities and missions secret; even when the interdictions were lifted, they were still prisoners of invisible walls and fences, and could not open up and behave naturally. Only in these meetings at Danielle's house could those amazons speak freely and spend a few hours with other secret warriors who understood their feelings and their reluctance to share their memories with friends and family.

Today Danielle lives in a sprawling house surrounded by a tropical garden, near Tel Aviv. Once in a while she appears on stage under a pseudonym, guitar in hands, and sings European songs and hits from distant yesterdays.

CHAPTER 15
Erika

Two Women and a Terrorist

AFTER THE LILLEHAMMER TRIAL, YEHUDIT NISSIYAHU, NOW head of the Manpower department of the Mossad, flew to Oslo and visited Sylvia Rafael in prison. On leaving, she asked Sylvia:

"Is there anything we can do for you?"

"There is only one thing I want," Sylvia replied, "Close the account with Ali Hassan Salameh! I can no longer do it, so it's up to you."

*

"Georgina Rizak!" the Master of Ceremonies roared. "Miss Universe Nineteen seventy-one!"

The public filling up the splendid ballroom of the Fontainebleau hotel in Miami beach, erupted in applause and cheers. The bunch of pretty girls on the stage rushed to the gorgeous young woman in the center, and almost smothered her with hugs and kisses (tinged with a lot of envy). The contest director placed on Georgina's head a sparkling crown. That was how the breathtaking Lebanese beauty, Georgina Rizak, was elected the most beautiful woman in the world.

Georgina, the daughter of a Christian Lebanese father and a Hungarian mother, was only eighteen when she arrived at the Miss Universe beauty contest in Miami. The contestants were beauty queens from all over the world. Between the formal stages of the one-month contest, some of them became close friends. Georgina got very friendly with Miss Israel, Esther Orgad; and when two Lebanese diplomats tried to rebuke her for "fraternizing with the enemy", she threw at them: "This is a beauty contest and not a political one ... The conflict is a matter for the governments, not for me."

After the election, the new world queen went on a tour in the United States and met with several state governors. One of them was future President Jimmy Carter. She declaimed everywhere the trite formulas about "her desire to work for world peace", and after an enthusiastic welcome in her native Beirut, plunged in professional activity – modeling, movies, television, fashion, and frequent travels overseas. She was not only beautiful, but also pleasant, well educated, and highly intelligent; Beirut adored her. Her social life became full of dazzling events, receptions, parties and public appearances.

*

While Georgina was painting Beirut red, a 24-year-young woman arrived in Israel. She enrolled in Hebrew University in Jerusalem. Her name was Erika Mary Chambers, born in February 1948 in the Holland Park neighborhood in West London. She was the daughter of a Jewish well-to-do family. Her mother, Luna Gross, had been born in Czechoslovakia, and had escaped to England on the eve of World War II. Most her relatives who stayed behind perished in the Holocaust. During the war Luna married Marcus Chambers. Their daughter, Erika, inherited her father's addiction for car races. He managed automobile clubs, organizations, and sporting events, and once won the famous French race "The 24 hours of Le Mans". His family was respected and well connected. His father had been a Royal Navy captain, and his son Nicolas, Erika's older brother, was about to become a brilliant attorney, a London judge, and a recipient of a Queen's honorary distinction.

Erika's parents separated and she moved in with her mother. From Luna she heard horrible stories about the Holocaust and all her massacred relatives. Still, she grew up as a good natured, curious girl, bursting with vitality. A reporter maintains that for quite a while she babysat the children of Labor MP Tony Benn. But she did not like the life in London, and escaped to Southampton where she studied geography in the local university. Some of the students remember her racing her small Mini Cooper car in the city streets. After a while she moved to Australia and studied Hydrology at Melbourne university. She participated in car races there as a full-fledged contestant, the proud daughter of Marcus, the races master. She disliked Melbourne and finally, in June 1972, arrived in Israel, hoping to complete her studies in the Geography faculty, and get a Ph.D. degree in hydrology.

Shortly after her arrival in Israel, she was shaken by the news about the massacre of the Israeli athletes in Munich. At that time Shabtai Shavit, Chief of Operations and future Ramsad, was active in recruiting. "Somebody told me about an English girl who used to race cars in Australia," Shavit told a friend. "I said – a race car driver? That sounds interesting. Let's check her!"

*

Erika received an official letter that invited her to a personal interview in the Office of International Cooperation. She was a shrewd lady, and immediately guessed that it was "something hush-hush [secret business]". She came willingly. In the "Office" a few men were waiting for her. She did not know them and could not know that the main figure in the room was Mike Harari.

Mike was about to leave the Mossad. Some said he had hoped to become the next Ramsad, but the Lillehammer fiasco had shattered that hope. Still, he continued directing Caesarea missions, mostly defensive against terrorist plots and attacks; like in the past, he kept looking for foreign born warriors, and especially capable women.

When Erika walked in, he came to meet her with another man, a psychologist. He showered her with questions about her life, her identity, her past, and her future plans. At a certain point he asked her: "Do you know what we are looking for?"

"Yes", she said.

"Tell me!"

"I will not", the young woman replied.

"Why?"

"Because if I am mistaken, I'll look like an idiot."

"Tell me anyway", Mike insisted. Everybody was looking at her.

"I think", she slowly said, "that you're looking for people who would be sent under a false identity to the Arab countries."

Silence settled in the room. Mike Harari looked at her for a long time and seemed to be thinking. He finally spoke. "You're right."

That was how Erika was recruited to the Mossad. From that first day she was designed to become a Caesarea target warrior. According to the Mossad instructions she cut off her relations with her acquaintances, left her home and moved to a safehouse where she was trained, alone, by Mossad officers. Bit by bit, Erika felt as if she was being disconnected from the outer world; as if a glass curtain had enveloped her and she had stayed inside while the rest of the world remained beyond the curtain.

During her private course she got to know Mike Harari well. "You, all the warriors, are my children", he once said to her. "A hair on your head is more important to me than any mission."

When her course was over Erika was sent to England, to get a new passport, as her old one carried Israeli entry and departure stamps. Her superiors told her that she would be using her real name and passport. They explained to her that this involved a certain risk, but also a great advantage. "Your name does not sound especially Jewish, they said, "It sounds rather Catholic…and if you are in danger in an enemy country, you always would be able to go to the British embassy with your real passport and ask for help." Still, they ordered her not to get in touch with her family and friends and not enter England again.

But they had another request. "Your nose looks too Jewish," one of her instructors remarked, "perhaps you should need some plastic surgery?"

"A Jewish nose"? These words, in a Gentile's mouth, could seem an Anti-Semitic insult. But she did not mind and agreed. She had surgery and came out of it with a cute little nose, "absolutely gentile". Now she was sent to several exercises and missions in the Arab countries and performed smoothly. "I felt great", she told a Mossad friend. As time went by, Erika impressed her commanders as a tough, calm, meticulous woman, ready to undertake any mission and take risks without getting overly anxious. During her trips, she maintained her contact with her handlers by listening to short-wave radio broadcasts at certain hours, receiving "groups of five letters" and decoding them with "a book and a page" code in a popular book she carried. The encrypted message was broadcast in a code reserved for her only. No outsider could guess that Tolstoy's "Anna Karenina" she was carrying was her code book, and she would count the pages starting, for instance at page 30...

During Erika's training, an Air France liner on its way from Tel Aviv to Paris was hijacked by terrorists and landed in Entebbe airport, in Uganda. The elite *sayeret matkal* commando, supported by paratroopers, landed in Entebbe in the wee hours of the night, and in a short battle killed the terrorists and freed the hostages. A short while later, Mike Harari was awarded the Intelligence medal. Erika learned that before the commando mission Mike had flown to Entebbe posing as an Italian businessman, and collected important information about the airport, the Ugandan soldiers protecting it, and the old terminal where the hostages were kept. He made it back to Israel on time. He then commanded a special unit that was sent to Nairobi, Kenya, to receive the Hercules aircraft coming from Entebbe and carrying the hostages; the unit included a field hospital, doctors and nurses, that finally were not needed. The IDF aircraft only refueled at Nairobi airport before continuing their flight to Israel.

In the winter of 1978 Mike told Erika that a mission to kill someone in Beirut was being planned, and she would take part in it.

*

One evening, while Georgina was having dinner with friends in Beirut, a stranger approached their table. He was handsome, of average height but of athletic built, dressed in black. He looked at her intensely, shook her hand and introduced himself. "My name is Ali," he said, "Ali Hassan Salameh."

She did not know who he was, but he impressed her deeply, by his looks, his charm and his stories about his travels around the globe. Without a doubt, Ali was different from the young Lebanese men she had met. He was a man of the world, one of the leaders of the Palestinian community in Beirut, always surrounded by a suite of admirers and bodyguards. The mystery surrounding his activity thrilled her. She saw in him a strong, confident leader, completely devoted to the struggle for an ideal – the fulfillment of the Palestinian dream. It was not her dream and her ideal, but she was attracted to this man. He fell in love with her and so did she, without suspecting for a moment that Ali was a wolf in sheep's clothing, and his hands had spilled the blood of hundreds of innocent people. When he proposed to her in 1975, she agreed at once, although she knew he already was married and even had a son with his wife. But he was Muslim, and the Muslims could marry more than one woman, could not they? Besides, he assured her that he had cut all contacts with his first wife. Even so, the two of them decided not to have a big wedding, but a modest ceremony where only family members and a few close friends would be invited. Dressed in white, Georgina with a flower in her hair and Ali with a happy smile, posed for a photograph while cutting their wedding cake.

She did not know that Ali had opted for a discreet wedding for another reason. He knew that he was a target of the Mossad. Since the killings in Europe and Beirut, Black September had collapsed, but Salameh knew that only his death would close the organization's file in the Mossad archives. Since his wedding with Georgina he was haunted by a dark premonition. When he met his friend Shafik El Hut, the head of the PLO propaganda department, he told him frankly: "I know I'll die. I shall be assassinated or die in battle."

Ali Hassan Salameh was the last – but also the most important – target in the hit list of "God's Wrath". Since the fiasco in Lillehammer the campaign had been stopped and the Kidon warriors did not chase terrorist murderers in Europe anymore. But despite the halt of the operation, Black September had suffered a mortal blow and disintegrated completely. The mission, after all, had succeeded more than expected; after "Spring of Youth" Black September disappeared as if dispelled by a magic wand. Aharon Yariv, the Prime Minister's anti-terrorism adviser, admitted years later that he did not expect that after killing a few terrorist leaders in Europe, the Mossad would annihilate Black September. Yet, Israel had an open account with Ali Salameh, the most cruel and resolute of them all. That account had been frozen after Lillehammer. The Yom Kippur War, Entebbe, the Camp David peace agreements with Egypt seemed to have relegated the Salameh affair to the back burner.

In the meantime, Salameh quickly climbed the Fatah hierarchy. Yasser Arafat appointed him commander of the prestigious "Force 17" that assured the personal security of the PLO leaders. Arafat also made Salameh his intimate adviser, and the Red Prince joined him in his trips to Moscow and to the United Nations in New York. The New York trip caused an angry confrontation between Arafat and his close friend Abu Ayad, who watched with envy the meteoric rise of Salameh. On the eve of the New York trip he presented a hard choice to Arafat: me or Salameh. Arafat chose Salameh, and repeated, in public, his decision that Ali would be his successor at the helm of the Fatah, one day.

Arafat was not the only one who showed interest in Salameh. The American CIA [the Central Intelligence Agency] also regarded him as someone with a great potential. Robert Ames, a senior CIA official, and some of his colleagues, established a close connection with Salameh and recruited him as informant and adviser. They paid him large sums of money and guaranteed him and his men full immunity, if they would not carry out any operations on American soil or against American targets elsewhere. In 1977 Salameh was even invited to the CIA headquarters in Langley, Virginia. In Kai Bird's book "The Good Spy" Ames describes how the CIA people hosted Salameh and Georgina in a trip to the US. "Charles Waverly was assigned to accompany the couple to New Orleans, then to Anaheim, California to visit Disneyland, and finally to Hawaii." CIA operations officer Alan Wolfe flew down to New Oleans to meet him. Salameh was showered with gifts including a shoulder holster for his gun; and Ames bought him a leather briefcase with a hidden tape-recorder. The couple escort, Waverly, recalled the addiction of Ali to oysters, believing they had aphrodisiac qualities. "I was in the adjoining hotel room," Ames quotes Waverly, "so in the evenings I heard the results".

One can hardly sympathize with the blindness and the absurdity in the CIA behavior. In Salameh they saw an important intelligence asset, even though the same Salameh had conceived and commanded the execution-style massacre of western diplomats in Khartoum, including the American ambassador. But for the Fatah, that foolhardy attitude of the CIA was a bonanza. Yasser Arafat was aware of Salameh's love affair with the American spies and regarded it as a secret communication channel with the US administration. These bizarre relations between the US and one of the most dangerous Palestinian terrorists, led to a grave confrontation between the CIA and the Mossad, that saw Salameh as a fanatical, dangerous killer who should be put to death. The Mossad senior leaders, frustrated, furious and helpless, watched the development of warm relations between Salameh and the Americans. Apparently, the CIA warned Salameh, more than once, of the dangers for his life that the Mossad represented, and even considered supplying him with a bulletproof car to protect his life.

On March 11, 1978, PLO terrorists landed on the beach of kibbutz Maagan Michael, in Israel, hijacked a bus, massacred its 35 passengers and wounded 71. This attack was the most recent in a series of terrorist attacks on Israel, and the public opinion angrily demanded to hit the terrorist groups that were back on the warpath.

Almost six years after the Lillehammer fiasco Prime Minister Menahem Begin summoned the new Ramsad, Yitzhak (Haka) Hofi and ordered him to find and kill the Red Prince.

*

Mossad warriors carrying fake papers landed in Beirut and soon were on Salameh's tracks. Their reports to King Saul Boulevard in Tel Aviv described the daily routine of the Red Prince. They knew the exact time when he would leave his apartment at the Snoubra neighborhood in west Beirut, and the composition of his motorcade – a Chevrolet station wagon with two bodyguards preceded by a Land Rover jeep with another four armed Palestinians, and followed by a pickup Toyota with more bodyguards, armed with a heavy machine gun. The Mossad warriors also found out the itinerary of Salameh's motorcade, through Beirut's crowded streets, to Arafat's headquarters, where the offices of Force 17 were situated as well. When they returned to Israel, the warriors also reported about the Red Prince's daily journeys for lunch at home with Georgina, and then back to headquarters. They also had collected some information about his activity after work.

Three paragraphs in the report caught the attention of the Mossad commanders: Salameh's frequent meetings with Bashir Gemayel, the major commander of the Christian phalanges, and Israel's close ally; his habit to come home every day for lunch and rest with Georgina, before returning to headquarters; and his regular visits to the Continental Hotel gym, in West Beirut. He exercised there in Karate, a martial art he liked since his youth in Germany.

One of Caesarea's warriors, Dror, (fictitious name) arrived in Beirut under the cover of a European businessman and rented an apartment and an office. He was instructed to visit the gym, and so he did. He swam in the pool, toiled at the machines, sweated in the sauna – but did not find Salameh. He finally decided to change his exercise hours, got there in the late afternoon, and entered the sauna. One of the men sitting there emptied a bucket of water on the embers, and the small cubicle filled with steam. Dror watched the steam dispel – and suddenly, in front of him, he saw the Red Prince, stark naked!

Dror ignored Salameh, according to Mike Harari's strict orders not to seek any contact with the Red Prince. But the opposite happened. Salameh was the one who started a conversation with the stranger he saw exercising at the gym, and Dror had no choice but go along. The conversation led to unexpected results. They met a few times; Salameh invited his new friend to his home, and introduced him to his beautiful Georgina. Salameh, who all day long was surrounded by PLO terrorists, apparently enjoyed his meetings with a foreigner, who came from a different world and brought with him a whiff of a different life. Dror often played squash with Salameh at the gym, and became a frequent guest at Salameh's house. During his visits there he saw that in the living room, the bedroom and even the bathroom, Salameh had placed Kalashnikov submachine guns for his protection, beside the handgun he carried all the time. Dror admitted later that he had reached a state of schizophrenia. On the one hand, he had become a friend of Salameh, and liked him – but on the other he planned his killing, as the massacre of the 11 athletes in Munich was always on his mind. Dror even reported once that on his birthday, Salameh gave him a present – a Dupont golden lighter. After dining at his home that night, he went with Salameh, his wife and her gorgeous sister Fellicina to a Beirut discotheque, and danced with the pretty women till the wee hours.

But he did not forget his mission, despite the friendship that developed between him and the Red Prince. The Mossad asked: how can we kill Salameh? Using the contacts Salameh had with Bashir Jemayel was out of the question, as an operation of the kind could cost the lives of Lebanese Christians and could disrupt the special relations between Israel and Jemayel. In those days Lebanon was torn by a civil war and the connection between Jemayel and Salameh perhaps was a secret communication channel. Israel could not interfere in these relations.

The Mossad efforts focused on the sauna in the Continental gym, where Salameh used to wander, naked and serene. He could be killed there and Dror was supposed to play a major role in this operation. The plan was to plant explosives under the wooden bench of the sauna and blow it up when Salameh entered. The preparations were completed but it turned out that such explosion could cost the lives of innocents. The plan therefore was shelved. Only the third possibility remained. Georgina, Salameh's beloved wife, was unwittingly to cause the Red Prince's death.

*

In November 1978 Erika Chambers landed in Beirut and entered Lebanon with her genuine British passport, that had been issued in 1975. During her "private course" she already had visited several "target countries" for training purposes; she also had to establish a legend of a social worker, volunteering in the Middle East. She had frequently traveled to Germany, to build the cover of an Englishwoman living in Frankfurt. She spent the following four years in Germany, actually moving from one city to the other, leaving behind a wake of addresses in Munich, Frankfurt, Wiesbaden, Cologne; that way any hostile effort to verify her life story was bound to fail. Her mother had taught her German since her childhood and she spoke it well. At the same time Mike Harari and David Shimron, under foreign covers, created a phony British humanitarian foundation, that supported Palestinian hospitals and mostly focused on children. The foundation was called The Safe Home of the Tel El Za'ater Children.

Tel El Za'ater was a Palestinian refugee camp in the outskirts of Beirut. On August 12 1976, at the peak of the civil war, the Christian Phalanges raided the camp and massacred about 2,000 people, mostly women and old men. The children who survived were moved to another camp, in the center of Beirut, where local and foreign volunteers took care of them. Erika was a "Foundation volunteer" and as such had visited several Arab countries. She had started visiting Beirut at the beginning of 1978, but only in November she came for a long stay in Lebanon's capital.

*

Before leaving, Erika met Mike Harari. Mike told her that the Mossad has got precise information on the whereabouts of the "target" in Beirut. "At first, we have to find an apartment that would serve as a base for the kill." He fell silent, then he added: "You are going to kill the target."

Another silence, then Mike again: "How do you feel about it?"

"I do not know", she said. "I never killed anybody. I'll tell you later how I felt. But as of now, I am ready to do it."

She did not feel any inhibitions or hesitations and decided that in order to carry out her mission well, she must think of herself as "an instrument of Justice."

When she got in Beirut, she started working in the local branch – the biggest – of the Tel El Za'ater Children foundation. After work she looked for an apartment. According to her orders, it had to be close to Salameh's house and have an unobstructed view of his home and vicinity. The Mossad had given her the addresses of three apartments in that area. She did not know that these apartments had been chosen by Dror, who also had suggested the assassination plan to Mike Harari. Out of the three apartments, Erika rejected the first, because it was too close to Salameh's house. The second one had only a partial view of his home; but the third was perfect: a flat on the eighth floor of a corner building, at the intersection of two streets – Rue Verdun and Rue Madame Curie. Bustling Madame Curie was the permanent route Salameh's motorcade took to and from his office. It passed virtually under Erika's windows.

Before furnishing the apartment, Erika hired a couple of handy-men to plaster and paint her new home. They were Palestinians and showed her Salameh's apartment across the street. "You see," they proudly pointed, "this is Salameh's home, just here!"

Erika hung mesh curtains on the windows, so she could look out but nobody could look in. Now she started sitting by the window for hours chain smoking. She soon became known in the neighborhood as "Penelope", an eccentric woman, who used to roam the neighborhood, disheveled, in shabby clothes, carrying bowls of food for stray cats. Her neighbors claimed that she also kept cats in her home. She also used to sit in her room, facing the window and paint Beirut – its mosques, streets, and the sea glimmering close by. She used to proudly show her paintings to her neighbors who profusely praised her talents out of sheer politeness but would not dream of buying one of her dubious artworks.

They all regarded her as a lonely, poor, miserable woman, who found some solace in her painting, her cats and the children of Tel El Za'ater. That was fine with her. Erika quickly got used to that kind of life. She did not have any social life, and no romantic interests. When asked years later if she had any dates with young men in Beirut, she retorted: "May I be vulgar? It was … a quickie and that's it. In order not to create an emotional commitment." And so she sat alone in her home, month after month, many hours a day, smoking and watching.

Nobody could guess that neither the Beirut mosques nor the blue sea interested her, but a certain view in the busy street under her window. She meticulously noted the hours and minutes when Salameh appeared at his house door, entered his brown Chevrolet and set off on his way. She noted down that Salameh's motorcade passed under her windows four times a day: in the morning- from Rue Verdun, turning into Rue Madame Curie and continuing southward, to the Fatah Headquarters, at noon in the opposite direction, and in the afternoon again southward and back in the evening.

Erika kept watching the Chevrolet with powerful binoculars and often could discern the figure of Salameh sitting between two body-guards. His frequent daily trips proved that the meals with beautiful Georgina disrupted the strict security measures that Salameh observed in the past. He disregarded the golden rules that a secret warrior had to remember: never develop routine habits; never live too long at the same address; never use the same itinerary twice. Salameh sacrificed all this for the delight of spending the sweet afternoons with his wife. That's how Georgina became the Achilles heel of the Red Prince.

*

In early January 1979 Erika came to Israel, to train for her mission. Finally, Mike revealed to her the full details of the operation.

The plan was to park a booby-trapped car on the street where Salameh's motorcade was about to pass. The explosive charge would be activated by remote control on the very second when Salameh's car would pass by the rigged vehicle. That lethal and yet delicate task was to be carried out by Erika.

The Mossad technology experts had built a model for the training. Erika stood by a window, a remote-control device in her hand, and the moment she received a signal, she had to press a button on the device. The operation had been rehearsed before, with male and female Kidon warriors, training to activate the charge the moment a car sailed past a certain point. During the training Mike Harari had found out that the women were more accurate than the men; therefore, he had decided to entrust the task to Erika, despite the objections of some.

Facing the model, Erika spent hours, repeating the operation over and over again. "Once more", she would say to her instructors, "I still do not feel I am ready." The Caesarea instructors admired her thoroughness. Still, they feared that "as a woman" she was weak and vulnerable. She probably would get agitated when a deafening explosion would occur, and then she might lose her reasoning for a few minutes, especially in the critical moments after the explosion. They therefore took Erika to the Palmachim base, on the seashore, to rehearse the explosion of a big charge. The signal was given – a sudden burst of white smoke – and Erika pressed the remote button. A tremendous explosion shook the entire area. Erika did not wince. The Caesarea experts had to admit that the lady was not impressed by the shattering explosion. She was ready.

The last briefing was held in Germany. Mike gave Erika the final orders. She also learned by heart scores of codes for communication use and flew back to Beirut.

On January 17, 1979, a British businessman named Peter Scriver arrived in Beirut on a Swissair flight from Zurich. He presented to the Immigration officer his British passport No. 260896, issued in London on October 15, 1975.

"Purpose of visit?" the Lebanese officer asked.

"Business."

"Welcome to Lebanon."

(A few years later an Englishman called Peter Derbyshire would come to the offices of the British "Guardian" newspaper and claim that his passport had been stolen by Mossad agents and served for establishing a fake identity for Peter Scriver.)

Scriver checked in the Hotel Mediterranee, and the following day rented a Volkswagen Golf at the Lenacar agency.

At a prearranged rendezvous in the city, Scriver met another foreigner, a Canadian carrying passport No. DS 104227 on the name of Ronald Kolberg, a traveling representative of the cutlery company Regent Sheffield, based in New York. Kolberg checked into the Royal Garden Hotel and rented a Simca-Chrysler at Lenacar.

Lenacar was definitely a popular company with foreign secret agents these days. The following morning, Erika Chambers rented a Datsun at Lenacar. The eccentric English lady confided in the receptionist and complained that her nerves were in a bad shape and she wanted to escape to the nearby mountains. The receptionist suggested a couple of resorts. Chambers thanked her profusely and promised to follow her advice. But instead of the mountains, she parked the Datsun in a side street, not far from her home, and returned to her paintings on the eighth floor. She never met Dror.

A couple of days before, Dror had left Beirut and traveled to Jordan. At night, he drove south in the desert, close to the Israeli border. He met there with Shabtai Shavit and a squad of *sayeret matkal* who had crossed the border from Israel, carrying 100 pounds of plastic explosives. The explosives were hidden inside a massive wooden armchair. The commandos swiftly loaded the armchair in Dror's car, then they stealthily crossed the border back to Israel while Dror drove his car north, successfully crossed the border to Syria and then to Lebanon, finally reaching Beirut.

In Beirut, Kolberg and Scriver were waiting for him. He delivered the armchair and watched from afar how Kolberg dismounted the armchair and extracted the explosives. They were concealed in the headrests of the driver and the passenger, exactly identical to the Volkswagen headrests. Kolberg, who was a legendary fighter in the IDF Golani Brigade, replaced the original Volkswagen headrests with the explosive ones. He also connected the charge to an electronic device, that would activate the explosives following a remote-control signal. Dror was not allowed to speak to them, but could not refrain, and when he passed by Kolberg, muttered: "Give them hell, kiddos!" He left, while the two warriors parked the Volkswagen at Rue Madame Curie, facing Erika's window.

Scriver changed several times the parking place of the Volkswagen until he found the right spot. He got up to the eighth floor and spent three nights in Erika's apartment. He and Erika watched the Red Prince's motorcade going back and forth in the busy street.

On January 22, Kolberg left his hotel, drove to the seaside town of Junia, populated by Christians, and checked into the Montmartre hotel. Scriver took a flight out of Beirut. Mike Harari, who had flown to Lebanon to supervise the last stages of the mission, left as well that day.

That same day, at 3:25 PM Ali Hassan Salameh left his home with a guest who had come for lunch. On leaving, he caressed Georgina's belly. She was five months pregnant now.

"It will be a girl!" he said.

"I want a boy" she answered, "I want a boy that will look like you. I want another Ali."

"And I dream of a girl as charming as you", Salameh said, and left the house with his guest, who was no other but Abu Jihad, Yasser Arafat's deputy.

*

Erika saw Abu Jihad from her window but did not recognize him. She saw him part from Salameh and go his way. Erika had been watching Salameh's house since 10:00 AM. A light drizzle, this morning, had cleaned the air and the visibility had improved. Erika had been waiting for almost six hours until Salameh entered his car, with his bodyguards sitting by his sides. Jamil, the driver, started up the car. The other bodyguards climbed into the Land Rover and the Toyota and the three cars moved forward.

Erika watched from her window. In her hands she held a unique kind of remote control. It was a small radio set that she had brought from Israel. It was a regular radio, but when one stuck a metal pin in a tiny hole on the radio side, it turned into an activation system. When a red button, usually serving to turn the radio on and off, was pressed, it became a powerful remote-control.

And all of a sudden – an unexpected glitch. A truck, loaded with gas canisters, stopped near her house. Erika understood that she might have to abort the mission; if the explosives blew up while the truck was in the vicinity, the gas canisters would explode as well, killing hundreds! Erika fervently prayed God in her heart that the truck would go away; and her prayer bore fruit. The truck left. Erika's last thought before Salameh's car passed in front of her was about coping with this situation: "I must kill a man", she said to herself. "This must be a pure target, and my action must be devoid of any personal feeling. No hatred and no nothing."

She saw the Chevrolet approaching down the street. The traffic was sparse. Barely ten yards now separated Salameh's station-wagon from the rigged Volkswagen, squeezed between other parked cars.

Six yards. Five. Four. Two.

She pressed her face to the windowpane and opened her mouth to protect herself from the shock wave. The Chevrolet moved by the parked cars and smoothly sailed by the Volkswagen.

She pressed the red button.

A huge explosion shook the Madame Curie street. The Volkswagen turned into a ball of fire. The Chevrolet and the Land Rover, engulfed by the fire, blew up in turn. Fire and smoke spread all over the street. Chunks of metal from the burning cars, and splinters of glass from the neighboring houses' windows were projected upwards. On the sidewalks and in the middle of the street lay wounded and dead people. A few minutes later, the sirens of police cars and ambulances were heard. Out of the twisted remains of the Chevrolet the paramedics extracted three bodies – the driver and the two bodyguards. Ali Salameh suffered a gashing head wound as an iron splinter had pierced his brain. An ambulance carried him to the American University hospital.

The mission also had a painful, unfortunate result. Four passersby were killed, and eighteen wounded. They all were innocent victims of the explosion. Among the dead was a young woman Erika had crossed a few times in the neighborhood. Her face and her family's pain would haunt Erika for years to come.

Georgina jumped into her sports car and darted toward the hospital. But the doctors' efforts in the operating room were in vain. The splinter in Salameh's head caused his death.

Yasser Arafat, who was at a meeting in Damascus, burst in tears on hearing the news; he was immediately ushered to a secret hiding place, as his entourage feared that Israel intended to kill all the Fatah leaders. He came out of hiding only a few days later.

*

Erika disheveled her hair, adopted an expression of fear and disarray, and ran down the stairs. She had to run away, and her escape depended on her actions in the next ten minutes. She emerged on the smoke-filled street, among the wounded and the horrified passersby, looking as a dismayed, badly scared woman. She scurried down the street, reached the rented Datsun car, started it and drove away. She had to reach a prearranged meeting point, pick up Kolberg and drive to Junia, north of Beirut. In the meantime, the Mossad dispatched to the Beirut area a communication aircraft, manned by the veteran warrior Shlomo Gal. Erika reached the meeting point, and picked up Kolberg, who was equipped with a small walkie talkie.

While his plane was circling close to Beirut, Shlomo Gal tried to establish a connection with Erika, but without success. He called her "Michelle", to protect her identity. He called repeatedly but she did not answer. Kolberg did not receive Gal's call.

In the Mossad, the tension was rising. At her last briefing Erika was instructed that if any problem arose in her extraction process, she had to use an alternative escape plan: take a taxi to Dror's apartment, which was at about 7 minutes from her home. Dror kept a fake passport for her and a wig that changed her looks completely. He was supposed to travel with her to Damascus, with her posing as his wife, and there help her to get on a flight to Europe.

Gal tried again to contact her from the plane. Suddenly, he heard Michelle's voice. Everything was fine, and she was on her way to Junia.

The IDF Navy reported: the extraction plan was ready. Erika and Kolberg could get down to Junia beach. From afar Erika noticed a few heads bobbing up and down from the sea waves. Those were the commando fighters of Flotilla 13, Israel's Navy Seals, waiting for her. The Seals immediately brought Zodiac fast dinghies that took Erika and Kolberg to the open sea, where an Israeli missile boat was moored. It sailed south, to Israel. A young Flotilla 13 fighter saw the young woman boarding the boat and understood she had done something extraordinary. He was Yoav Galant, a future general and Minister in Netanyahu's cabinet.

Evening came. From the moment she boarded the missile boat Erika felt that the tension was fading away. Somebody brought her a telegram of congratulations from Mike Harari. She contemplated the Junia mountains, the starry skies ang the moon and thought – what a romantic way to end a career! It was clear that her warrior days were over, for she could not step on Arab territory after that mission.

Dror was not in Beirut anymore. Immediately after Erika's departure he drove his car to Damascus. It was strange, he recalled years later, the dangerous, cruel city of Damascus had suddenly become a safe haven for me.

When the Lebanese security forces broke into Erika's apartment, they found there her personal effects, her field glasses and her genuine passport.

*

Four months later Georgina gave birth to a son and called him Ali, after his father. When he grew up both he and his brother from Salameh's first wife refused to take part in the violent struggle against Israel, and publicly expressed their support for a peace solution. Young Ali also visited Israel after the 1994 Oslo agreements and enjoyed warm hospitality wherever he went,

Georgina, devastated, painfully mourned her husband, but went on with her life and remarried. Years later, in Cairo, she met the Israeli journalist Semadar Peri and shared some of her memories with her, even helping, by Semadar's intermediary, Bar-Zohar and Haber who wrote a book about the Red Prince.

Erika Mary Chambers vanished from the face of the earth. Various rumors placed her in the South of France, where she allegedly managed a small hotel. The Mossad officers who knew her protected her secret, and her new identity was not revealed. All that Aliza Magen said about her was: "If you saw her, you wouldn't believe that this was the warrior who pressed the button. She is a nice, plump lady, resembling a pleasant aunt..."

In 2019, forty years after the mission, Erika suddenly appeared on television, her face blurred, and frankly answered the questions of reporter Alon Ben David, in his program "Hit List." She described her actions and feelings in those far-off days, and at the fatal moment when she pressed the red button. Today, she said, she was living a happy life.

Erika and Georgina were the two women who caused the demise of the Red Prince.

The one, Georgina – with her love.

The other, Erika – with her daring.

Erika was awarded a Medal of Valor by the Mossad. "She was in Beirut for long months almost completely alone," said a former Ramsad in an interview with "Yedioth Aharonoth". "And she was the one who had to decide when to press the button and slay Salameh."

*

Mike Harari left the Mossad in 1980 and went into private business, but not for long. He returned to the Mossad, then left again and started a new career as the unofficial Mossad envoy to Latin America. His career culminated when he became the personal adviser of Panama's dictator, Manuel Noriega, and wielded great power in the country. He was aware of Noriega's dark affairs in money, drugs and violence, but was not involved in them. On the demand of the US Secretary of State, George Shultz, Mike tried to mediate between Noriega and the US government, but failed. Still, when President George H. Bush decided to invade Panama, the two most wanted men by the American military were Noriega and Harari. Noriega was captured, tried, and died in prison; Mike Harari escaped, and after a dramatic odyssey in the South American maze, was back in Israel and settled down in Tel Aviv, surrounded by his wife, children and grandchildren. But retirement was not for him. He returned to the Mossad for a last time in 2005, took part in one of the most sophisticated missions in Iran, and was decorated by the great Ramsad Meir Dagan. Mike Harari died in 2014, warmly remembered by his ladies.

Part Four

Crystalline Waters,
Virgin Beaches –
and a Secret

CHAPTER 16

Yola, Gila, Ilana

A Divers' Paradise, far, far away

Yola

The beautiful yacht "Yemanja" sailed into the port of Eilat, on the Red Sea, stirring admiration and curiosity. Built of teak wood in a classical style, it was the biggest yacht in Israel. On her deck stood the owners, Yola (Yolanta) Reitman and her associates. Yola, a curly, blue eyed blonde, was born in Germany, and had been barely two years old when she immigrated to Israel with her parents.

Her mother had given her the name of a legendary princess, the heroine of Tchaikovsky's last opera. Her parents spoke German at home and for Yola it became a mother's language. She was addicted to the sea since her teens as a high school student, dreaming of the day when she would sail the seven seas on board of her own boat. She admired the great Portuguese sea masters, like Vasco da Gama and Ferdinand Magellan, who sailed the seas in their absurd cockleshells in search for Eldorado.

After her military service Yola spent two years studying architecture in Paris, but the addiction to the oceans did not fade away. When she heard that a New Zealand family living in Caesarea was selling an amazing yacht, she mortgaged her home in Kadima village, and bought the stunning boat. She also named her Yemanja, after the Brazilian sea goddess that protected the Bahia fishermen, or so the legend went.

Yola swiftly established her routine in Eilat, taking tourists to Coral Island and the Sinai golden beaches. Between sailing expeditions, she worked as a flight attendant in "El Al", and in her free time took a diving course. Her instructor, Ruby Eviatar, would often disappear for a few weeks from the Divers Club. She was not interested in his trips but he was interested in her; one day in 1982 he introduced her to his friend, a handsome, suave man named Danny Limor. They asked her a lot of questions and even made her go through a detailed security scanning. They did not give her the reason for that impromptu interrogation, but she guessed a lot. Many of her friends were in the past commando fighters in Flotilla 13 and *Sayeret Matkal*, and some of them were today members of the Shabak; she surmised that Ruby and Danny were connected to the Mossad.

She did not know, however, that Danny Limor was a Mossad warrior in the "Bitzur" department that dealt with the immigration of Jews from the Arab and Muslim states to Israel, and also took care of the protection of Jewish institutions throughout the world. At one of their meetings, Danny asked her if she would like to join them. She did not ask to what purpose, did not inquire if there was a danger involved, did not want to know what her salary was going to be, or – the major question – where they wanted to send her. She just said "Yes".

Her born curiosity and her adventure streak made her agree even without knowing anything about the mission. She understood she was being recruited for Israel's defense, and the offer suited her deep Zionist feelings. "It was for the good of our country," she told reporter Oren Nahari years later. "So it was obvious that I should be there."

There was another reason for her quick decision. It dated from her youth, when she was at the twelfth grade. One day two IDF officers came to her high school and described to the boys the various army corps where they could serve, when drafted. She rebelled. Why only to the boys? Why not to the girls? At that early age she already slammed into the glass ceiling, that prevented women to carry out missions exactly like the men. And when she said Yes to Ruby and Danny, she saw the opportunity to prove that a woman could carry out a mission like a man, and perhaps even better.

Yola did not know anything about the mission they had in mind. Before another meeting with Ruby and Danny, she casually leafed through an old copy of the National Geographic magazine and saw an article about Soudan in Africa. When she entered their room, she nonchalantly tossed the open magazine on the table, and asked, half-jokingly: "It's there, right?"

The two men were stunned. They assailed her with questions: "How do you know? Who told you? Who leaked this to you?" Her explanations did not help. It took her a considerable time and efforts to convince them it was a wild guess, and nothing else.

But indeed – the objective was Soudan.

Danny Limor asked Yola to manage a divers' resort on Soudan's beach. Soudan, a Muslim nation, was one of the biggest countries in Africa, and Israel's sworn enemy. Yola thought that the offer was strange – why did not they appoint one of the more experienced Mossad warriors? And why a woman and not a man? It turned out that Danny saw in Yola the ideal candidate and had to fight all his superiors in order to get her the assignment. Mike Harari had left the Mossad a couple of years before, but it seemed that Danny Limor, unwittingly, had taken his place as a fighter for the Mossad amazons.

The head of Bitzur at that time, Efraim Halevy, objected to Limor's idea. Send a woman, alone, to an enemy country? No way. The confrontation fired up and reached the Ramsad. Hofi did not object but told Halevy: "Check her!" Hofi's successor, Nahum Admoni, would have a similar reaction, when he would become Ramsad.

Halevy met Yola in a café. They plunged in a long conversation. "What do you know about secret activity?" he asked.

She replied: "Only what I read in spy novels."

"What novels?"

"John le Carre's."

Le Carre apparently convinced Halevy and he told Yola that she would get the assignment. From that moment on he supported her all along her service in the Mossad.

Yola was sent to a crash course. According to the Mossad compartmentalization rules, the course was divided into small groups;

Yola's group included her and four men. The course included exercises and tests, beside long sessions with a psychologist and a psychiatrist. The psychologist gave Yola a hard time. He admitted finding in her a great potential, but her gender bothered him. She fought back. "Why you, men, always know what is good for the women? What is the problem with my gender? That my wet dream is not washing a baby's diapers?"

Finally, the psychologist surrendered and gave her the green light. Out of the five course participants only two reached the finish – Yola and one of the men. Now the process of recruitment to the Mossad was completed, and Yola could learn the secrets of her mission.

A few years before, shortly after he was elected Prime Minister, Menahem Begin summoned the Ramsad Yitzhak Hofi and told him: "Bring me the Jews of Ethiopia." That was how a unique Mossad operation started, code-named Operation Brothers.

Hofi dispatched his deputy, Dave Kimche, to Addis Ababa, and he negotiated a deal with the Ethiopian ruler, Mengistu Haile Mariam: Israel would supply Ethiopia with arms, and Ethiopia would allow the immigration of Jews to Israel. That arrangement did not last, and was canceled by Mengistu after Moshe Dayan, the Israeli Foreign minister, leaked the deal's details. Many thousands of Jews who were about to immigrate, became prisoners in their country. The project seemed doomed when a brave Jewish-Ethiopian maverick, Ferde Aklum, met the Mossad envoy Danny Limor; the two of them conceived an alternative immigration plan. The Jews would illegally cross the border into neighboring Soudan, would cross the desert by foot, reach the international refugee camps around the capital, Khartoum, and from there would proceed to Israel by one of several possible ways.

And so, the Ethiopian exodus started.

Thousands of Jews left their villages, crossed the border and walked toward Khartoum. The desert was merciless. The long march under the brutal sun, snakes and scorpions, wild animals, armed robbers, decimated the defenseless convoys of men, women and children. Thousands died in the march, turning it into a tragic saga on the courage and the yearning of an entire community to reach the Promised

Land. But even when the survivors reached the refugee camps, they found out that the major portion of the road to the coveted Jerusalem was still ahead. Mossad warriors secretly arrived in Khartoum and tried to send groups of Jews carrying fake passports to Israel via Europe. But the Soudanese secret services discovered the ploy and prohibited the flights. Another solution was necessary, urgently. The Ethiopian Jews were hunted in the refugee camps, beaten, stabbed, arrested and tortured. Some of their daughters were abducted and never seen again. Something had to be done.

Danny Limor thought of the Red Sea. His idea was to bring the Jews to Soudan's coast, load them on rubber boats that would carry them to big ships in the high sea; the ships would sail to Eilat, Israel's southern port.

Operation Brothers was back on track.

In Soudan, Danny Limor posed as an anthropologist, who researched the mores of the tribes spread along the coast. He set out on a unique kind of journey with one of the greatest warriors of the Mossad, Jonathan Shefa. Their plan was to explore the beaches, hundreds of kilometers north-east of Khartoum, and find a bay from which the Ethiopian Jews could sail to Israel. To their immense surprise, they discovered a ready solution. By a splendid Red Sea cove Limor and Shefa found an abandoned tourist resort. The place was called Arous. Nobody lived there now, except for a guard by the name of Abu Medina. The sweet old man gathered twigs, lit a fire, ground coffee beans with a couple of stones, made coffee for Limor and Shefa and told them the resort's story. The picturesque tourist village had been built on the seashore by Italian investors – but they went bankrupt and left Soudan. Danny immediately reported the find to Halevy and the Mossad was back in business.

Danny was known to the authorities as anthropologist – he even gave a lecture in Khartoum university on the Soudanese tribes. Now he metamorphosed into a businessman. He was helped by the Soudan-born Jewish tycoon Nessim Gaon, who set up a bogus company for him in Switzerland. Danny, as a representative of the company, got in touch with the Soudanese government that was now the owner of the resort. He asked to rent the place for three years, and establish there an "International diving center." He willingly paid the price of 320,000 US dollars. The Soudanese government was delighted to earn some foreign currency and supported the project. And the Arous diving center resort was born.

The Arous bungalows could host 40 people. Local workers refurbished, painted and equipped the lodges. Mossad technicians arrived, with phony passports, and brought modern equipment including air conditioning units; the inscriptions in Hebrew had been diligently erased. Limor bought a generator for electricity supply; water could be brought in containers from sources four hours away. In the village the Israelis found a small desalinization plant, a gift to Soudan from Saudi Arabia. When they checked it, the Mossad officers found inscriptions in Hebrew; it had been made in Israel! Danny and his comrades bought motorboats and kayaks, trucks and a Toyota jeep. Radio communication sets were also smuggled to Arous and concealed in oxygen bottles. For the proper functioning of the village, the Mossad envoys hired 18 local employees – three cooks, waiters, a driver, a technician, and chamber maids from Eritrea. The diving instructors were veterans of Flotilla 13, under Anglo-Saxon cover.

And of course, the manager – Yola Reitman, under the name of Angela, carrying a German passport.

The opening of the village was publicized in Europe. A Swiss travel agency organized divers' groups and the resort was on its way. It was not very easy getting there: a commercial flight from Europe to Khartoum, then a local flight with the Soudanese airways, that the Israelis nicknamed "Inshallah airways" out of the hope – Inshallah – that the flight, even if delayed by one or two hours or even a whole day – will finally take off. The plane would bring the passengers to Port Soudan, then the Arous vehicles would take them another 70 kilometers on the bumpy dirt roads to the resort. This *via dolorosa* apparently enhanced the divers' feeling of an exotic adventure.

But then they would reach Arous and discover a piece of paradise.

And paradise it was. Yola arrived to Arous while it was still in the process of refurbishing. Efraim Halevy, who cared about her safety, sent her first to Zurich in Switzerland, where she waited two days and then flew to Soudan with her German passport. The moment she entered Arous, she fell in love with the village and the bay. She saw a row of little houses, painted in bright colors with red roofs, arched passageways, and an astounding view of the ocean. The pristine beauty of the area moved her deeply. In the early evening she looked at the sea – and saw that "the entire shore was moving"! It turned out that tens of thousands hermit crabs, in tight formations, were crawling on the sand and creating the illusion that the beach was moving toward the water...

Yola quickly took matters in hand – she organized the diving schedules, established the work rules for the locals, prepared the menus of the dining room while juggling with the limited supply of food from the city, bought an ice box for the products, made yoghurt out of milk powder, took care of a continuous supply of fish from the sea and most – created close relations with the inhabitants of the area. She also bought large quantities of fuel, as the village needed a barrel a day, and on top of all this, took on an unofficial job; protecting the chambermaids from the Soudanese men in her team.

And of course, she prepared for her secret function: help managing the missions that were carried once a month.

The missions were code-named "home haven". Jonathan Shefa, also known as "Prosper" recruited some of his former Mossad comrades, like Emmanuel Allon, code-name "Julian", and others; the journalist Gadi Sukenik, a former Flotilla 13 fighter, also joined the team. A few days before a mission, warriors would come in from Israel, settle in the village, and one evening would get on the trucks, and tell the local employees that they were going to meet the Swedish Red Cross nurses in a nearby town. Actually they drove the village vehicles to Khartoum, 500 kilometers away, arrived at a prearranged meeting area out of town, loaded on the truck and jeep hundreds of Ethiopian Jews – sometimes 200 or 300 at a time, and drive them to "Marsa Fijab", a secluded cove north of the resort. These journeys lasted a few Days; but the convoy moved only in the dark, and only in moonless nights; during the day the vehicles and their human load hid in some wadi by the road, and resumed their journey after sunset. Those days Soudan was torn by a civil war, and the army was setting roadblocks on the highways. Danny knew how to buy his passage, by bribing the soldiers with packs of cigarettes and white bread; the vehicles were allowed to continue and reached the cove in the dark of night.

On the beach the seals of Flotilla 13 were waiting. They had landed in Bertram boats, ("Swallows"), checked the coral reef, and set up lighting on the beach. The missions always took place on a Friday, as it was the Muslim day of rest; the locals' vigilance decreased that day. On the previous night, the local employees of Arous were assembled, as usual, around their fire, when they would suddenly see Yola and her friends run toward their boats and set sail in the dark. They were familiar with that custom of the "crazy" foreigners, to go diving at night.

They could not guess that it was not diving but sailing to the cove where the mission was to take place. When the vehicles arrived at the cove, the warriors gently transferred the Ethiopians to the "Swallows" that sailed to an IDF Navy boat, "Bat Galim" waiting at the high seas. Most of the Ethiopians had never seen the sea, and some even tried to drink of its water. Aboard the ship a warm welcome and a hot meal were in store. After the ship sailed to Eilat, most of the Mossad and Flotilla 13 fighters left Soudan and Yola remained alone with two Mossad warriors.

During the "waiting periods" between the missions Yola adopted a strict daily routine – sport, jogging and swimming, books, and even astrophysics' studies at a British Open university. Every two or three months she flew to Israel for a two weeks' furlough.

The diving resort soon became famous. Arous turned to be the playground of the Khartoum high society, of diplomats, officers and senior civil servants. In the holidays all the who is who in Khartoum arrived, beside the divers who flew in from Europe. Often, in the evenings, all the guests joined in dancing parties. Rich men from Saudi Arabia came to hunt in the desert with falcons. The wife of the Egyptian ambassador covered Yola with compliments for the impeccable service. The French military attaché unwittingly revealed to

Yola and her Mossad warriors top secrets on the Soudanese army, and dispelled their concern that the IDF Navy boats might be discovered by electronic means. Soudan does not have naval radar stations, he declared.

Yola established close relations with the government officials in the area. The governor of Port Soudan erased the red tape in local rules concerning the village and was properly remunerated by free stays for him and his staff in Arous. The police commander gave the village vehicles permits for free travel, and regularly received whisky bottles that Yola smuggled for him despite the Soudanese laws strictly forbidding alcoholic beverages. A Soudanese general who had fallen in love with Yola, put at her disposal the only decompression unit in Soudan; and in return, he asked that the Arous diving instructors would train the Soudanese naval commando, whose courses had been canceled for lack of funds. So, the Flotilla 13 divers from Israel trained the Soudanese special forces... The general also gave Yola a special radio communication set by which she could summon his private helicopter, in case of emergency. Every Thursday Yola sent to the general fresh lobsters from the bay.

She became well known by the local tribes, that often asked her to mediate between their hostile clans. She got the title "Mudira Kabira" – Great Commander; some called her Golda, because of her golden curls, other named her The Iron Lady, after England's prime Minister Margaret Thatcher. Despite her promise to Efraim Halevy, she traveled by herself, driving the Arous jeep, all over the immense area surrounding the village. She was confident and fearless and felt at home in the wild Soudanese desert. "You have to conceal your identity," she said later to the journalist Ishai Hollander. "You're in danger, the adrenaline is flooding you... The background story and the fact that you are all alone add a whiff of mystery to your experience." She used to travel to the Bedouins of the Hadandawa tribe, who could not believe their eyes when they saw a white woman driving all alone in the desert. "My name was already famous", she said without false modesty. "And in Port Soudan I was an attraction. And I used it."

She had excellent contacts and yet, the Soudanese authorities suspected Yola and her friends. They did not know what exactly the resort managers were doing, but mostly they suspected them of smuggling. Several smugglers' gangs operated in the region, in close contact with their partners in Saudi Arabia, across the gulf. Yola herself was arrested once but was released after a short interrogation.

The owner of a manor, perched on a hill across the bay, probably was in the contraband business as well. Yola befriended him and supplied him with fresh rolls from the village bakery. His house was an ideal lookout on the bay area. The gift of rolls paid off. One evening the man warned Yola of a forthcoming raid of the Soudanese army on the village, that very night. Yola and the Mossad warriors immediately buried all the compromising equipment in preset hiding places, and stuck the bottles of alcohol in a barrel that they submerged in the bay. At dawn, indeed, a squad of heavily armed soldiers appeared in Arous, headed by a young officer who ordered a search of the village. The search started in Yola's room and she cordially invited the officer to get in and check the place for himself. The officer was embarrassed – to be alone in a room with a woman, and, even worse, a European! But Yola calmed him down with a pleasant conversation that ended in an exchange of greetings and the officer's promise to come to the village again, this time as a guest.

The really grave incident happened shortly afterwards. During one of the missions, while the Ethiopians were being transferred to the ship, a Zodiac with four Mossad warriors got stuck on the coral reef. Even before the rubber boat was disengaged, a Soudanese military unit suddenly appeared on the beach. The soldiers, armed with Kalashnikov submachine guns, trained their weapons on the foreigners, and one of them was about to fire on the Mossad officers. Danny Limor, who commanded the operation, pulled himself together, hurled himself on the soldier and pushed his weapon aside. Then he yelled, in English, at the soldiers' commander: "Are you out of your mind? Are you going to fire on tourists? Don't you see we run diving here? We bring tourists from all over the world to show them the beauty of Soudan, and you want to shoot them?...Who is the idiot who made you an officer?" He threatened to lodge a complaint against the squad commander in Khartoum. The Soudanese officer, who understood English, was stunned. He apologized to Limor, explaining that he had assumed the people in the boat were smugglers. He ordered his soldiers to leave the place.

The incident was closed without further problems. But ironically, the only case when the secret of Arous was exposed, happened when young Henry Gold came to the resort village. Gold was a Canadian Jewish volunteer working in the refugee camps. Exhausted, he decided to take a couple of days off, to swim, dive and tan on the beach. He had no clue about the secret activity of Arous; but shortly after arriving, he got the feeling that something was very strange there. He had the impression that the place was run by...Mossad agents.

The staff seemed very weird. "They had a strange, unnatural accent...At dinner, they served us a very thinly chopped salad. Now, I have been in many places all over the world, but I ate such a salad only in Israel." Gold had been a volunteer on a kibbutz and was served that chopped salad for breakfast; the Israelis called it "Arab salad." The following morning Gold went straight to the diving instructor and asked him in Hebrew: "What are you people doing here?" The guy, astounded, collapsed on a chair, Finally, he asked Gold, also in Hebrew: "Who are you?"

The secret was out but not for long. Danny Limor was urgently summoned to the resort. He held a long conversation with Gold and convinced him, by various arguments, to keep the story to himself.

*

Since the moment when she was stepping on Soudanese soil, Yola, the Israeli girl, was becoming the German businesswoman. "I was forgetting who I was. I forgot my friends; I played my role. If you had asked me then who I was – I definitely was that girl from the Arous diving resort."

She was not ready, though, for the challenge that suddenly emerged. One day, two German engineers who worked in a Soudanese quarry, arrived in Arous. They were delighted to meet a soulmate; a young German like them. One of them was attracted to Yola and followed her everywhere. He did not miss an opportunity to engage her in long conversations, to revive old memories from Germany, even sing children's songs with her. She did not fail and explained the difference in their accents by their different places of birth: he came from the north of Germany, and she, "from the south".

As the incidents and the suspicions of the Soudanese police and army increased, the Mossad leaders started envisaging other ways of continuing the "Brothers" operation. Yola did not fear of being unmasked, and was prepared for any hazard, even though her escape plan was not the best. Her handlers in Israel had told her: "If the secret of the village is exposed, sail to the high seas in a Zodiac and take with you a "Rina" (a satellite communication device that could alert the Mossad antennae in Israel). "I was supposed to hope", she said later, "that our helicopters would find me before the Soudanese".

She loved her life in Soudan. "I stayed in Soudan for long periods, for I have a good detachment capacity. Even before Arous, when I was on trips abroad, I did not feel the need to call home."

When she would come to Israel for short vacations, she had a strange feeling, and was losing patience at meetings with her friends; she would meet people and not recall who they were. Her friends did not know where she had gone, and the only hint for her whereabouts was that she would come home deeply tanned. Some of her friends spread the rumor that she had found a rich lover, who was taking her sailing to faraway oceans. Her worried father looked for her all over the world and thought she had left the country.

After almost three years of running the resort, Yola came back to Israel. This chapter in her life was closed, and she did not stay in the Mossad, like some of her comrades. She returned to El Al airlines and was appointed head of the flight attendants' department. She also fulfilled an old dream, when she was sent to a faraway country, to bring over a friends' boat to Israel. She studied Physics and Biochemistry, and settled again in Kadima, with a boyfriend, an adopted daughter, three dogs and six cats.

*

Gila

"My name is Gila Waxman.

"I was studying computers at the Haifa Technological Institute. On the row next to mine, right before me, sat a tall, handsome guy. He would disappear once in a while for a week or two, and return happy, relaxed, smiling, with a superb tan. It was mid-winter, storms and rains were raging outside, and he was sunburned!

"I could not stand it. I took a pencil, shaved it to needle point sharpness, then I bent over, pressed it to his jugular, and said: "I do not know what you're doing, but I want the same."

"He smiled."

*

Perhaps the tanned guy, Yariv Gershoni, got scared of Gila's pencil and perhaps not. Anyway, the two of them had a long conversation. Yariv, a former combat pilot, brought a couple of friends who questioned her over and over. Then, following his suggestion, Gila was invited to a "course on security matters". She did not know then that the course was organized by the Mossad. It was held at the Mandarin hotel in Herzliya, near Tel Aviv. The participants were nine young men and Gila. When she met the men, they stared at her in disbelief. What was a woman doing in a men's course?

She thought that perhaps the course was organized by the IDF. She had heard rumors about IDF experts who were training the army of Chad, in Africa. Perhaps Yariv got his tan in Chad? And perhaps she would be sent there too? The mystery attracted her, "When I was young," she said, "I loved all kinds of thrillers and crime novels, like Agatha Christie...My friends claimed that I spoiled the whodunit movies we saw together, as in the second scene I knew who the murderer was, I like to solve mysteries, I like being a part of the mysteries, okay?"

Born in Poland, Gila had immigrated to Israel with her parents at the age of four. The family then moved to Australia where she studied in a Jewish religious school, as her father wanted her to acquire a quantum of Judaism. She was the only secular girl in the school – but joined a left-wing Zionist youth movement, returned to Israel in 1970, served in the Army, then went to study biochemistry. Her uncle, Selman Waksman, had invented the Streptomycin and got the Nobel prize. She dreamt of getting the second Nobel prize in the family, but after a couple of years "...I had enough of mice and wanted people instead." She went to study computers at the Technion and there she met the sunburned Yariv Gershoni.

*

The course in Mandarin hotel lasted a few months and she learned a lot about secret warfare, operations, signals, Morse, handling weapons, servicing dead-letter drops...Only two of the cadets graduated from the course, Gila and one of the men. Her instructor told her that she was accepted in the Mossad.

Yariv took her to the Caesarea department, where other men questioned her over and over. Mostly, they wanted to know if she was able to work alone, and face unexpected challenges, knowing that there was nobody nearby who could help her. Her answers apparently satisfied them and she realized that she was about to become a Mossad warrior. Another man briefed her about running a resort.

She realized that she would be sent to run a village of the "Club Med" kind somewhere very far. At first, they sent her to a country club in Herzliya, then they introduced her to somebody "who would teach her how to run a resort". A few days later she was flown to London to learn the ropes of the hotel business. Why London? She was told that "a cousin of a warrior" owned a hotel there. "It was not a hotel but a motel," she told me, "quite close to the notorious Brixton jail." The prison guards used to drop at the motel for a drink after work. "I did not learn how to run a hotel, but I learned how to serve beer. The hobby of the guards beside beer drinking was using dirty language and pinching my ass. After three days I returned to Israel."

At last she was informed that she would be sent to Soudan. Gila flew to Soudan, using a foreign passport. But on the flight to Khartoum she had to deal with an unexpected problem. A few years before, she had volunteered in kibbutz Mishmar Hasharon for a few months. In the kibbutz she met a charming Swiss girl, also a volunteer. The two of them became great friends and spent a lot of time together.

Years went by, and now Gila boards a plane in Geneva, bound for Khartoum. And on the plane she sees her Swiss friend, sitting by the aisle! What should she do? What if the Swiss girl recognizes her? Gila is flying under a false identity, with a fictitious name, to an enemy country. She shivered at the thought that she might be recognized and arrested.

The long flight turned into a nightmare, as Gila tried to hide from her friend. It almost was a mission impossible, as the Swiss girl sat in an aisle seat on the way to the restrooms…But luck was on Gila's side, and she got out of the aircraft without her friend noticing her.

Yariv was waiting in Arous, He introduced her to Yola and a wonderful friendship sprouted between the two women. Gila spent three weeks with Yola, who taught her how to run the resort. In Soudan Gila received a new name, "Janet". At first, she replaced Yola during her leaves; but after a while Yola left for good and Gila became the "Mudira Kabira".

She quickly adapted to life in the resort. "What you needed was – ingenuity and self-control. You are alone, and you have to find your way in conditions of total lack of knowledge." Unforeseen glitches could happen at every step of the way. One of the diving instructors, who posed as Anglo-Saxon, spoke English with a bad accent. A guest from New Zealand was puzzled and complained to Gila. "This guy," he said, "doesn't have an Anglo-Saxon accent." She retorted: "And you, do you have a New Zealand accent?" The man calmed down.

A worse crisis erupted in 1984, when the Soudanese government applied the Sharia law on the entire territory of the state. Many European countries immediately instigated harsh sanctions against Soudan and reduced the fuel exports to the country. Arous used to buy 30 barrels a month from "Agip", the major supplier to Soudan. When the number of barrels in the resort was down to fifteen, Gila would send the driver, Ali, to Port Soudan to bring another 30 barrels on his truck. But one day Ali came back from Port Soudan and announced: "Mudira, no fuel, they do not give." She jumped in his cabin and drove to Port Soudan. She entered the office of the company manager and sat down in the waiting room,

An Arab was sitting beside her. "Who are you?" he asked.

"I am the Mudira of Arous. And you?"

"I am The commander of the Fatah training camps in Soudan."

The guy was a real enemy. He was training Fatah terrorists to attack Israel!

"What are you doing here?" she asked.

"I need two barrels of fuel a week, for illumination during night exercises."

He got into the manager's office and came out delighted. "They authorized a barrel a week!" he declared, jubilant.

"He got one barrel a week," Gila morosely thought, "and I need thirty a month," She entered the manager's office, and even before she said a word, the man sighed and moaned: "How I hate those Palestinians!"

Her mood improved. On his desk she saw his family's picture and asked about it. She also asked if they had visited Arous. No, he said, On the spot she invited him and his family to be her guests in Arous. A pleasant conversation ensued, and at the end of their meeting, she came out of his office, proud of his commitment to supply her with as much fuel as she needed, as long as she needed,

All the time, she was aware of her double life in Arous. The place was "a paradise for divers", one of the most beautiful places in the world. Divers and tourists arrived from all over the world, "the food and the drink were excellent, the village standard was like two Michelin stars" – and at the same time Operation Brothers was at its peak, as if it happened elsewhere, in a parallel world.

During the two years she spent at Arous Gila was very proud of her mission – bringing a Jewish tribe back to its ancestors' land. "There was something amazing – while we had a good time in the village, drinking and dancing at a party for our guests – at that very moment, behind the village, a convoy of trucks carried Jews on their way to the beach and to the boat bound for the promised Land."

She learned to overcome crises and dangers, all by herself, and devise creative solutions to impossible situations. She had to deal with sudden raids of the Soudanese army on Arous; with recalcitrant Mossad warriors who questioned her authority or failed in adopting foreign identities; with a tightening net of suspicions and draconian measures by the new fundamentalist government.

One night, the village truck broke down on the road and Gila received a crash alert from the Mossad: "Prepare, they [the Soudanese] are coming!" She took immediately all the necessary measures, then called a diver who had recently arrived from Israel. He was badly scared. "Tonight you will sleep in my room", she said. In her room there were two beds. At about three AM they heard heavy thumping on the door. She looked by the peephole and saw a uniform. The diver cringed in his bed. She undid her pajama buttons, exposing her cleavage, ruffled her hair, and opened the door. Outside stood a Soudanese officer. Embarrassed, he diverted his eyes.

"I am here with a truck of soldiers", he said gruffly, avoiding looking at her.

"What do you want?"

"We are out of gas. Will you help us?"

You bet, she thought. She gave the officer fuel, also gave him and his soldiers a great breakfast. "We became good friends", she concluded her report.

Gila returned after two years and decided to stay at the Mossad. In her Mossad missions she loved changing her identity and playing the roles of different characters. "If you want me to be Janet – I'll become Janet", she teased a television reporter, "If you want me to be Sara – In five minutes I am Sara. Those were my moments on the world stage."

*

Ilana

The dreamworld of Arous evaporated in minutes, when Ilana Peretzman, the third Mudira, got into her jeep for the last time.

A year before, Ilana was studying Marine Archeology and Biology at Haifa University. She was a certified diver, addicted to the ocean and the world of silence thriving under the waves. One day a schoolmate approached her. "Would you like to join the Mossad?" he asked, straight to the point.

She hesitated. "This sounds rather interesting," she finally said. "But what's it all about?"

"It's about good things," he smiled. "Saving Jews."

Several months later, after a crash course, Ilana landed in Soudan. Yola met her in Arous and initiated her in the art of running the resort.

When she took over, the journey of the Ethiopian Jews to the Promised Land was no more by sea but by air. The original formula, of bringing the Jews to the coast and taking them to Israel by boat, became dangerous. Thousands of Jews were brought to Israel in Operation "Home Haven". But because of the growing suspicion of the authorities it was decided to continue the Ethiopian immigration by air. Israeli Air Force Rhinos (Hercules aircraft) started landing on improvised runways in the desert. The Mossad trucks brought the Ethiopian Jews to the landing areas; the Rhinos swallowed hundreds of Jews in their bellies and took off at once. Repeatedly, the flights were discovered by the Soudanese, and the planes landed elsewhere. In the meantime, Efraim Halevy left the Bitzur department and was replaced by a gifted Mossad officer, Aharon Sherf. Sherf ordered to continue and even double the airlift of Ethiopian Jews from Soudan. There were nights, when two or three Israeli Rhinos were simultaneously landing in various locations, and taking off, laden with hundreds of Jews. Not even once did the Soudanese army succeed to bring down or capture an IAF aircraft.

the commander of the secret airlift was Yariv Gershoni. He toured the desert and found areas that could serve the heavy IAF Rhinos. Arous turned into the advance headquarters of these secret flights, and the naval activity was stopped.

Ilana stayed in Arous less than Yola and Gila, and was in the village when a military coup took place in Khartoum. The fanatics and radicals took over, and the Mossad made a hasty decision – evacuate Arous immediately.

Ilana and three warriors packed the sensitive equipment, loaded it on a pickup and a jeep, and told the local staff that they were going on an excursion and will be back in the afternoon. When they were about to leave, a couple of divers arrived and Ilana gracefully showed them their room and the amenities, then left. The little convoy headed for the landing zone, and at 8:00 PM, exactly, a Rhino landed. The two vehicles drove into its belly and the Rhino took off in a matter of minutes.

That was the end of Arous. Only later the Mossad leaders realized that leaving the resort was a major error. It could have kept functioning, as the flights continued and even increased in the following months.

Still, the escape of two other Mossad warriors from Khartoum was not a mistake. They were wanted by the Soudanese military. They escaped their safehouse and rushed to the US embassy. At the gate, they whispered the secret passwords given to them beforehand by the CIA; the Americans packed them in two big crates and smuggled them out of Soudan as "diplomatic mail."

*

Ilana, on her return, went her own way, away from her secret adventure.

As for Gila, she stayed in the Mossad. For years she participated in many operations abroad, even though she married and started a family. "I still participated in undercover missions abroad while seven months pregnant," she recalled.

There were times, when her assumed identity took over. Arous had grown up on her, with its beauty, the ocean, the desert, the starry sky, the diving in its crystalline waters... In spite of the risks and the dangers and the crises – her life in Arous, this small paradise, had been like a dream. She often recalled that balmy evening, when she walked on the virgin beach of Arous, with" Tony", a Mossad warrior. "Tony", she said, "whom do you love more? Tony in Arous or David (his real name) in Israel?"

"And you?" he asked.

"We both could not answer this question," she said years later, "what we preferred to be – who we were in Soudan or who we are in Israel?"

*

Yola, too, had loved her life in Soudan. As time went by, she kept reminiscing her Arous days.

"I could have stayed and lived there forever," she confessed. "I am the woman who was there, that was the real Yola. I was a part of history. I learned what it means to overcome obstacles, find ingenuous solutions, extend myself to the edge. And yes, contribute to my country."

Danny Limor summed it all up in seven words: "Without Yola it would not have happened."

Part Five

Aliza Magen
and Friends

CHAPTER 17

Aliza, Liron, Sigal and Rina

The little girl who broke the glass ceiling

As TIME WENT BY, ALIZA MAGEN FELT THAT SHE SHOULD assume a more responsible position. In 1975 she went to see Yitzhak (Haka) Hofi, the new Ramsad. Hofi told her, half-joking: "Listen, I just was vaccinated against the flu, and I feel quite weak. You can get whatever you want." She asked to be appointed head of a major Mossad branch in West Europe, that operated in Germany as well. She got it.

Two years later she transferred that job to her friend Linda Avrahami, and was appointed Deputy Chief of the advanced headquarters of "Tzomet" ("Crossroads") in Europe, and soon afterward – Chief of Tzomet, the agents' handling department. That was a top position and Aliza was the first woman to get it, like most ranks she had attained so far. Some criticized that choice, pointing out that her main job would be recruiting Arab agents; in the Arab society, they said, men would not accept orders and instructions from a woman. But "Lizchen" overcame that obstacle. In her new position she recruited agents in Europe and in the Arab countries, and became a frequent visitor, under various aliases, in the enemy capitals.

In a friend's house she met a charming tourist guide, Avraham Halevi. She married him after her Mossad friend briefed Avraham about her employment, but not about her exact functions. Her husband adapted to her way of life, and while she was in Europe, he got a job in another European country. They used to spend the weekends together, and afterwards each of them went his own way. Avraham died in 2011.

After Tzomet Aliza spent "a wonderful year" in the National Security College. Back in the Mossad, she was appointed Head of the Human Resources Department, and promoted quite a few women to senior positions. In 1990 she reached the conclusion that she had exhausted every possible avenue at the Mossad, and time had come for her to retire. But then, when she went to see Ramsad Shabtai Shavit, he made her an offer she could not refuse: become head of the coveted Department for Operational coordination and accede to a rank that no woman ever had reached: Deputy Chief of the Mossad, the highest grade after the Ramsad. This was a status that only very few of the best Mossad warriors could dream of; and she was the first woman – and the only one till now – who reached that level. Both she, and her Mossad colleagues, did not regard her appointment as "breaking the glass ceiling", but as a very natural promotion.

In her new position Aliza kept taking care of the Mossad women. When Mirla Gal, one of the brightest young warriors came to her office, Aliza's first question was: "How do you think you'll be able to command a bunch of macho-men?"

Mirla shrugged. "I do not see any problem in that."

After a while, when she was about to promote Mirla to Branch head, Aliza asked her the same question – and got the same answer… And indeed Mirla performed well and rose to a senior position in the organization.

Aliza remained Deputy Chief under two more Ramsads – Danny Yatom and Efraim Halevi. She was involved in hundreds Mossad operations, including the famous "Kaniuk" mission for the capture of Mordechai Vanunu, "the atom spy" (See chapter 17)

Aliza retired after 39 years of service. Like Sylvia Rafael, Yael, Erika,

Rina and others, she gave up the dream of normal family life and bearing children. She later frankly admitted that "in my time, there were not many women in senior positions, not because the Mossad was against, but because women would not accept the compromises stemming out of the job requirements. [On the contrary] the Mossad always looked for women, knowing that women could get to places where men did not fit. The shortage of women was a result of women's preference to have a family and bear children."

After retiring, Aliza devoted herself to the family and children of her niece, and to another new hobby that excited her – golf.

Long after she left the Mossad, many of the senior officers of the organization kept talking about her amazing knack for intelligence work. She also understood the conflicting feelings of the warriors who set out on missions abroad, often in glamorous capitals, stay in five star hotels, wear expensive clothes and hold meetings in gourmet restaurants. She often spoke about the dramatic reversal, when the warriors come back home, overflowing with adrenalin – and now have to return to a modest way of life, and a dull, often frustrating everyday routine.

Ilan Mizrahi, who also would become Deputy Ramsad one day, remembered well what Aliza told him once, when he came back awash with pride and elation after a successful mission in Europe. "Ilan", she said, "You're going abroad on your missions, and every time you come back, here is what you're going to do. You'll enter the bathroom, stand in front of the mirror and say: "I am Ilan from Giv'ataim (a workers' suburb of Tel Aviv)."

*

Aliza was very proud of helping women to move up the ladder in the Mossad. She also instructed and directed a young generation of amazons, who achieved astonishing results in Tzomet, Keshet and Caesarea.

One evening, the phone rang at the Baghdadi residence, in an enemy Arab capital. Nihal Baghdadi (fictitious name) picked up the receiver. The caller was a woman, speaking a heavily accented English.

The caller, Claudia (fictitious name) said that she was calling Nihal from Europe; she was organizing an international conference, she said, and was about to launch a feminist magazine. Nihal asked Claudia to email her the details about the magazine and its contents.

"Do you happen to travel to Europe?" Claudia asked.

"Yes, once in a while."

"Great, perhaps we could meet."

Nihal gave Claudia her email address and ended the conversation. She was a staunch feminist, married and a mother of three and a known socialite; she was involved in the university activities in her city, but also closely connected with the government of her country. She had just returned from an international convention.

In the following weeks Claudia and Nihal exchanged mails, had long phone conversations, and became quite friendly. They met in September of that year, when Nihal flew to a Bookfair in Europe, and Claudia came to see her. Their friendship became very personal, and Nihal even revealed to Claudia that beside her husband, she also has a lover in Damascus. She did not know, of course, that Claudia was not Claudia, but "Sigal", an intelligence officer of the Mossad, and their connection was Sigal's first mission in her new functions.

Sigal was a special kind of woman, pretty, sharp, confident, born and grown up on a farm. "I even know to drive a horse cart, and a tractor in reverse gear," she boasted to her friends; she spent years in a youth movement and after her military service in AMAN, got a phone call from the Mossad. They offered her a position as secretary, and she refused. She went back to school and got a university degree in Psychology and Philosophy. After a couple of years, the Mossad called again, with a new offer, but she refused again. "I am writing now my Ph. D. thesis," she said. "You have a year to complete your doctorate," the Mossad recruiters told her, "and then you're coming to us." She completed her thesis, and joined the Mossad. The basic operational course was hard. In the meantime she got an offer to complete a post-doctoral course abroad, and agreed willingly, as she was sure she'll fail the Mossad course. But to her surprise – she made it.

Soon after, Shabtai Shavit became Ramsad. "Why do not we train

women to became Katza?" he asked his aides. Katza was an abbrevia-
tion of "Intelligence-gathering officer". The experts explained to him,
as before, why it wouldn't work – Katzas work with Muslim agents
and those would refuse to be handled by women, etc, – but Shavit was
a stubborn fellow. And Sigal landed in a Humint course, and became
the first Katza in Mossad history.

After Nihal she participated in several challenging missions. In
Europe, she intercepted a nuclear scientist, Saddam Hussein's representative in the International Agency for Atomic Energy. She looked
good, and he courted her assiduously. She won his trust, when she
noticed that he was wearing a plastic rose in his lapel. She entered a
flower shop and at their following meeting stuck in his lapel a real
rose. When they agreed to have dinner together, he tried to enter in
her room, but she sent him to the hotel lobby where she "dried" him
up for a half hour. "These people want to go wild, as soon as they land
in Europe," she told a friend. But finally she succeeded to recruit him
as well.

Another "object" was another Middle Eastern scientist, who was
also sent to the conference of the Atomic Agency. She did her home-
work and when she bumped into him "by accident" at the conference,
she mentioned the name of his former university professor who had
spoken very highly of him. He was thrilled. She introduced herself as
a European, fascinated by atomic research, and hosted him for several
dinners. He became for her a great source of information, and at the
end of the convention she handed him an envelope full of money,
as "consulting fees". He was awkward and embarrassed but took the
money. That was the beginning of a beautiful friendship. They met
several times. He kept disclosing to her priceless information and
she kept bringing him presents for his children, perfumes for his wife,
and ... envelopes of money. He believed she was a European involved
in intelligence matters.

All of a sudden, a few days before their next scheduled meeting,
he sent her a mail canceling the encounter, and abruptly severed their
relationship. A secret inquiry revealed that a female scientist had been
arrested by the Iranian secret services after they discovered that she

was working for another foreign intelligence service. Sigal's friend got cold feet and decided to abandon the dangerous games.

*

Sigal's greatest achievement was "the officials' mission".

A high ranking delegation from an enemy Middle Eastern country arrived in a European capital. Sigal, who had just returned from a mission abroad, was urgently rushed over. She checked in the same hotel where the Muslim delegation members were staying. Sitting in the hotel lobby, she saw and memorized their faces. The following morning, at breakfast, she chose a table near the Muslim officials, ate yoghurts and tried to engage them in conversation, but failed. Day after day, at breakfast, she tried – and failed. Her mission was going to fail.

One night, when in her room, she suddenly heard a woman screaming, apparently from one of the lower floors. According to Mossad rules, she was not allowed to get out of her room and get embroiled in any kind of contact with official authorities or the police. But this time she decided to go out; in the hallway she met one of the Muslims who occupied the room next to hers. "I want to see what happened," she said and both of them turned to the staircase. At one of the lower floors, by the stairs, stood a young woman, stark naked, screaming and wailing. A few men had gathered around her and offered her towels, to cover herself. Sigal turned to her but the girl kept screaming. Finally, she noticed Sigal's soothing hand signals and went with her to her room. There she dressed and started speaking. She still was in tears. She told Sigal that she was a hooker, from Poland, and her client had stolen all she had – her car, her documents and all her money. Sigal calmed her down, then hurried to the hotel reception and asked the clerks to help the poor woman and call the police. Then she left the hotel, to avoid meeting the police officers. When she reported all this to her Mossad commander, he angrily scolded her, but when she got back in the hotel, early in the morning, the reception manager warmly thanked her for her help. He happily informed her that the grateful hotel would cover all her breakfast expenses.

She entered the dining room, and the Muslim officials, who so far had just ignored her – got up, applauded, and showered her with compliments. Who was she, they politely inquired. She said she was a businesswoman from another European country.

"And you?" she asked.

They gave the name of a Middle Eastern country.

"Wow, that's fascinating," she said. She added that she was very interested in the Middle East, and they agreed to meet her in the lobby that same evening and talk about their country. In the evening she made up her face, put on a truly short black dress and met the group in the lobby. Some took seats beside her, and one of them assailed her with questions, as in a police interrogation. Who are you? Where do you live? Why are you here? What is your profession? What do you think about the Arab-Israeli conflict?

He probably was their security officer, Sigal thought. She sailed through the interrogation unscathed. The man and some of his friends got up and left, and she remained with two of them. They had a long, pleasant conversation, and they invited her to their room, where, they said, they kept delicacies they had brought from home. She politely declined the offer.

She met them repeatedly in the following days. At first, they did not realize that they were unwittingly participating in a process of recruitment by a foreign secret service, and were turning into informants of a Mossad officer. The connection with one of the senior Muslim officials. triggered by "the night of the Polish hooker" lasted for a long time and was very fruitful.

*

During her missions, Sigal found out that sometimes a real friendship might emerge out of her convoluted ties with "targets" in enemy countries. "In the final report about one of my missions, I wrote about a special, warm relationship I created with the family of an agent. Some of my commanders thought that I had crossed the line, but the Ramsad Meir Dagan loved it."

Sigal was aware of the price she was paying in her personal life. She had got married in the early stages of her employment at the Mossad, and since, kept traveling all over the world, almost always missing the birthdays of her three sons. Only years later, when she retired, did her older sons glimpse an inkling of her secret past. Her eldest son was enormously proud of his mother, when he learned the real reason for her frequent disappearances.

Sigal, like many of her comrades, led a double life in Israel and abroad, and enjoyed this. She was constantly aware of the importance of her missions, and knew she was contributing to Israel's security. "When I'll be ninety-five," she said to a friend, "I'll be able to say to myself: I am a part of a small group that accomplished great things. They write books about us!"

After leaving the Mossad Sigal went back to intensive college studies, determined to achieve a new goal – teaching at a school in some poor, neglected neighborhood. Once in a while she is called to "reserve service" by the Mossad, and is sent to missions abroad. That creates a problem. "How can I tell my Arab professor at the college – that I have to miss school for a few days because I am leaving on a mission for the Mossad?"

*

When women started populating the operational teams, they still had to overcome many obstacles. The main was psychological – commanders and warriors wouldn't easily believe that women could accomplish daring and complicated tasks as the men. But gradually they found out that women had sangfroid, courage, technical capability, acting talents, knowledge, and a great improvisation gift. And they were not stuffed with the male "machismo" that sometimes could endanger a mission.

One amazon, Orna Sandler, found out during a mission that women tend to notice small details better than men. She was sent with her team to watch a PLO office in a European city and follow some couriers who were supposed to arrive. And indeed, a couple arrived by bus, a beautiful American girl in an elegant long dress, and a bearded young man who stopped for a moment and lit his curved pipe. They indeed entered the PLO office and spent a long time there.

According to a source report, the two were to get to the airport after meeting the PLO officials. Sandler's team spread out at the airport, waiting for them, but the young couple did not show up. The only couple that approached one of the counters were an ugly, neglected woman and an old man. They are not our targets, the warriors concluded. The team members felt that they had failed in their mission. They were about to leave the place, when Orna noticed the old man sticking his hand in his pocket and taking out a curved pipe...

Orna knew that another obstacle to women's service at the Mossad was the physical one. In the fifties, a woman who wanted to have children thought twice before joining the Mossad. At that time women had to promise not to marry and not to have children for a certain period. The Mossad veterans remember the case of two friends – Mirla Gal and Tzipi Livni, who graduated from the perational course of the Mossad with flying colors, and started carrying out secondary missions. But Tzipi Livni refused to promise giving up motherhood and resigned fron the Mossad. Mirla Gal simply refused to sign the papers stipulating that she wouldn't bear children. Despite that mini-rebellion she married and had two children, and yet became one of the best Mossad amazons ever. (Livni went into politics and became Deputy Prime Minister in Ehud Olmert's cabinet).

That draconian measure did not last long and starting at the seventies the only amazons who did not have children were women who wanted to devote their whole life to the service. Orna Sandler, like Liron and Sigal and many other amazons of her generation, had two daughters while serving in the Mossad.

But life in the Mossad took its toll. Orna's home was in Paris, but her cover was of a Dutch company employee, and she also kept an apartment in Brussels. Every Monday she would leave her Paris home and take the fast train to Amsterdam, returning only at the weekend. Her husband was taking care of their daughters. But the two girls badly suffered from their mother's absence. For a while they suspected that she had a secret affair and was spending the weekdays with her lover. The complaints of her children and a heart wrenching letter she received from one of them made her burst in tears in her train compartment and decide to come back to Israel and to a more normal life. Like some other amazons, Orna was later employed by the Mossad at research, training and planning.

Another Amazon, Rina [fictitious name] refrained for many years from getting married. Extremely beautiful, slender, blue-eyed, she was known for her courage, her calm and her inventive senses. She spoke six languages and was a born actress. "Isn't your beauty an obstacle to your undercover work?" a friend asked her, as she attracted attention wherever she went. "A woman controls her beauty," she said. "When she wants, even the most beautiful woman can turn into a mouse."

Rina married very late; but she never had a normal family life. Her thumbprints could be found in many of Keshet's successful missions. One that failed was the quest for the Nazi criminal, Dr. Josef Mengele, nicknamed "the Angel of Death" by the concentration camps inmates. Together with a veteran warrior, Danny [fictitious name] she followed Rolf, Mengele's son, who seemed to maintain a secret relation with his father. Rina and Danny planted a listening device in Rolf's desk, at his office in Freiburg; but soon after the young man moved to Berlin. They followed him there as well, and again concealed listening bugs in his desk, hoping that his father will call him on March 16, when both had their birthdays. But nothing happened, and the mission did not bear fruit. Only years later they found out that while they were tailing Rolf, his father was already dead of a stroke while swimming at Sao Paolo's beach, in Brazil.

Ram Ben Barak, a former Deputy Ramsad, recalled a mission with Rina in a European capital. "We penetrated an office where important intelligence material was stored," Ben Barak recounted. "Suddenly we heard the approaching steps of the guards. I needed a few more seconds to complete the task and escape. I stressed out and started sweating. Rina calmed me down, she even produced a handkerchief and wiped the sweat off my face. She calmly, confidently, whispered to me: "Everything is fine, you should go on, you can do it!" Such cool headedness is critical in such missions. I continued working and we successfully completed the mission."

Rina, extremely cautious, was never captured. She claimed that the worst enemy of the Mossad warriors was "the old lady at the third floor" in any target city. "That kind of old woman has trouble sleeping," Rina said. "So she sits every night by her window and stares out, attentive to any change in the nightly scene. That old lady is the one that would notice suspicious characters moving in the street and would call the police." That indeed happened on several occasions. Rina kept warning the young warriors setting out on their missions: "Beware of grandmothers at the third floor!"

Rina rose in the ranks, reached the position of Department head, and was regarded by her peers as the "Grand Dame" of the service. She retired with the rank of general. With other veterans she now devoted her life to volunteer work in the Ethiopian Jewish community.

"I loved my missions," she resumed her Mossad years, "and I did something for the country. And this is a great satisfaction."

*

As time went by, all the restrictions on women's family life were lifted, and they could start families and raise children. The numbers said it all: in the last few years, between forty and fifty percent of the warriors in the operational units were women, who participated in all the missions, including assassinations of terrorist leaders and enemy experts developing weapons to be used against Israel.

In a notorious mission, attributed to the Mossad, a Hamas leader named Mahmoud al-Mabhouh was killed in Dubai. He was the go-between the Hamas in Gaza and the Revolutionary Guards in Iran. Several amazons participated in the Mossad mission in Dubai that ended with Mabhouh's death.

But this was not the first time when the Mossad tried to kill Mabhouh. A few months before that operation a team of Caesarea arrived in Dubai and located Mabhouh in one of the hotels. While he was sitting in the dining room, having breakfast, a waitress passed by his table. She actually was a Mossad warrior. She feigned to trip, and the tray she was carrying fell on the floor, its contents breaking or scattering around. Mabhouh turned toward the waitress and looked at the broken china at her feet. At that moment a Caesarea warrior passed by his table, behind his back, and emptied a tiny bag of poison into his coffee. The poison was supposed to kill Mabhouh in a few hours. He indeed drank the coffee, collapsed, spent a few days in bed – but did not die, and returned to his dangerous missions. After a while another mission was conceived and he was killed in his hotel room.

But those killing missions were only a tiny part of the Mossad activities. The Ramsad Tamir Pardo maintains that they are less than one percent of the Mossad missions, that count in the thousands a year. "The Mossad is not an assassination organization", Pardo stresses.

The participation in dangerous missions abroad often brought to romantic ties between men and women, and quite a few of them got married and started families together. Ilan Mizrahi, when a young warrior, traveled every week or two to a neighboring island, to command a continuous mission of local agents. One day the island immigration officers asked him: "What exactly are you doing here? Why do you come so often?" He mumbled a vague answer, but on his return, reported the conversation to his superiors. They found an original solution to the problem. "We'll send a young amazon with you on all your future trips. Your cover story will be that both of you are married to other spouses, but you are having an affair and you're flying away every weekend to spend time together." Ilan was "paired" with Michal, a charming amazon and the daughter of Ya'akov Caroz, a former Deputy Ramsad. The trips together triggered a real love affair between the two, and finally they got married.

*

While Aliza was on her way out, some Mossad senior officers started looking for a likely worthy successor for her job, and perhaps even more. Soon they noticed the performance of a young amazon, Liron, in one of her early missions as a "Keshet" warrior. Her goal was to obtain the home key of a reclusive Frenchman, Jacques Tournon, who maintained suspicious relations with Islamic extremists. All the past efforts to get access to his house, by the border – failed. The assignment of Liron and another amazon was to get the key and bring photographs and charts of the house interior.

And in a stormy winter night, in 1994, two charming but very distraught young women knocked on the door of Tournon's secluded house. In broken French they introduced themselves as tourists. Their car, they said, was stuck on the highway nearby, because of a flat tire. They did not know how to replace a wheel. Could he help? Tournon hesitated but finally agreed to help the damsels in distress. He left the house, locked the door and followed the two ladies down to the highway. He called, on his mobile phone, a friend who lived nearby, and asked him to come and help.

The two men had started working on the spare wheel, when one of the women turned to them, sounding uneasy. She must go to the bathroom, she said, perhaps…

Tournon had no choice but to agree. He gave her the house key and instructed her, in detail, where the bathrooms were situated. She ran up the path to the house, unlocked the door, and once alone inside fished from her handbag a miniature device for key duplicating. She also photographed the interior. While feverishly darting between the house rooms and clicking her camera she prayed inwardly that Tournon wouldn't come back.

But he did. She suddenly heard steps outside and Tournon's angry voice as he spoke to her friend: "What's going on? How long is she staying there?" She heard the voice of the other man too, and he sounded upset.

Liron thought she was lost. But her friend invented a reason, connected with the female body, and Liron gained a few more seconds. She completed her task, left Tournon's key by the door and ran out. In the meantime, the car had been repaired by the two men, and after thanking them profusely, the two women departed. The mission was a success. Another team used the key and the photos to penetrate, undetected, Tournon's home a few days later.

That was Liron's real baptism of fire.

*

Liron, 20 years old, had served in the famous IDF 8200 Sigint unit; at the Mossad initiation course, she was the youngest cadet. For her, the course was extremely difficult, and there was a moment when she thought about dropping out. She brewed some coffee at the compound kitchenette and held an inner debate with herself. "What should I do? I want to quit. Okay, fine. But then I said to myself: 'Liron, what's that decision to quit? If everybody quits, who is going to defend the state? Aren't we all here out of choice, out of Zionist faith?"

She stayed and made it. At the end of the nine months course an "assignment ceremony" was held. She heard the name of one of the course graduates and his assignment: "Keshet."

"Keshet", she said to herself. "Wow, that's scary! That also is very dangerous. Thank God, I'm not there." Fifteen minutes later she heard her name. "Liron" – and her assignment: Keshet!

She was afraid, but she got over it. And after "The Frenchman's Key" mission, she felt the adrenalin flowing through her veins. "Adrenalin of elation" she called it. She had enjoyed the thrill. "There indeed are moments of fear," she later described her feelings during her perilous missions abroad, "perhaps they'll catch me! But the fear is like 'adrenalin of challenge', a sudden capability of accomplishing the impossible. In the middle of the operation I suddenly stop and look at the mission as from the outside.

"Often I think – what are the qualities of a good Mossad warrior? Personal charm, balance, cool-headedness – but also an adventurous streak. Without adventurism I wouldn't have been there."

That was how her dramatic life in "Keshet" started, mission after mission, endless flights to foreign lands, with foreign passports, hotels, teamwork, assuming responsibility, defining goals but conceiving sudden changes if conditions on the ground change... She learned to live in two worlds, the real world in Israel and the one created around her current mission. "Before the plane lands in a foreign airport, I start assuming my new identity. Every morning I wake up in some hotel room and I ask myself – what the hell am I doing here? Sometimes we carried out two or three missions abroad, one after the other, and I would wake up in the morning, unable to remember where I am..."

"And so was born the commandment: 'Just a moment!' Before I check in a hotel or going through immigration in some country, I would stop for a moment and think: 'Who am I? What's my name? What's my date of birth? Just a moment!"

During one of her flights, a stewardess came to her, beaming, and handed her a glass of champagne: "Congratulations!"

"For what?" she asked, surprised. She had forgotten that today was her real birthday.

She realized that "Keshet" was carrying out scores of missions every month. One of the experiences she really enjoyed was a mission in a major European capital where Mossad male and female warriors, in perfect synchronization, got "stuck" and blocked six different intersections with their cars for one minute, allowing their colleagues to penetrate an Iraqi strategic office without being spotted by the police cars touring the neighborhood,

She also recalled moments of crisis. She participated in a team mission in Europe, trying to establish a connection with an important "target"; but they suddenly found out that the local services were also trying to contact the same person, at the same place and the same time. The presence of "Keshet" warriors close to the target could result at a clash with the locals and their capture. The Israelis had to run away and escape the country instantly.

*

One of her most important missions took place in an African capital. She was urgently sent over with a male warrior, after an important Arab delegation from an enemy country had arrived there. The two warriors landed at the airport, without knowing a thing about the country, except for the fact that it was a Muslim nation. They did not know where they would stay, how much money they could bring, how they should answer the immigration officers' questions: "Who are you? Why did you come?" And in the hotel or the street they were assailed by other questions: "Where are you going? Why? Whom are you going to meet?" Two white travelers in an African country naturally attract attention; the locals know everything about them, where they are at every moment, what they are doing, where are they staying.

The days passed, and they did not make any progress. At any given moment, the Arab delegation could leave the country. And they had not established contact yet.

Liron took the initiative. When she learned that the enemy delegation was staying in a certain hotel, she walked in, and asked to see a room on an upper floor. The reception clerk led her to a room, and while they were entering, the neighboring door opened and a member of the Arab delegation came out. Right away, Liron rented the room, despite the strict orders, forbidding an amazon to reside, alone, in a target's vicinity.

It was the right thing to do. She and her Mossad partner met, as if by chance, in the hotel lobby. They devised a plan for acceding the delegation's documents. For the mission, Liron had to stay, alone, in the hotel for the following three weeks, while the hotel staff was watching her, local and foreign guests were trying to pick her up, the police was following her everywhere. At night she was all alone with the "targets", and one evening, while she was sitting in the lobby, a wild party was held around her, and the delegation members, with many locals, danced in front of her shouting at the top of their lungs: "Allahu Akbar! Allah is the greatest! Islam will prevail!"

Every day she passed by a decrepit prison and kept saying to herself: "If I enter this place – I'll never get out."

But finally, she succeeded establishing the right connection with the delegation members; she and a freshly arrived team penetrated into their rooms and obtained all they needed. That mission duly impressed her commanders. But in the following weeks, she had nightmares where she was running for her life, pursued by the vengeful targets.

But she liked her work. She felt that the best men, the smartest brains, served in the Mossad. And yet, she loved the Friday nights, when she visited Tel Aviv's discotheques with other Mossad amazons; and nobody they danced with had the faintest clue what was their real job at "the Defense Ministry".

*

In her missions Liron discovered that a beautiful, intelligent woman has an advantage over male warriors. A woman's way of thinking was also different, she realized. "As women have less physical force than men, they rely more on their brainpower. A woman's way of thinking – and a man's strength – form an amazing combination, and then the sky is the limit."

*

"Liron, get to the airport right away!" The voice in the phone receiver, in the wee hours of that night, carried a note of urgency. A few hours later she landed in a German-speaking European city. Her team also landed there. She had been briefed before takeoff and knew that the success or failure of her mission depended on her actions in the next hour or so. After getting through immigration she rushed to the baggage claim hall, and saw the target waiting by one of the carousels. Now it was her turn.

At that time the Mossad was on the tracks of an Egyptian general who was often flying to a faraway, hostile Asian country. What was he doing there? All their efforts to find the answer to that question had failed so far. They failed to get even a glance at the documents he carried in his attaché case. One day, in 2017, a source flashed a short message to Mossad Headquarters. The general was on his way back to Cairo, he was flying to Europe and would spend a night at the airport hotel.

The Mossad team flew to the European city and spread through the airport. The team commanders assumed that after the general checked into the hotel and entered his room, the warriors wouldn't be able to get to his attaché case, and the mission would be aborted. They had to establish contact with him before he entered the hotel. That was a question of minutes. Their only hope was Liron.

When the general got out of the terminal, on his way to the adjacent hotel, he saw a pretty woman walking at the same direction and crying. He politely addressed her and asked if he could help. She shook her head. "No!" she managed. Between two bouts of crying, she said that her boyfriend had just left her, after years of living together. A short while ago she had landed, coming to meet him; he was there, waiting, but he had told her that he did not want to see her anymore, ever. That was the end, he said. She was now all alone and desperate.

The good general wanted to help that poor woman; besides, she was gorgeous. When he heard that she was on her way to the same hotel, he suggested that they meet at the hotel bar, downstairs, have a drink and calm down. She hesitated, but finally agreed.

The two of them reached the hotel, checked in and went to their rooms to leave their luggage. Half an hour later they met at the bar and ordered drinks and snacks. While they were there, some warriors sneaked into the general's room, found his documents, photographed them and vanished. After about an hour the young woman recovered her poise, and the general returned to his room unaware that somebody had been there during his absence.

In Tel Aviv, the Mossad analysts examined the photographs, and found out that the general was involved in illegal and unauthorized activity in the Asian country, that was engaged in a secret project of developing forbidden weapons. A western power that uncovered the weapons' development, blocked the project and the plan was abandoned.

*

Liron took part in 146 missions. She was the first woman to be appointed, at 29, chief of an operational team. At the first meeting she attended in her new functions, the representatives of IDF Intelligence, 8200 and other departments were baffled by the presence of this young woman and could not believe she was a team commander. But the Mossad chiefs stood by her. "At the Mossad I soared like a meteor," she said later, "I got fantastic support all along the way. I never said I wanted to be promoted. I enjoyed every moment." The department head Avi and all the Ramsads, Shabtai Shavit, Danny Yatom, Efraim Halevi, Meir Dagan, Tamir Pardo, the Deputy Ramsad Ram Ben-Barak, the future Ramsad Yossi Cohen – they all gave her their full support. When she got married, all the Ramsads were at her wedding. Prime Minister Olmert did not want to expose her by his presence, and his "mazeltov" phone call reached her at the beauty salon before the ceremony.

Liron married at 33, and was accepted for postgraduate studies at

Harvard, but chose to stay in Israel. When on maternity and studies leave, Ramsad Meir Dagan called her and asked her to manage the operational section of the Sigint department. She could not refuse; it was a "fantastic" job. Three years later she was promoted to a grade equivalent to a two-star general.

But in the meantime her three children were born; besides, "the sparkle in my eyes had faded away". Nine years after her marriage she resigned from the Mossad; by doing so she disappointed many of her colleagues who saw in her the best candidate for becoming the first female Ramsad.

CHAPTER 18

Cindy

A Honey trap with no Honey

L ONDON, SEPTEMBER 1986.
 He saw her in Leicester square, in the throngs of tourists that inundated London during this golden September. She stood in front of a newspaper kiosk, a pretty, willowy blonde, who reminded him of Farrah Fawcett, the star of the TV series "Charlie's Angels." She is really angelic and gorgeous, he thought. He stared at her for a long moment, and when she turned, their glances met. She smiled, somewhat embarrassed, and he smiled back. And she know that this exchange of glances would bring her a great success – but also wreck her life.

At first, he turned to go. She wouldn't even look at him, he thought. He was gloomy. skinny and balding. But then he stopped, gathered all his courage, and went back. He addressed her, politely, and she answered with a smile. He asked her for her name. "Cindy", she said. As he kept asking she told him she was a beautician from Philadelphia, and that was her first vacation in Europe. She agreed to have a light drink with him at a nearby café. Their chat was pleasant and relaxed, but he was suspicious, "Are you from the Mossad?" he asked.

"No, no" she giggled. "Not at all. What is Mossad?"

She then asked: "And what's your name?"

"George", he said. That was the name he had used at the hotel.

She cast him an amused look. "Come on," she chuckled, "you're not George."

So, she said, and she knew what she was saying.

*

She knew that his name was Mordechai Vanunu. She even carried his photo in her handbag. She also knew that he was wanted by the Mossad and an order had been issued, to capture him at all costs. She was not "Cindy", but Cheryl Hanin-Bentov, a Caesarea amazon. She had been sent to London urgently with other warriors as soon as their commanders learned that Vanunu was there.

"Cindy" had been born in Florida. Her father, Stanley Hanin, had made his fortune in the automobile tire business. She grew up in Orlando, and after the divorce of her parents in 1977, immigrated to Israel, and served in the IDF where she met her future husband, intelligence officer Ofer Bentov. They married in 1985 and settled in Netanya, a seaside city north of Tel Aviv.

Before her wedding she had been summoned to an interview at the Mossad. She was gifted with an impressive IQ (Intelligence Quotient), English was her mother's language, and she was highly motivated. These were three good reasons for the Mossad to become interested in the young lady. Mike Harari was back at the Mossad for a short while but played only a marginal part in Cheryl's recruitment. She was sent to a two-year course, passed the tests with flying colors and was accepted in Caesarea. The first challenging mission where she participated, was "Operation Kaniuk", the abduction of Mordechai Vanunu.

Before flying to London, to join her Caesarea comrades, Cheryl was briefed about the man they had to locate and kidnap: Mordechai Vanunu, an Israeli, a former technician at the Dimona nuclear reactor, the most secret and the most closely protected site in Israel.

Since the sixties, foreign governments, spies and reporters from all over the world had been trying to pierce the secret surrounding the Dimona reactor in the Negev. Strong rumors claimed that Israel was using this reactor to produce nuclear weapons.

All of a sudden, in September 1986, the Mossad learned that a grave breach of security had occurred: Vanunu, the former technician in the top-secret Dimona Institute 2, had left Israel with a bunch of photographs that revealed the dark secrets of the nuclear compound. After spending a while in Australia where he had converted to Christianism, Vanunu had flown to London with his photographs. The "Sunday Times" had lured him with promises of a down payment of 100,000 US dollars, high percentages of forthcoming deals with other media throughout the world, perhaps a Hollywood movie where Robert de Niro would play Vanunu's role. The Ramsad, Nahum Admoni, was instructed by the Prime Minister to bring Vanunu back to Israel at all costs. The man was about to betray his country for money.

"Cindy" realized her assignment's importance, especially when she found out that Shabtai Shavit, the Deputy Ramsad, oversaw the mission. Shavit appointed Caesarea's head Beni Ze'evi as the direct commander of "Kaniuk". Ze'evi was a legend in the Mossad. He had participated in many risky missions, and in the "Wrath of God" hits in Europe.

Cindy joined one of the search units that spread through London in an effort to locate Vanunu. One of the units posed as a TV crew filming the protest of the Sunday Times print workers, who happened to be on strike. After a couple of days, they saw and photographed Vanunu, when he entered the building. Other teams acted according to the "comb" method conceived by the famous Zvi Malkin, the warrior who had captured Eichmann. They "combed" the areas that their target might visit, so they were in place before he arrived. Even if he took measures to shake off any tails, he could not identify the team that was already waiting for him. Cindy was in the unit lying in wait in the famous Leicester square, that sunny September 24, 1986. Her task was not to establish contact with him, but only shadow him. But he saw her, liked her, started talking to her – and that was a game changer. From that moment on the Mossad mission proceeded in a totally different way from the one planned beforehand. Cindy had to play a role for which she was not ready.

Since they met at Leicester Square Vanunu did not let Cindy go. He was lonely and morose, badly in need of female company and affection, and Cindy was a godsend. They had coffee, then they strolled to the Soho, and stopped at a café again. Gradually he opened, and told her about himself. He revealed his real name, told her he was Israeli, and had come to London to close a deal with the Sunday Times about the secrets of Dimona.

She knew the man was a traitor who was selling the vital secrets of her beloved country; but she also knew how to conceal the disgust she felt. She acted as if she had no idea what he was talking about and pretended to hear the name Dimona for the first time in her life. She advised him, however, to fly to the US and offer his material to one of the American newspapers; she added that she knew some good lawyers who could help him. He refused and stuck to his fabulous arrangement with the Sunday Times. Yet, he seemed to her stressed and nervous. At the end of their meeting he escorted her to her hotel but did not leave before she promised to meet him the following day.

Once alone, Cindy hastened to report to her commanders. Her report triggered a surge of enthusiasm. The mission commanders immediately decided to change the plan and adapt it to the great opportunity – creating a direct contact between Cindy and Vanunu. Thanks to Cindy they discovered the Achiles heel of Vanunu – the loneliness and the urge to create an intimate relationship with a woman. It turned out that the Sunday Times editors who realized Vanunu's need to protect his personal security, did not discern this other need of his. Wendy Robins, a Sunday Times reporter, questioned Vanunu for hours on end, and understood what he yearned for. "He really needed love, a woman's love," she said later. "Then he met Cindy. Perhaps if I had kept a closer contact with him, he would not have needed to fill that vacuum." The Mossad officers discovered the vacuum and charged Cindy to develop their relationship. They encouraged her to establish an intimate rapport with Vanunu.

It seemed that the way was now open for the capture of Vanunu. But things were not as simple as that. The Mossad had a limited freedom of action in England, and for a good reason. A few months before, the German police had discovered in a Frankfurt phone booth a briefcase containing eight fake British passports. The briefcase carried the nametag of an Israeli embassy employee. That event stirred a lot of anger in London, and the confused Mossad had to promise not to carry out any other action that could harm British sovereignty. Besides, Prime Minister Shimon Peres knew well "the Iron Lady", British Prime Minister Margaret Thatcher, and did not want to get in trouble with her. The Ramsad Admoni, after consulting the Prime Minister, ordered his men to find another way to whisk Vanunu out of England; and in the meantime – get him involved with Cindy.

And indeed, for the six days that followed, Vanunu spent most of his time with Cindy. These days, he later said, were the happiest in his life. Cindy and "Mordy", as she called him, strolled in the parks of London holding hands. They hugged and kissed, again and again; they went to the movies and watched Woody Allen's "Hannah and her sisters", and "Witness" with Harrison Ford. They also went to a musical, 42nd Street, and Cindy even dragged him to a museum. He spoke to her about his leftist views, his Moroccan origins, that allegedly were the reason why he had been rejected from the Air Force academy and fired from the Dimona reactor. He also described his childhood in Morocco and his travels to the far provinces of the globe.

But he did not breathe a word about the instability and lack of confidence that stuck to him as a shadow; he did not tell her that years ago he had been religious, a traditional orthodox, and an extreme-right militant; afterwards he had switched to the radical left, started engineering studies, then moved to Economy, then Philosophy, and finally dropped out of the university. He had become a vociferous left-wing activist; yet he was cleared for working in Institute 2, the sanctum sanctorum of the Dimona reactor, together with 150 other technicians who were the only ones among the 2700 reactor employees to know the truth about Israel's nuclear weapons. He smuggled his camera into the reactor, without the security personnel noticing, then used the lunch breaks when the labs were empty to photograph the underground floors of the structure.

In 1985, Vanunu was fired after nine years in Dimona. He did not tell Cindy that his dismissal was not connected with his political activities but was part of budgetary cuts at Dimona. He received a 150 percent severance package and traveled the world – Greece, Russia, Thailand, Nepal...In Nepal he almost converted to Buddhism, but finally changed his mind and in Australia converted to Christianity instead. All this time he carried in his rucksack the photographs of Dimona's entrails, but did not use them. Only when a Columbian friend, Oscar Guerrero, heard about the trove he kept in his poor lodging, he convinced Vanunu to sell them to a newspaper. The Australian papers did not believe his story and rejected his offer, but finally Guerrero hooked the London Times. By the time he came to London, Vanunu was terrified, obsessed by fear that the Mossad was after him.

Vanunu did not know that his offer to the Australian papers was the one that had sounded the alarm in Israel. One of the Sydney editors contacted the Israeli embassy to check Vanunu's credibility, the embassy contacted Jerusalem, and the news reached the "Prime Ministers Club" – the present Prime Minister Peres and the former Prime Ministers Rabin and Shamir. They were astounded to discover that a terrible negligence of the reactor's security officers enabled that technician to photograph the reactor's most secret labs, and then leave the country with his sensational film. The publication of the photographs, they agreed, could trigger a tremendous international pressure on Israel, to immediately stop its dangerous activity at Dimona. On the Prime Minister's order, the Mossad dispatched a team to Australia, but too late. Vanunu was already in London, negotiating with the Sunday Times. There he was tracked down by the Mossad warriors.

*

Vanunu now boasted before Cindy about the great deal he had got from the Sunday Times. Yet, he said he was frustrated by the slow progress of his talks with the newspaper editors. They had delayed the publication of his story, and kept troubling him with endless questioning sessions, in nerve racking detail. He was fed up, he said, with the way they treated him. Beside the boasting and the frustration Cindy also noticed a lot of stress and tension in his behavior. He admitted being very tense before the final closure of the deal with the Sunday Times; there was no time, he said, the Israeli Mossad could find him at any moment. She spoke to him tenderly and succeeded to calm him down.

Their conversations were pleasant; but what really excited Vanunu were the kisses. He did not stop hugging and kissing the blond woman. She complied, but deep in her heart she felt anger and revulsion. That was not what she had come to London for! Vanunu's kisses and hugs sickened her and caused her a mental and physical disgust. She was married, patriotic, and now ordered to play a role she loathed. But she was disciplined and obeyed her commander's demand that she maintain and even develop her connection with Vanunu. Operation Kaniuk was now completely focused on the romantic bond between Vanunu and Cindy.

But Vanunu wanted more, and for him kisses were not enough. He wanted to sleep with her. Cindy stubbornly refused. She told him she could not invite him to her hotel, because she shared a room with another girl; she also refused to come to his hotel room. "You are tense and edgy", she kept saying, and added a few words that her commanders insisted on. "It won't work. Not in London." When his pressure increased, she added another well-rehearsed argument: "Why do not you come with me to Rome? My sister lives there, she's got an apartment, and she always leaves for the weekend... We can have a real good time, and you'll forget all your troubles..." She added that she, too, wanted to be with him.

At first, he hesitated. But she was determined to go to Rome. She even bought him a business class ticket.

And he fell for it.

If he were a more reasonable man, he would have realized right away that he had fallen into a "honey trap" – the term used by the secret services for seduction of a target by a woman. He should have coldly analyzed what was happening to him: he met a girl in the street, she was swept off her feet, and was ready to take him to Rome, just for sleeping with him and even paid for his flight ticket... She could not sleep with him in London, but would be delighted to sleep with him in Rome...

A serious man would have realized that Cindy's story was very suspicious. But the Mossad psychologists knew exactly what Vanunu wanted. They assumed that he would be entranced by the sweet kisses and the enticing promises of this stunning, sexy woman.

Vanunu, these days, was not a reasonable man. But Peter Hounam of the Sunday Times certainly was one. When he heard about Cindy, he felt something was wrong. He tried to convince Vanunu to stop seeing her; but Vanunu had fallen in love and nothing in the world could make him think again. Once he asked Hounam to drive him to the café where he was to meet Cindy, and Hounam got a fleeting glimpse of her. When Vanunu told him, he was going to go away for a couple of days, Hounam again tried to dissuade him, but in vain. He advised Vanunu not to leave England. He could not imagine, though, that Vanunu would fly to Rome just in order to sleep with sweet Cindy.

Rome was chosen by the Mossad as the convenient place where Vanunu could be captured. The relations between the Mossad and the Italian secret service, the SISMI, were close. The Ramsad Nahum Admoni, and the SISMI chief, Admiral Fulvio Martini, were friends. And with the traditional disorder reigning in Italy, it seemed certain that the SISMI would never be able to prove that Vanunu was kidnapped on their soil.

*

And so, on September 30 1986, Cindy and Mordy boarded British Airways flight 504 to Rome. At 9:00 PM they landed in Leonardo de Vinci airport. A charming Italian was expecting them with a big bunch of flowers and took them to his classy car. They drove to Cindy's sister apartment, and on the way they kept kissing and hugging. Vanunu was blissful, virtually on cloud nine. He could not wait, he wanted to get to the promised bed!

The car stopped by a small house in a quiet Roman suburb. A young woman opened the door. That was another Mossad amazon, posing as Cindy's sister. Vanunu was the first to enter. Suddenly the door was slammed shut behind him and two men jumped him, hit him hard, and threw him to the floor. One of them was blond. They tied his hands and feet, while the woman bent over him and plunged a needle in his arm. He fainted.

The unconscious Vanunu was immediately carried to a commercial van, that headed to the north of the country. The van traveled for several hours. Vanunu's abductors, the two men and the young woman, sat beside him. The woman was a doctor, in charge of keeping Vanunu sedated. After a while he woke up and got another injection.

Cindy vanished. According to standing orders, she left Italy right away and returned to Israel. Vanunu did not see her anymore. The van brought him to the port of La Spezia. His kidnappers strapped him to a stretcher and took him on a fast speedboat to the open sea, where an Israeli freighter was moored. It was a ship often used by the Mossad for special missions. According to eye witnesses, two men and one woman carried an unconscious man aboard the ship; the crew members were ordered to enter the crew lounge and stay inside. Some of them, who were on duty, however, saw that the strangers brought a stretcher to the first mate's cabin, and locked the door. The ship immediately sailed toward Israel.

Vanunu spent the trip locked in the small cabin; he did not see Cindy anymore. He was worried about her and did not know what had happened to her. He did not believe she was a part of the kidnapping team. He did not stop asking about her.

Cindy was in Israel. On October 6, 1986, while Vanunu was on his way to Israel, she learned that the Sunday Times had started publishing the series based on his revelations. The articles, enriched by drawings and photographs, revealed that the previous assessments of Israel's nuclear arsenal had been mistaken. The experts throughout the world believed that Israel possessed between 10 and 20 primitive atomic bombs. The information brought by Vanunu, however, proved that Israel had become a nuclear power, and had produced so far at least 150 to 200 hi-tech weapons. Vanunu got scared by his own revelations and feared that the Israelis would kill him; he also feared for Cindy.

Nobody thought of killing Vanunu. He was charged with espionage and treason and sentenced to 18 years in prison, out of which he spent 11 in solitary. Israel regarded him as a traitor who had sold his country's most vital secrets for money. But overseas he was not considered as a traitor. Associations in his name sprouted in Europe and America, and worshipped him as a bold fighter for peace, a martyr who had risked his life to stop Israel's nuclear project. Of course, he was nothing of the kind, and had not realized the importance of the photographs that he had carried for almost a year in his rucksack, till he found out that they could make him rich.

And Cindy? Even many years after his release from prison Vanunu still was obsessed with her. In his first interview, 11 years after his release, he said: "She was not a Mossad agent but an American CIA agent…I saw the pictures that were published…That was not the real Cindy. She was a 26-year-old woman from Philadelphia. I spent a week with her and I know her well…"

He added: "I met her in the street, in London. I initiated the conversation with her. We talked a lot. I did not fall in love with her. I told her that our relationship could develop a little. At the first moment I told her that she was a Mossad agent, but later I forgot about it. She was not the only one who tried to bring me down. You have no idea how many Mossad girls were at every corner there."

"When did you realize that the affair with Cindy was a trap?" the interviewer asked.

"Only when the Mossad agents jumped me at the house in Rome, I understood…And even there I still thought that she, too, was a victim…After the three days I spent in the ship that took me to Israel, I reached the conclusion that she was a part of the plan."

"Cindy" had singlehandedly brought Vanunu to Rome and delivered him to Israel. That was a huge success for the young woman. Yet, at the same time it was the end of her Mossad career.

It turned out that because of the urgency of the operation, the Mossad had had no time to build a foolproof cover for her. She had used her sister's name, Cindy Hanin, and her passport, and that helped British and Israeli reporters to discover her real identity, Cheryl Bentov, nee Hanin. Foreign papers also published her sketch, based on the description given by Peter Hounam, who had seen her once, and other London sources. Cheryl, a gifted Mossad amazon, had to give up her dreams of serving in the Mossad for years to come.

After the foreign media had discovered Cindy's real name a couple of reporters knocked on Cheryl's door in Netanya. They asked her questions about the abduction; the exposure hurt her deeply. Newspapers throughout the world now printed her photograph that had been taken without her consent; they described her as a "seduction woman", a secret agent whose task was to entice Vanunu by sexual means; in Israel, too, several articles appeared about that girl sent to London to seduce Vanunu with her sexy looks, promises, and behavior. Some even portrayed her with harsh, humiliating terms. All this was untrue. Cheryl had encouraged Vanunu's courtship on her commanders' orders and despite her feelings. She brought the Mossad a great victory, but the image that stuck to her pained her awfully. And besides, she was "burned" as a warrior and could not pursue her Mossad career.

She left Israel with her family and returned to Orlando. She settled in a nice home by a golf course, and started a real estate agency. Before Vanunu's release from jail she got into a "Vanunu alert", fearing that his supporters might try to hurt her or her family. Therefore, she stayed at home for a while and even took a time off from her job.

"For me the Vanunu story is a black hole", Cheryl said to a friend, "and I want to delete him from my life and forget him completely." For years she did not recover from the trauma of "physical closeness" that she was told to establish with Vanunu in London. In the middle of her mission, she was told to hold him and kiss him repeatedly, to keep "the affair" going; that left a painful scar in her soul. His incessant efforts to sleep with her, also distressed her deeply.

After a few years, she decided to demand damages from the Mossad.

In her request she claimed that she had not been previously informed that she had to seduce Vanunu by physical means. She described in detail all the cases during their meetings in London, when she had to establish physical contact with him until all the preparations for his abduction were completed. She also described his efforts to sleep with her and all the evasive moves she had to conceive and use.

After a thorough review, all of "Cindy"'s requests were approved by the Mossad and she received an important sum of money. One of the former Ramsads told us that "her request was fully justified ... The mission caused her trauma and distress. I met her several times after the operation. At every meeting she spoke of the abduction and of the pain she was feeling since ... I believe she felt that a great wrong had been done to her, because she had been misled about the role she had to fulfill as a seductress ... That's why I approved the compensation she deserved." Aliza Magen also approved of the settlement.

"She was appalled", a close friend said, "by the reporters entering her house and questioning her about the abduction. Many nights she could not sleep, fearing she might be attacked. This was very disturbing, and she felt she had to escape from Netanya to Orlando. Since this affair all she wants is a normal, quiet and ordinary life."

CHAPTER 19

Linda

The day the Ramsad wept

T HE MOSSAD AMAZONS CAME FROM ALL OVER THE WORLD.
Sylvia Rafael came from South Africa, Waltraud and Yola from
Germany, Yolande and Marcelle from Egypt, Shula Cohen from
Argentina, Isabel Pedro from Uruguay, Aliza Magen and Ilana from
Israel, Marianne Gladnikoff from Sweden, Erika Chambers from
England, Gila from Poland via Australia, Danielle from France,
"Flamenco" from Holland, Yael from Canada, Cindy from the US,
and Linda Avrahami from the inferno of the Holocaust.

*

April, 2018.

"When I was a baby my mother wrapped me in rags and threw me
over the Ghetto wall", Linda said.

Her audience froze. It had never crossed their mind that this pretty,
blue-eyed woman, that had spent all her adult life in the Mossad, had
experienced the horrors of the Holocaust. And more was in store for
them.

They were about twenty senior Mossad officers, who had set on
a trip to Auschwitz, together with select groups of the IDF and the
Shabak. The Mossad group was headed by the Ramsad Yossi Cohen,

and the entire delegation – by Israel's President himself, Reuven (Ruvi) Rivlin. Before entering Auschwitz, the Mossad delegation met in a building close to the death camp, and their guide suggested that each of them told his comrades a little about himself. Some of them spoke about their youth in the kibbutz or the Moshav, of their military service in IDF elite commandos, or their participation in the rare Mossad missions that were not secret anymore.

When Linda's turn came, she could have described her past in the IDF Operations Department and later in the Mossad. She had started her Mossad career as a field intelligence officer, first as a *bat-levaya*, that had operated abroad undercover from 1965 to 1971. Two of her three children had been born abroad. Because of her vast experience she was the first woman to receive a "desk" of a European country when she returned to Israel. She became deputy, then head of a division at "Tsomet", later was appointed head of a Mossad branch in Europe that operated also in Germany, during the years 1982–1986. That position had been held, before, by her good friend Aliza Magen. Linda married David Avrahami and had three children. After a year of classified studies at the National Security College, she joined the Mossad operations department.

When she faced her companions, that day in Auschwitz, she thought of her childhood, not far from the death camp. She hesitated, as she had never spoken about that chapter from her past; perhaps because of the place and the event, she unlocked that sealed episode in her life.

For years, she said, she knew nothing about her family. Later she found out that after the eruption of World War II, her family had escaped to the Soviet occupation zone in Poland. Soon after, her affluent father had been arrested by the Soviets and disappeared forever. Her young mother was pregnant. When she was born, in 1940, her mother was seized by an intense, blinding urge to reunite with her family. She returned to the German occupation zone, where her family still lived. It had been a complicated operation, that included forging documents and payment of bribes to smugglers, clerks, and officers. But only when she was trapped in the Warsaw ghetto with her baby daughter, did she understand how horrible her mistake had been. When the Nazis started sending the Jews to the concentration camps, she understood that her death was near and she had to save the little girl's life. She had a secret treasure – a diamond. She succeeded to establish contact with a young Pole, who lived outside the ghetto, and struck a deal with him: he would save and raise the baby in exchange of the diamond. And on the day they had agreed upon, at exactly the time and the place set up – a far and deserted corner of the ghetto – she wrapped the baby in rags, layer upon layer, till it became a big and heavy bundle, slipped the diamond inside, and threw the bundle over the ghetto wall. Outside the wall, at the convened point, the Pole, Yanek, (fictitious name) was waiting. He caught the bundle in his arms and disappeared.

A few days later, indeed, her mother was sent to her death. And young Yanek brought the baby girl to an elderly couple, probably his grandparents, who raised her. They were poor, bitter people, who managed and serviced a destitute housing project in a distant suburb of Warsaw. They were living in a small, miserable flat in the building. They gave the little girl a new name – Stefa Kosmolova, and the old woman embroidered the name and her address on the smock the child was wearing every day. The girl arrived at their home when she was two months old and lived there till the age of four. Her childhood was grim, hard, loveless. She vaguely remembered "unpleasant things" that the old man did to her.

And one day, while the old couple was busy, she ran away. She ran by the unpaved streets to the main road where a large crowd was walking to an unknown destination. The old couple ran after her, to bring her back, but she mixed with the crowd. She suddenly saw a hand stretched toward her. An old, nice woman took her by the hand and they walked together. What happened then? She could not remember. Her memory came back to her much later at an orphanage at Raba, a town near the city of Krakow, at a distance of more than 300 kilometers from the house she had escaped. She never recalled how and when she did manage to cover this huge distance and resurface in the orphanage.

She stayed there for a while, and one day was called to the office, where she saw the manager of the orphanage and two men, one tall and skinny, the other plump and smiling. "With whom would you like to go?" the manager asked. She stared at the two of them and chose the plump one who seemed nicer. The man took her to Krakow, to a house facing the church. There she met his wife. They did not have children and adopted her. She called them Mother and Father, and got a new name – Krisha (Christina) Markovski. They were devout Catholics, and took her to the church, where she learned all the prayers, learned to cross herself and light candles. She also got a present she cherished: a golden chain with a pendant representing Jesus on the cross.

The Markovski couple treated her well, with one exception: they beat her up every day. "With the Poles, those days, educating the children was by beating them". Linda told a friend years later. After all her vicissitudes she was wetting her bed, that's why she was entitled to some trashing every morning.

Two years later, when the world war was over, a strange woman suddenly knocker on their home door. She was pretty and well dressed. Linda – Stefa – Krisha was ordered to stay away from her, but when the woman saw her she burst in tears. "This is our girl!" she managed. Later the six-year old child learned that the pretty lady was Jewish and her name was Mrs. Sarah Bernstein (fictitious name). She demanded to get the child, claiming she belonged to her family. The Markovskis refused. "She is ours," they said, "we adopted her legally." The confrontation reached the court of law, and the judges ruled in favor of the Markovski couple, as there was no proof whatever that the child was Jewish.

But the Bernstein family did not give up, and appealed to a higher court. A long and costly investigation located the orphanage where the child had been hosted; the name and address embroidered on her smock guided Bernstein to the home of the old couple, where the little girl had been raised after she was thrown over the ghetto wall. A new trial was ordered and the judge, this time, ruled differently. He showered the Markovski couple with compliments about the way they had treated the child, but pointed out that they already were in their fifties, and if the girl stayed with them, she soon would be an orphan again; while the Bernstein couple were in their thirties and they would be her loving parents for many years to come. And so, the little girl finally left Krakow with her new parents, and took the train to Warsaw, her new home and new family...

The Bernstein couple brought the child to their pleasant home, surrounded by a garden. They told the little girl that they were her real father and mother. At their home she met an older girl, about eight years old. "This is your sister", Sarah Bernstein said. After a while Krisha got a new name: Linda. She took her Jesus pendant off her necklace, stopped praying to him, and slowly started acquiring her Jewish identity. Her parents spoiled her, treating her with warmth and love, but the kid felt that something "was not right". One day she entered the kitchen and saw her photograph on the table. She turned the picture over and saw an inscription on the back: "The daughter of Marisha and Yaffim." Really? she thought, and who were Marisha and Yaffim?

Those days many people, single or families, were returning to Poland after surviving the war in Russia or elsewhere, and the radio daily broadcast greetings or messages to lost relatives. That day the Bernstein couple were sitting in the garden. Linda ran to them and said: "The radio just said that Marisha and Yaffim are looking for their daughter Linda." The Bernsteins were dumbfounded. They did not react, but when she went back to the house she heard her "mother" whispering to her husband: "She knows."

But she learned the truth only when she immigrated to Israel with the family in 1950. She was ten years old. The couple revealed to her that they actually were her uncle and aunt, and Sarah Bernstein was her mother's sister. At last she found her real identity. But her life with the Bernstein family was full of love and care; and their older daughter remained her "sister" for the rest of her life. "For me, Israel was Paradise", Linda said later. Everything around her was perfect: the home, the people, the children at her school who were so nice and friendly to her; some of them became her friends for life. The only "problem" was her name. When her teacher heard the name Linda, she was very upset. "This is not a Hebrew name!" she declared, and the girl received her grandmother's name, Shulamit.

The main result of the via dolorosa that Linda had endured until arriving in Israel, was a deep, overwhelming desire to do all in her power for Israel's security. In her military service she was employed in the IDF Operations' department, and afterwards joined the Mossad. "Somewhere", she said, "deep in my heart, a great pain for my mother is engraved for her remaining all alone in the ghetto, in her terrible quandary. And yet, I feel an intense gratitude for her determination to give me life ... And as about my work at the Mossad – I found what I was looking for since I was in IDF Operations at the General staff. I am proud of belonging to the Mossad."

*

Linda concluded her story.

Much later, when they boarded the plane that would take them back to Israel, Yossi Cohen sat beside her and said: "I told your story to President Rivlin. He was deeply moved."

But Linda did not tell him that back in Auschwitz, when she finished her narration, she raised her eyes – and to her amazement she saw him, the tough Ramsad Yossi Cohen – wipe a tear from his eyes.

CHAPTER 20

Dina and Sammy

A night in Teheran

Just one of many stories, Teheran 2018.

That night, Sammy and Dina (fictitious names), two young Mossad
warriors, set out on an extremely dangerous mission in Teheran. They
got out of a car in the city outskirts and walked in the black streets of
Shurabad, one of the most neglected neighborhoods of the Iranian
capital. That was not the first time that Dina was sent to that area.
She glanced at Sammy, who looked Iranian with his short beard and
collarless shirt. He was wearing a threadbare jacket and faded jeans.
Dina was impeccably dressed in long. loose black clothes and a *hijab*.
She spoke several languages, including Persian. They had committed to
memory a logical explanation for their presence in this neighborhood,
if interrogated by police. Actually, Dina had visited Shurabad many
times, every time with somebody else, dressed differently and bearing
different ID papers. Once, during the day, she had photographed the
area with a concealed camera in her bag, and especially focused on a
yellow building, watched over by a single guard. The following night
she had come back again, dressed well, and wearing a different hijab.

But tonight was different. Midnight approached. The employees
in the workshops and the industrial warehouses in the area had left
long ago. The streets were empty, with very few passersby still walking
in the dark. Dina cast a look at the warrior walking beside her. She

relied on him and knew that he trusted her as well, and felt secure when they operated together. They had paired in several missions in enemy countries.

Like at any mission in that neighborhood Dina felt a rising tension. At any moment, suddenly, a Revolutionary Guards squad might emerge, or a team of the Modesty Guards, perhaps even a police or army night patrol. She felt that a terrible danger was hovering over their heads, and their smallest error might end in only one way: a public hanging from a tall crane, positioned in the city center.

She recalled the first time when she saw the structure that her friends called "the warehouse" – a ramshackle building with dirty walls whose yellow paint had faded away long ago. The roof was slightly arched, the door made of corrugated iron. On the right was a poorly shaded parking lot for a couple of vehicles; in summer the guard used to squat there, seeking refuge from the scorching heat. She did not know what was kept in that warehouse. But when she would return from her tours there and deliver the photographs to her commander. she always had to report – are the doors of the building open? Are people entering and exiting? And if they did – when? Are they loading or unloading equipment on or off vehicles outside the building? How many guards are positioned there permanently? Did she see soldiers or police patrolling the neighborhood?

Indeed, she had been in Shurabad before, but this time the mission was different, unique. Her commander explained to her that she should photograph the "Warehouse" and its surroundings with concealed stills and film cameras she carried in her bag. Dina also carried a special, sophisticated device that could transmit the films, in real time, to the command post at Mossad Headquarters. It is very important, her commanders told her, to also photograph the entrance to the building and its environment and transmit the film immediately to headquarters.

An abandoned house, at the street corner, seemed to suit their purpose. Dina and Sammy had discovered it in one of their former missions. The house was surrounded by a fence and offered a view of the buildings on both sides of the street and of the yellow warehouse.

The two warriors knew exactly what to do. They had trained on a model that was built in the safehouse, and now they had to photograph and transmit without being spotted by a living soul.

Dina knew she was not the only one who had toured the place before. During the last few months – some said the last two years – several Mossad warriors had scouted the warehouse and its surrounding area. Dina was told that other warriors filmed the transporting of crates, big bags and heavy equipment into the yellow building. They had focused on the people coming in and out of the building, prepared detailed timetables of the police patrols in the vicinity, and the most important – they noted the time, at night, when the guard was leaving, and the morning hour when he was back. They knew now exactly how many hours, at night, the place was totally deserted.

Yet, Dina's commanders did not tell her what was so special in the yellow building – and she did not ask. In such a complex operation like this one, compartmentalization was vital. And yet, she understood that the warehouse, despite its shabby and neglected facade, concealed something of utmost importance. Apparently, she thought, the dilapidated appearance of the warehouse covered something top-secret – perhaps weapons or nuclear research equipment, Otherwise, why would the Mossad risk some of its best warriors in such a long and complicated mission, in the very heart of a cruel enemy country?

Now the two warriors passed by the yellow structure, heading for the house at the intersection. Here and there old trucks stood on the street, some of them parked for the night, others abandoned by their owners after their last breath. Dina was tense and anxious. If a police patrol appeared suddenly and made her open her bag – only God Almighty could save her. Iran was the most dangerous place on earth for her, a Mossad amazon. A real war was being waged between Iran, her army, her Revolutionary Guards and the fanatic Ayatollahs – and Israel and her far-reaching Mossad. So far the Mossad had the upper hand and its warriors entered Iran, carried their risky missions and left the country undetected. But what would happen tomorrow?

Dina and Sammy reached the wall surrounding the abandoned house. With quick, expert motions, Dina took out the filming assignment. She liked working with the computerized electronic equipment, after long engineering studies. Her heart pounded in her chest like a hammer, but her hands were steady.

They rapidly concluded their task and moved away. Now they chose to return by side alleys and backstreets. The car was waiting for them by a junction, as agreed. Adrenalin flowed through Dina's veins, and an intoxicating taste of success made her feel lightheaded. They had touched the lion's mouth and survived. The Mossad driver who had been waiting for them in the escape car briefly smiled and turned on the engine. They did not exchange a word until they reached the safehouse.

A wave of excitement swept the Mossad Teheran safehouse, when the warriors watched the photos and the films. In Mossad headquarters in Tel Aviv the organization senior officer watched with bated breath the footage of an empty street, and the close-ups on the yellow warehouse. The place was locked, and a large padlock was hanging on the outside door. No guards could be seen, no police patrols, no pedestrians. Former reconnoitering reports stressed that during the day a police car was appearing occasionally in the street; in the evening the guard was going home and nobody, ever, had unlocked the door before sunrise.

*

The Mossad operations in Iran, that focused on that country's nuclear project, had actually started in 2003, when an Israeli analyst discovered Natanz in a satellite photograph. Natanz was a huge compound in a secluded area, 315 kilometers away from Teheran. It had been built in utmost secrecy and was Iran's major nuclear center. Step by step, the Mossad spies found out that the nuclear project had started seventeen years before. In a small and discreet office in Dubai, Iranian envoys had signed a top-secret agreement with Pakistan. At that time Pakistan had become a nuclear power, thanks to the contribution of Dr. Abdul Qadeer Khan. The good doctor used to work in Europe, in the industrial company "Eurenco" and at the first opportunity stole the company's blueprints of state-of-the-art centrifuges. Thanks to these centrifuges, arranged in cascades (chain rows). Khan had succeeded to enrich uranium till it had reached the grade needed for the construction of atomic bombs. The greedy scientist shared his invention with North Korea, Libya and Iran, for fabulous sums of money.

According to the Dubai agreement, Dr. Khan supplied the Iranian nuclear project with centrifuges, uranium, know-how and experts. The nuclear project was not situated in one place, but was divided into secondary sections that operated in Teheran, Natanz, Qom, Isfahan, Fordow and several other sites throughout the country. The project directors had learned the lesson of the 1981 Israeli bombing of "Osirak" Saddam Hussein's nuclear reactor outside Baghdad. Determined to prevent the eradication of the entire project in one bombing, the Iranians erected secret compounds in various sites, in faraway regions. In one base their experts toiled on activating the centrifuges; in another they developed the bomb that will contain the nuclear core; in another installation engineers worked on building a missile warhead capable of carrying the nuclear bomb to its target. Select labs at Teheran university and other academic institutions served a group of scientists for carrying out advanced research connected with the atom.

The Iranian project was discovered by the Mossad only 17 years after its launching. That was a major failure of the Mossad. But even after the exposure of Natanz and its secrets, the Mossad failed to convince the United States that Iran had initiated a secret nuclear venture. The satellite photographs, the written reports and memorandums, as well as the testimonies of Israeli master-spies were rejected by the Central Intelligence Agency, and considered as "Israel's efforts to involve the US in a hazardous conflict with Iran". The Americans changed their minds only after a dramatic event on a television live show. In the middle of an interview on the Pakistani television, Dr. Khan burst in tears and confessed that he was selling centrifuges and know-how to the "axis of evil" nations and especially Iran. Now, finally, Washington agreed to cooperate with Israel against the Iranian project.

The Mossad was very worried by Iran's nuclear ambitions, as the Ayatollahs' regime did not miss an opportunity to declare that it intends to wipe Israel out of existence. The incitement and the blind hatred of the Iranian regime had no limits; and Israel feared that if Iran succeeded to produce nuclear weapons, she wouldn't hesitate to use them against the Jewish State. General Meir Dagan, who was appointed Ramsad by his friend Ariel Sharon in September 2002, focused the Mossad major efforts on the battle against the Iranian project. He knew that the Mossad alone could not prevent the completion of the project; but he also knew that he could delay the Iranian venture for a long time. And he did not spare efforts, time and means.

The Mossad warriors penetrated Iran. With the support of the US Central Intelligence Agency and the British MI-6, they started operating against the Iranian project. Iranian military planes, carrying scientists and senior officers in domestic flights crashed mysteriously. Fires burst in labs of atomic research; cascades of centrifuges exploded after being assembled with defective components supplied to Iran by Israeli straw companies. Some foreign sources claim that the explosion on the launching pad of a Shahab missile, of the sort intended to carry the lethal nuclear charge to Israel, was also the Mossad doing. Elusive viruses like "Stars" were planted by Israeli and American engineers in the computing system of the Iranian project and paralyzed its activity for several months. Another virus, "Stuxnet" was embedded into the activation organism of the Natanz facility. Scientists and senior officers, like Ali Reza Asgari, the former Deputy Defense Minister of Iran, suddenly vanished; some of them defected to the West with Israel's help. Other scientists, who played major roles in the project, were assassinated in Teheran's streets.

The results were impressive: The Iranian project was in trouble. Dagan appeared before the Defense and Foreign Affairs Committee of the Knesset and drily declared: "The Iranian nuclear project is delayed because of technological difficulties."

The Mossad missions described in the world press amazed the cynical commentators in the Israeli media. When Dagan was appointed Ramsad, they mocked and derided him. "Dagan who?" quipped a popular pundit. But now the headlines changed. "The man who restored honor to the Mossad", cheered the newspapers, after some successful missions of Dagan's warriors in Iran.

Even "Al Ahram", the major Egyptian daily, usually very hostile to Israel, could not remain indifferent. In January 2010 it published an article titled "The Superman of the State of Israel" by the famous columnist Ashraf Abu Al-Haul. Al Haul wrote: "If not for Dagan, the Iranian nuclear project would have been completed years ago ... The Israeli Ramsad, in the last seven years, has dealt painful blows to the Iranian nuclear program ... The Mossad is responsible for several daring missions in the Middle East ... All this has made Dagan the Superman of the state of Israel."

"The Iranians," Al-Haul added, "know that [Dagan] is the man behind the assassination of the nuclear engineer Masoud Ali Moham-madi."

Masoud Ali Mohammadi was killed in the explosion of his car outside his home in Teheran, on January 12 2010, at 7:50 in the morning. Iran's President, Ahmadinejad, claimed that he had been killed by the Mossad. But Mohammadi was not the only one.

*

On November 29 2010, at 7:45 in the morning, a 45-year-old nuclear scientist, Dr. Majid Shahriyari was on his way, in his car, to his lab in Northwest Teheran. His wife sat beside him. Shahriyari was a leading figure in Iran's nuclear project, and was considered to be an expert in uranium enrichment. Suddenly a motorcycle emerged behind him. Its two passengers were dressed in black, and their faces were concealed by bikers' helmets equipped with blackened plastic visors. When the motorcycle passed by Shahriyari's car, the backseat passenger stretched his hand toward the vehicle's back and stuck a limpet charge there. Shahriyari apparently did not notice that. The motorbike darted forward and disappeared. Less than a minute later the charge exploded and the car turned into a black, smoking wreck. In the debris police officers found the body of Shahriyari. His wife was seriously wounded but survived.

The motorcycle sped in the city streets, entered side alleys and reappeared in clogged boulevards. The biker kept glancing in his rearview mirror, to make sure he was not followed. He got to the city outskirts, turned to a deserted dirt road and reached a dusty square. The escape car was waiting, engine running. The two bikers jumped off the motorcycle and ran to the car. Another man who was waiting there poured gasoline over the motorcycle and set it on fire. The two bikers got in the escape car. The driver looked at them in his rearview mirror. He gasped when he saw the bike passenger, the one who had stuck the limpet bomb to Shahriyari's car, take his helmet off – and a mass of long black hair cascaded on his shoulders. This was a woman, a Mossad female agent!

That same day the two bikers left Iran. Like them, another couple of Mossad officers took off that afternoon. They had attacked, in a very similar fashion, the car of another nuclear scientist, Dr. Fereydoun Abassi-Davani. Like Shahriyari he was a member of the board of the nuclear scientists' association. The Mossad attack on his car took place on Atashi Street, in South Teheran, but it failed. Abassi was badly wounded but survived. The London Sunday Times that reported the bombing, revealed that three years before, Mossad warriors had poisoned the 44-year-old Professor Ardeshir Hosseinpour who worked in a secret installation in Isfahan. He was in charge of a team of technicians, in white coveralls and foolproof face masks, who converted raw uranium to gas. That gas was fed into the centrifuges that enriched it to a dangerous level. The causes of Hosseinpour's mysterious death were never officially established.

Most of the Mossad operations in Iran were not intended to harm civilians. The scientists' assassinations had two goals: interrupt their dangerous research and also scare them and their families. It turned out that they were very effective, as they spread acute demoralization among their families and relatives.

The biker who killed Shahriyari was not the only woman to participate in a dangerous Mossad mission in Iran. Other women arrived to Teheran in various disguises, and carried out missions of spying, surveillance, planting listening devices, covert breaking into government facilities for gathering intelligence or planting electronic recording devices. "The Mossad women," told us one of the Ramsads, "are about 50 percent of the organization employees. The Amazons take part in missions in Iran, Syria and in any enemy country, according to our needs. They participate not only in executing the missions but also in planning, activating and coordination."

*

At a certain stage, when the Iranians were quite close to obtaining enough enriched uranium for assembling nuclear weapons, Israel considered attacking the project bases throughout the country, in a massive raid by the Air Force. But finally, mostly because the objection of the IDF, the plan was shelved. Prime Minister Benyamin Netanyahu made a huge effort to raise the world public opinion against the danger of an atomic Iran, and to motivate the world nations to stop the project.

Netanyahu only partly succeeded. He indeed influenced the world leaders to try blocking Iran's nuclear ambitions. But they refused to take resolute steps, like requiring of Iran to disband all her nuclear centers. They chose, instead, to sign a ten-years agreement with Iran that only delayed the nuclear project. "Not on my watch!" President Obama declared, which meant – Iran would not become an atomic power as long as he was president.

But after?

The agreement with Iran was signed in Vienna on July 14, 2016, by Iran and the members of the United Nations Security Council. Shortly after, the International Agency for Atomic Energy (IAAE) declared that Iran is implementing the agreement, not to enrich uranium beyond a certain grade. The sanctions against Iran were lifted, and the American and British agents packed their belongings and returned home. Israel was left alone against Iran, as in the first year after the discovery of its nuclear project. Israel did not believe for one moment that Iran had given up its nuclear project; it also refused to accept "the big lie" of Iran's leaders that their country had never tried to develop atomic weapons, and never had had such an intention. But in order to refute that lie in the eyes of the world Israel needed tangible proof.

And that was how the Nuclear archive operation was born.

*

Iran had accumulated a huge archive on the nuclear project secret activity, before the agreement with the big powers had been signed. The Project heads were determined to hide the secret archive for two reasons: first, because it could prove that their declarations that "they never had tried to develop nuclear weapons" were a lie; and second, because it contained plans, formulas and blueprints that would be used as soon as the ten years moratorium stated in the agreement was completed, and the nuclear project was revived.

But where would they conceal the archive? It was obvious it could not be buried in the cellars of government buildings or one of the universities. It was also clear it could not be hidden in a military base, as the military installations were under scrutiny by the UN observers. Finally, the heads of the nuclear project chose the third option: to hide the archive in a location where nobody would look for it – in a dilapidated, shabby building in a far-flung district of Teheran, among scores, perhaps hundreds of similar ramshackle structures, dreary workshops and garages, with zero security, as nobody would suspect that something of value was kept there.

And indeed nobody suspected... except for the Mossad agents. According to the foreign press, only five men in Iran's government knew where the archive was hidden. The Mossad, probably using electronic devices and spies' findings, discovered the building where the archive was kept. Informers with good sources reported that the documents were stocked in thirty-two steel-plated, impregnable safes. The Mossad soon found out exactly which safes contained the most important material.

As soon as he was appointed Ramsad, Yossi Cohen concentrated his efforts on a daring, apparently impossible mission: to steal the nuclear archive. That was to be a giant operation, the biggest and the most complicated in the history of the Mossad till this very day. The preparations lasted about two years with the participation of about one hundred warriors, amazons and agents. That mission was also the closing of a personal circle for the Ramsad. According to Dr. Ronen Bergman, a young Katza had brought to the Mossad, many years ago, the blueprints of the first centrifuges built by the Iranians. His code name was "Alan" and his real name – Yossi Cohen.

Thus was born Dina and Sammy's mission.

The operation developed in several stages. First – finding the address, then examining the outer routine – security, hours of guard presence and police car patrols, door padlocks. Next stage: inside – the location and the type of the safes; preparing the burners that could shoot spurts of fire reaching 2,000 degrees, for the piercing of the steel armor of the safes; outside – preparing the vehicles and the paths for smuggling the archives through one or several of Iran's borders; buying or renting safehouses and concealed parkings along the roads to the border, where the trucks carrying the archives could hide if they did not reach the border on time. The Mossad officers prepared everything down to the smallest details. They also established escape routes for the multitude of warriors and agents, once the mission was over.

The date chosen for the mission was January 31, 2018, at night.

*

But the weather, too, had its say.

On the night of January 27, four days before the mission, Iran was swept by a mighty snowstorm. It hit large parts of the country and Teheran was buried in snow. Roads were blocked, airports, schools and government institutions were closed. Thousands of drivers were stuck in the blizzard, electricity and water were cut, adventurous youngsters climbed on frozen waterfalls; heavy chunks of snow-covered sidewalks and piled up on parked cars. Teheran was used to extreme cold in winter, but such snow was a very rare occurrence. Only in the evening life started to return to normal after the snow had been removed from some parts of the city.

On January 28, at night, Dina and Sammy returned to Shurabad.

Their mission had been delayed by 24 hours because of the storm but tonight, as the blizzard had moved away, they had to go. She put on the long black dress, an old sheepskin coat and the hijab. Sammy donned a frayed black coat. The car carried them to the outer edge of Shurabad.

Dina remembered the first time she saw the decrepit yellow building. A veteran amazon had told her once that years before she had participated in a vaguely similar mission. She had been sent to take photos of a modest workshop that produced electric clocks, named "Kalaye Electric Company". After the operation had ended it turned out that this was the secret factory where the Iranians had built their first centrifuges. After collecting tangible proof, the Mossad had alerted the IAEA in Vienna. But by the time the foreign observers were allowed to enter Iran; and after they got the permission to visit the workshop; and after the Iranians "lost the keys" and delayed the opening of the doors by another day or two – the honorable IAEA experts found an empty building with recently painted white walls…

*

After her first visit to Shurabad Dina had come back a few times. Tonight she and Sammy were told that they had to photograph the place for the last time before the operation. Dina's commander told her that beside taking photos, she had to remove all pieces of evidence proving that the yellow building had been watched by the Mossad for a long period.

She walked beside Sammy in the dark, deserted street. The freezing winds still howled in the courtyards; the snow was melting, and the streets were strewn with large puddles of murky water. The trees whipped by the wind and the desolated buildings cast eerie shadows on the street. It was very cold. They passed by the yellow warehouse that looked deserted as usual, reached the nearby corner and the empty house that had served them as the observation point. In a few moments, Dina and Sammy took their photos, then packed the devices they had installed in the place. On their way back, they trudged between the puddles to the meeting place, a few blocks away. The escape car was waiting. The mission was accomplished.

Because of the strict compartmentalization, Dina did not know – till a few days after – how important her missions had been.

*

The break-in started at 10:30 PM, after the last workers and guards had left the area. Mossad warriors and agents surreptitiously approached the building from different directions. According to the Ramsad order, they had six hours and 29 minutes to accomplish their task. They had to leave the place by 05:00 AM, two hours before the arrival of the guard and the beginning of the police car tours.

Everything was executed according to plan. The warriors neutralized the alert system, broke down the outside door and an inner armored door, located the safes where the important documents were kept, and opened them using their powerful burners. Yossi Cohen's orders were clear – take all the thousands of documents and blueprints. As a general practice, the Mossad warriors used to photograph or copy the documents and put them back in place in order to mislead the enemy. But this time, the decision to steal the archives was taken on purpose; this time the Iranians could not claim that the documents had been forged by Israel. Cohen's order was to scoop all the documents from the major safes into containers and take them away.

The Ramsad and his senior staff watched the operation on huge screens in the Mossad situation room. The activity in the warehouse was transmitted directly by the warriors. Suddenly an unexpected message arrived: the agents discovered in the safes, beside the documents, a large quantity of compact discs. What should we do? The mission commanders asked. Cohen answered – take all the discs. At that moment he could not know that the discs contained a golden trove of information, memos, videos and plans, about the Iranian project.

In a few hours the Mossad team took out hundreds of files, containing 50,000 pages and 183 discs storing another 55,000 electronic files. The materials, weighing about half a ton, were bagged and loaded on several trucks. According to various reports, the trucks crossed Iran's border and their precious load was successfully shipped to Israel.

The break-in was discovered only at 07:00 AM, when the guard came to the yellow warehouse. Some say that the blizzard had been very helpful, as the confusion and the power shortages caused by the foul weather slowed down the Iranian efforts to spread a net of search and pursuit throughout the country. The Mossad participants in the mission – and they were many – left the country without any problems.

In Israel, the operation was kept secret, while translators and experts worked on the analysis of the material. "The Big Lie" of the Iranians came to light almost immediately. The nuclear weapons project had started with a venture named "Amad". The project was closed in 2003, and the Iranians presented tangible proof about that to the world organizations. They only did not reveal that immediately after Amad's closure they launched a new project, "Spand" with the same materials, the same people and the same goal. The Mossad operation in Shurabad proved that Iran continued working on the nuclear project in the following years.

In March 2018 Prime Minister Netanyahu and the Ramsad Cohen flew to Washington where they met Defense Secretary James Mattis, Secretary of State Rex Tillerson, and the National Security advisor Raymond McMaster. Netanyahu also met with President Donald Trump. The Israelis presented the Americans with the major findings in the archive; soon after, they sent copies of all the materials found in the documents and discs. Some claim that the amazing discovery made President Trump decide to retire from the agreement with Iran, on May 8, 2018.

Iran did not react on the theft of the archive and kept total silence about it. On April 30, Netanyahu appeared before the media, described the mission and presented the documents, blueprints and detailed plans that had been found in the yellow warehouse. While governments around the world were shaken by the meaning and the authenticity of the documents, the deputy foreign minister of Iran declared:" Netanyahu's appearance was a childish and ridiculous game, that was planned to influence Trump's decision on the agreement, on the eve of the May 12 deadline."

"In this material," Netanyahu said in his speech, "we found incriminating documents, presentations, assembly plans, photos, footage etc., proving that Iran secretly continued developing nuclear weapons and lied to the world and the International Agency for Atomic Energy."

The operation also proved that Yossi Cohen's Mossad, with its male and female warriors, succeeded in carrying out a mission impossible, without precedent in the world history of espionage. The films and books on James Bond and his colleagues, that millions regarded as the ultimate symbol of covert activity, paled in comparison with the Teheran mission.

Dina and her friends took a huge risk and carried out a challenging and dangerous mission. Dina' s story was just one of many. On the eve of Independence Day, the Israel Security Prize was awarded to the Mossad team that broke into the Nuclear archive. A few Mossad warriors, men and women, were chosen to receive the prize from President Rivlin in Jerusalem.

In 2020, according to foreign sources, the Mossad missions in Iran continue. Centers for Research and production of centrifuges are blowing up, strategic facilities and labs are consumed by fire, and the world media insist that Israel's war against the Iranian atomic bomb is attaining new heights and intensity.

On November 27, 2020, the head of the Iranian nuclear project, Mohsen Fakhrizadeh, was mysteriously assassinated by persons unknown.

Epilogue

In a speech on July 1, 2019, the Ramsad Yossi Cohen said:

"Men and women from all segments of the Israeli society serve in the Mossad. We intentionally act to enlarge the social circles from where the Mossad officers come. Our force comes from our diversity; this is operationally logical, but it also carries moral power. Women have served in the Mossad, in every function and every profession, since its creation. We need women, today more than ever, in every position and every grade. We need women at senior command positions and in the last few years we act intentionally and in depth to get more women as commanders and directors in the organization. Today, women already serve in major command positions in the Mossad, and I hope that in the future we'll see a woman as Head of the Mossad. Our experience along the years has proven to us that mixed teams of women and men succeed to accomplish their complicated tasks much better. 40 percent of the Mossad employees are women, 26 percent of the commanders are women. This is a very high percentage in an operational security organization, but we still strive to improve it."

The Mossad also initiated a special effort to make it possible for women to marry and have children, and still carry out their missions. For that purpose, when a woman is recruited by the Mossad, its officers interview her spouse as well. Will he agree to a family life when his wife will have to be absent from home? Will he agree to take care of the children during these absences? For the Mossad, there is no difference between the life of such a couple and the life of a doctor or a nurse who have to be absent from home days and nights because of their profession.

As about the arguments against recruiting young women because they get pregnant and have children, the Ramsad said to a friend: "How long is a maternity leave? Six months? Let's say even, in special cases, nine months? And how long is a leave for studies in the university, where we send the Mossad warriors to get a degree? At least a year and a half or two years. So what is the problem with a female warrior who wants to have a child?"

In 2019, women were 47 percent of the new recruits to the Mossad. 30 percent of the unit commanders were women, and in a specially challenging course that took place in the fall of 2019, the graduates were two men and five women.

ABOVE: An advertisement recently published by the Mossad
Wanted: Women of Strength
We do not care what you have done – We care who you are!

Bibliography and Sources

The Mossad Amazons is based on a large variety of sources, books documents, newspapers, articles and interviews. As it deals with exclusively secret materials, the importance of reliable, solid sources is crucial. Most of the sources in Hebrew were unpublished documents and in-depth interviews with many of the major players in that world of shadows. We also used a great number of sources in English, after trying to separate the genuine information from the fantastic inventions of fertile minds. We hope to have succeeded in this endeavor.

As for the Hebrew books and articles mentioned in the references, their titles were translated into English. The sources marked with an (H) are in Hebrew.

Introduction: Liat – A *Lohemet* Speaks
Interview with "Liat" by Michael Bar-Zohar and Nissim Mishal

CHAPTER EXTRAORDINARY: TRIO: Nina, Marilyn and Kira
Interview with former Heads of the Mossad and Mossad high officials
    by Michael Bar-Zohar and Nissim Mishal
"An End to Ambiguity: How Israel Attacked the Syrian Nuclear
    Reactor", Aluf Ben, *Haaretz*, 21.3.2018 (H)
Bar- Zohar Michael, Mishal Nissim, *Mossad*, from North Korea with
    love, Ecco, HarperCollins publishers, New York, 2012, pp. 279–290

PART ONE: VANGUARDS

Chapter 1 – Sarah: Death on Mount Carmel
"Women in the Mossad", Yos'ke (Joseph)Yariv, talking to Yeshayahu
    Ben Porat, editors Niza Zameret & Uri Neeman, *Mabat, Israel*

Intelligence Heritage & Commemoration Center (IICC) no. 17, January 1998 (H)

"Our woman in Beirut", Amira Lam, *Yedioth Ahronoth*, 3.9.2015 (H)

Mossad, op. cit., chapter 4, A Soviet mole and a body at sea, pp. 38–49

Chapter 2 Yolande – Her Shoulders Were Padded with Secrets

"Yolande, An Unsung Heroine" Dan Wollman (Documentary) movie
https://vimeo.com/297561106

"Yolande Gabai Harmer: Israel's Secret Heroine", Prof. Livia Bitton-Jackson, *Jewish Press*, May 17, 2013

"Yolande, The Egyptian Woman Who Spied for Israel", Lea Falk, *Jewniverse*, July 21, 2015

"Extraordinary tale of Alain de Botton's heroine Grandmother", Alain de Botton, *The Observer*, June 7. 2015

"An Israeli Secret Agent in King Farouk's Court", Anne Joseph, *Times of Israel*, July 4, 2015

"Yolande Harmor", *Israel Intelligence Heritage & Commemoration Center* (IICC) (H)

"An interview with Alain de Botton", Shlomzion Keinan, *Haaretz*, 10.1.2007 (H)

Sharett Moshe, *Private Diary*, Maariv publishers, 1978 (H)

Interview with Yaakov (Kobi) Sharett

Interview with Ora Schweizer by Michael Bar-Zohar

Interview with Prof. Dan Segre, by Michael Bar-Zohar

Chapter 3 Shula – Monsieur Shula, Codenamed "The Pearl"

Golan Aviezer & Pinkas Dani, *Shula: Code Name the Pearl*, Kinneret Zmora-Bitan, Tel Aviv, 1980 (H)

Yachin Ezra, *The Song of Shulamit, the Story of a Zionist spy*, Jerusalem, Yachin Ezri publisher, 2000 (H)

Lapid Ephraim, *Secret Warriors, the Israeli Intelligence, a look from within*, Yedioth Sefarim, 2017, p. 91 (H)

"Grandmother Jams Bond" – the Zionist spy in Lebanon, Ofer Aderet, *Haaretz*, 25.5.2017 (H)

"Shula Kishik-Cohen, A Zionist spy in Beirut", Hadar Perri, *View-Point*, 21.4.2019 (H)

"The Royal Party Which Gave Birth to a Spy", Tova Kaldes, *Mabat*, (*IICC*), *Journal, no.78*, July 2017, pp. 12–13 (H)

"A Secret Warrior", Hanna Zemer in *100 Men and Women of Valor*, edited by Bar-Zohar Michael, Magal and Defense Office publishing house, 2007, p. 104 (H)

"Our Lady in Beirut", Joseph Arenfeld, *Israel TV, Channel 7*, May 25, 2017 (H)

"Monsieur Shula", Yariv Peleg, *Israel Hayom*, 6.5.2017 (H)

"Interview with Moti Kfir", by Roni Daniel, Friday studio, *Israel TV*, 23.7.2010 (H)

"Shulamit Kishik – Cohen", *Israel Intelligence Heritage & Commemoration* Center (*IICC*), Video (H)

"Shula Cohen's story", *YouTube* (H)

"The Israeli Spy in Lebanon is Dead", Itamar Eichner, *YNET*, 22.5.2017 (H)

"Memoir, This Woman was My Mother", Isaac Lebanon, *Haaretz*, 18.12.2018 (H)

"The Beirut Spy: Shula Cohen" – The Best Documentary Ever, Loren Gusikowski, (BR Docs) December 6, 2017

"Israeli Spy Who Lived Undercover in Lebanon for 14 Years Died At 100, Shulamit – "Shula" Cohen-Kishik who was codenamed "The Pearl," died Sunday at Hadassah Medical Center in Jerusalem. By JTA, *The New York Jewish Week*, May 22, 2017

Interview with Isaac Lebanon by Michael Bar-Zohar

Interview with Sami Moriah by Michael Bar-Zohar

Conversations with Shula Cohen by Michael Bar Zohar, 1982–1990

Chapter 4 Marcelle – Better Death than Torture

Conversations with Marcelle Ninio (1985–2020) by Michael Bar-Zohar

"To Live on Another Planet", Hanna Zemer, *100 Men and Women of Valor*, op.cit. p. 108 (H)

Mossad, op.cit, pp. 169–170

Bar-Zohar Michael, *Ben Gurion*, Am-Oved, Tel Aviv, 1977, volume 2, p. 1049 (H)

Jackont Amnon, *Meir Amit, the Man and the Mossad*, Yediot Sefarim, Tel Aviv, 2012, pp. 154, 242, 243 (H)

"The Affair, Life in prison", nidoneykahir.org.il (H)

Golan Aviezer, *Operation Suzanna*, Idanim, Tel Aviv, 1976 (H)

"Cairo Prisoners": Marcelle Ninio a Special Prisoner, nidoneykahir .org.il (H)

"Identity-Card" – The Mission and Fall of Max Bineth, www.maxbineth *(H)*

Yossi Cohen, Head of the Mossad, Eulogy for Marcelle, *Yedioth Ahronoth* 27.10.2019 (H)

Chapter 5   Waltraud – The Mysterious Mrs. Lotz

Avneri Arie, *Lotz, The Spy on a Horse*, Y. Gutman publishers, Tel Aviv 1968 (H)

Lotz Wolfgang, *A Mission in Cairo*, Maariv publishers, Shikmona Tel Aviv 1970 (H)

"What Do I Tell Mother", Yossi Melman, *Haaretz*, 27.2.2007 (H)

Waltraud Lotz (biographical details), *Palestine Information with Provenance* (PIWP Database)

cosmos.ucc.ie/cs1064/jabowen/IPSC/php

"The Champagne Spy", Nadav Shirman, *Documentary*, 11.2.2007 (H)

Meir Amit, the Man and the Mossad, op.cit., pp. 148,156, 242–243(H)

Conversations with Wolfgang Lotz by Michael Bar-Zohar

Conversations with Marcelle Ninio (1985–2020), by Michael Bar-Zohar

Chapter 6   Freedom!

Bibliography to this chapter is taken from the above three chapters.

PART TWO: LITTLE ISSER IS RECRUITING AMAZONS

Chapter 7   Yehudit – Flamenco in Buenos Aires, A Girl from Jerusalem

Shen A., *Moroccan Jewry Past and Culture*, Hakibbutz Hameuchad, Tel Aviv, 2000, p. 10 (H)

Harel Isser, *The house on Garibaldi street*, Zmora-Bitan 1975, Kinneret, Tel Aviv, 1990 (H)

Palmor Eliezer, *The Lillehammer Affair, an outsider's diary*, Carmel publishers, Jerusalem, 2000 (H)

Man Peter, Dan Uri, *Eichmann in my Hands!* Masada Publishers, Tel Aviv, 1987, pp. 144–200 (H)

Malkin Peter Z., Stein Harry, *Eichmann in my Hands!* Grand Central Publishers, April 1991 (Kindle edition), chapters 19–20

Klein Aaron, *Mike Harari, The Master of Operations*, Keter publishers, Jerusalem, 2014, p. 25 (H)

Melman Yossi & Raviv Dan, *Spies Against Armageddon*, Yedioth Sefarim, Tel Aviv, 2012, pp. 115–117 (H)

"The Only Woman in the Operational Team", Itai Ascher, *Maariv*, 17.8.2003 (H)

"Yehudit Nissiyahu is Dina Ron, The Woman Who Kidnapped Adolf Eichmann", Uri Blau, *Haaretz*, 19.9.2008 (H)

"A Jewish soul", The TV movie about Yehudit Nissiyahu, *documentary division, Israel Broadcasting Authority (IBA), Channel 1*, 22.2.2017 (H)

Mossad, op. cit. pp. 59–87

"My Dark Bureau" (Photographer Sara Eyal), Ofer Aderet, *Haaretz*, 15.2.2019 (H)

"Yael Pozner, a Woman at the Top of the Mossad", Talma Admon, *Maariv*, 28.11.1990 (H)

"I Am Not a Superman", Yochi Weintraub, *Mabat*, (IICC) no. 51, February 2008, p. 8 (Yael Pozner) (H)

"Silence suits them", Yochi Weintraub, Limor Klipa, *Mabat*, (IICC) no.51, February 2008, p. 4–7 (H)

"Aliza Magen – A Confidante", Asaf Liberman, Tali Ben Ovadia, research Mali Kempner, *Real time, TV* chapter 6, Kan 11 (H)

"Super Heroines", Carmit Sapir-Weitz, *Maariv*, 1.5.2017 (H)

"Things You See from There" – Minister Rafi Eitan 'Identity-Card', Ephraim Lapid, Yochi Erlich, *Mabat*, (IICC), no. 51, February 2008, p. 4–7 (H)

Interviews with Aliza Magen by Michael Bar-Zohar

Interviews with Moti Kfir by Michael Bar-Zohar

Interviews with Isser Harel for the book *Spies in the Promised Land*, by Michael Bar-Zohar

Interview with Malka Braverman for the book *Spies in the Promised Land*, by Michael Bar-Zohar

Conversations with Yaacov Meidad (Mio) By Michael Bar Zohar

Interviews with Rafi Eitan for the book *Mossad* by Michael Bar Zohar and Nissim Mishal

Chapter 8 Isabel – High Heels in Cairo

"Our Woman in Cairo: The story of an Israeli Spy who Penetrated Egypt in Nasser's Times", Shlomo Nakdimon, *Haaretz*, 1.9.2011 (H)

Interview with Isabel's sons: Eilon and Asaf Kaplan and her niece, Ruth Aner, by Michael Bar Zohar

"Her Michael: Yitzhak Shamir's Mossad Agent", Dalia Mazori, *Maariv* NRG 2.7.2011 (H)

"Alone in a Strange City", Jacki Hugi, *Galei Zahal*, 27.4.2012 (H)

"Unknown Affairs, presentation about Isabel Pedro", Gideon Mitchnik, *Cinema City*, November 2018 (H)

Chapter 9 Nadine – A Tragic Love Story

Caroz Ya'acov, *The Man with Two Hats*, Defense Office publishing House, Tel Aviv, 2002, pp. 239–246 (H)

"Double Identity", Marina Golan, *Israel Defense*, 30.8.2013 (H)

Interviews with Sami Moriah, Isser Harel and Ya'acov Caroz, by Michael Bar-Zohar

Part Three: Mr. Mike Harari and his Ladies

Chapter 10 Mike

Mike Harari, The Master of Operations, op.cit.

Conversations with Mike Harari, by Michael Bar-Zohar

Chapter 11 Sylvia (1) – The Most Famous of Them All

Oren Ram with Kfir Moti, *Sylvia, the Life and Death of a Mossad Warrior*, Keshet publishers, Tel Aviv, 2010 (H)

Oren Ram, Kfir Moti, *Sylvia Rafael: The Life and Death of a Mossad Spy*, (Foreign Military Studies) University press of Kentucky, Kindle edition, 2014

The Lillehammer Affair, an outsider's diary, op.cit.

Mossad, op.cit. The quest for the red prince, pp. 186–213, 205–208

Bar-Zohar Michael, Haber Eitan, *The Quest for the Red Prince*, William Morrow, New York, 1983

Shavit Shabtai, *Head of the Mossad*, Eulogy for Sylvia, 1.9.2010, Yedioth Sefarim, 2018, p. 311 (H)

Dan Uri, *Terror Incorporated*, Masada, Tel Aviv, 1976, pp. 138–148 (H)

"Sylvia Rafael", *Mabat* (IICC), no. 41, June 2005, p. 42 (H)

"A Foreign Woman", Gad Shimron, *Bamahane*, 29.8.2008 (H)

Mike Harari, The Master of Operations, on Mike Harari, op.cit.

Bergman Ronen, *Rise and Kill First*, Random House, New York, 2018, pp. 110–112, 179,183

"Terrorists Threatened to Murder the ex-Mossad Agent, Sylvia Rafael", Esther Edelstein, *Maariv*, 9.5.1989 (H)

"Fresh-faced, I fell into the Honey trap laid by Israel's Mata Hari", Jon Swain, *The Sunday Times*, 21.2.2010

"Israel's legendary spy Sylvia Raphael returns to the spot life", *The Jerusalem Post*, 4.11.16

"The spy who fell into a trap", Stephen Appelbaum, *the Jewish Chronicle*, 18.8.2016

Interviews with Moti Kfir by Michael Bar-Zohar

Conversations with Aaron Scherf by Michael Bar-Zohar

Chapter 12   Yael – A Screenplay About an English Adventuress

Mass Efrat, *Yael, The Mossad Combatant in Beirut*, Hakibbutz Hameuchad, Tel Aviv, 2015 (H)

"The first digger in the Holy Land, did what women were not supposed to do at that time", Shirly Sydler, *Haaretz*, 22.5.2015 (H)

"An interview", Yuval Malchi, Historical chapters, podcast, The Mossad, chapter 189 (H)

"Eileen – A Mossad Warrior who took part in Operation: Spring of Youth", Hadar Peri, *Point of View*, 27.4.2019 (H)

"Our Woman in Beirut", Amira Lam, *Yedioth Ahronoth*, 3.9.2015 (H)

"Yael – The story of a Mossad warrior", Mina Berman, *Mabat*, (IICC), no. 74, April 2016 (H)

"First time in the History of Israel, 5 Mossad Women Warriors are interviewed", Vered Ramon-Rivlin, *Lady Globe's*, 11.9.2012 (H)

"Operation Spring of Youth, the untold story", Ronen Bergman, *Yedioth Ahronoth*, 10.5.19 (H)

"Lady Hester: Queen of the East by Lorna Gibb", Paula Byrne, *The Telegraph*, (BST) 30 April, 2005

Conversations with Mike Harari by Michael Bar-Zohar

Conversation with Yael and John by Michael Bar-Zohar

Chapter 13 Sylvia (2): Fiasco

Bibliography from chapter 10

Bird Kai, *The Good Spy: The Life and Death of Robert Ames*, Crown Publishers, Broadway Books, New York 2014, (Kindle edition), pp. 93–94, 173, 180–182, 198

"The warrior who left the Mossad to grow flowers, looked for Ali Hasan Salameh", Ofer Aderet, *Haaretz*, 6.8.2015 (H)

"The Protocols of the Fiasco in Lillehammer Uncovered", Yossi Melman, *Maariv online*, 2.7.2013(H)

"Not Yet the Time to Reveal the Historical Truth", eulogy for Sylvia Rafael, Yossi Melman, *Haaretz*, 16.2.2005 (H)

"Marianne Gladnikoff", in a TV interview by Amnon Levi, *True Face*, Channel 13, 16.2.2017 (H)

"Marianne Gladnikoff, details emerge in Boushiki Murder Trial", *Jewish Telegraph*, 9.1.1974

Chapter 14 Danielle – Two Spies in Love

Interview with Danielle by Michael Bar-Zohar

"First time in Israel, Five Mossad Women Warriors are interviewed", Vered Ramon-Rivlin, *Lady Globe's*, 11.9.2012 (H)

"Coming Home the Hard way, From the Mission to Egypt to Despair", Yossi Melman, *Walla News*, 25.9.2012 (H)

"Dead End, a Blue and White story about Espionage", Yossi Melman, *Israel Forbes*, 3.6.2017 (H)

Chapter 15 Erika – Two Women and a Terrorist

"Hit List", The killing of Hassan Salameh – (interview with D, and Anna) Alon Ben David, *Channel 13, Israel TV*, 22.12.2019 (H)

"The Mossad for Special Services", Amir Shoan, Amira Lam, *Yedioth Ahronoth*, 15.12.2017 (H)

The Quest for the Red Prince, op.cit.

Dietl Wilhelm, *A Mossad Agent, Operation Red Prince*, Bitan, Tel Aviv, 1997 (H)

"Erika Chambers, The story of a Mossad Warrior", Hadar Peri, *View Point*, 16.5.2019 (H)

"The top QC, his Vanished Sister and the Mystery of Mossad's First British Hitwoman", Tom Rawstorne, *The Mail*, 20.2.2010

Rise and Kill First, op.cit., pp. 214–224

Mossad, op.cit. pp. 210–212

Mike Harari, The Master of Operations, at Mike Harari, op.cit

PART FOUR: CRYSTALLINE WATERS, VIRGIN BEACHES – AND A SECRET

Chapter 16 Yola, Gila, Ilana: A Divers' Paradise, far, far away

Interview with Yolanta Reitman by Michael Bar-Zohar

Mossad, op.cit., from the land of the queen of Sheba, pp. 317–332

Shimron Gad, *Mossad Exodus* (Bring Me the Ethiopian Jews), Hed Arzi Tel Aviv, 1998 (H)

"The Mossad – Cover Story", Duki Dror, Yossi Melman, Chen Shelach, chapter 3 (Women) *Israel TV, Channel 8*, 2017 (H)

"Desert Queen", Yishai Hollander, *Makor Rishon*, 5.8.2016 (H)

"The Mossad Ran a Fictitious Diving Site in Sudan. The Story Behind It". Alison Kaplan-Somer, *Haaretz*, 14.5.2018 (H)

"The Mossad Agent and the Resort in Sudan, The Secret Operation to bring the Ethiopian Jews", Oren Nahari, *Walla news*, 16.4.2017 (H)

"Heritage Story, The Rescue of Mossad People in The Middle of the Desert", Shai Levi, *Pazam, MAKO*, internet site, 18.6.14 (H)

"Sudan's Secrets", Ronen Bergman. *Yedioth Ahronoth*, 26.7.2019 (H)

"Operation Brothers: Diving Site in the Red Sea", Rabi Shraga Simons, *AISHRAEK*, Internet site, 1.10.2017 (H)

Interview with Gila Waksman by Michael Bar-Zohar
Interview with Ilana Peretzman by Michael Bar-Zohar
Interview with Dani Limor by Michael Bar-Zohar
Interview with Yariv Gershoni by Michael Bar Zohar
Conversations with Aaron Scherf by Michael Bar-Zohar

PART FIVE: ALIZA MAGEN AND FRIENDS

Chapter 17 Aliza – The little Girl Who Broke the Glass Ceiling

Interviews with Aliza Magen, by Michael Bar-Zohar
Interview with "Liron" by Michael Bar-Zohar and Nissim Mishal
Interview with Ilan Mizrachi by Michael Bar-Zohar and Nissim Mishal
"Silence Suits Them", Yochi Weintraub, Limor Klipa, *Mabat, (IICC)* no.51, February 2008, p. 4–7 (H)
"Things You See from There" – Minister Rafi Eitan 'Identity-Card', Ephraim Lapid, Yochi Erlich, *Mabat, (IICC), no. 51,* February 2008, p. 4–7 (H)
"Aliza Magen- A Confidant", Asaf Liberman, Tali Ben Ovadia, research Mali Kempner, *Real time, TV* chapter 6, channel 11 (H)
"Super Heroines", Carmit Sapir-Weitz, Maariv, 1.5.2017 (H)
Interviews with former Heads of the Mossad and high officials in the Mossad by Michael Bar-Zohar and Nissim Mishal
Interview with "Sigal" by Michael Bar Zohar and Nissim Mishal
Conversations with Ram Ben Barak by Michael Bar-Zohar and Nissim Mishal
Interview with Sima Shein by Michael Bar Zohar and Nissim Mishal
Interview with "Rina", by Michael Bar Zohar and Nissim Mishal
Interview with Orna Sendler-Klein, by Michael Bar Zohar and Nissim Mishal
Interview with Mirla Gal, by Michael Bar Zohar
"Our Woman in Beirut", Amira Lam, *Yedioth Ahronoth,* 3.9.2015 (H)
"The Mossad – Cover Story", Duki Dror, Yossi Melman, Chen Shelach, chapter 3 (Women) *Israel TV,* Channel 8, 2017 (H)
"The Double life of a Mossad Agent (Orna Sandler)", Rina Mazliach, *Mako News, channel 12,* 26.2.2016 (H)

Sandler-Klein Orna, *The Woman Among the Shades*, Gaya, Tel Aviv, 2015

"A High official in the Mossad (Sima Shein): "I never though the Iranian threat was existential", Limor Even, *Globes*, 10.6.2016 (H)

Yossi Cohen, Head of the Mossad, Speech in Herzliya Convention, 1.7.2019

https://www.idc.ac.il/he/whatsup/pages/herzliya-conf-day2.aspx (H)

Chapter 18   Cindy – A Honey Trap with No Honey
Mossad, op.cit. pp. 239–253

"Sophisticated, Israelis and not so Discreet, the Mossad in the Service of Hollywood", Amir Bogan, *YNET*, 5.10.2017 (H)

"From Australia to being tempted by Cindy, how Vanunu was Kidnapped", Yossi Melman, *Haaretz* 25.8.2011 (H)

"History Catches up with Mossad Seductress Who Trapped Vanunu", Donald Macintyre, *Independent News, World – Middle East*, Wednesday 21 April 2004

"Vanunu Speaks for the First Time after 30 Years to an Israeli Media", Danny Kushmaro, *TV Channel 2*, 2.9.2015 (H)

"Cindy: For me the Vanunu Story is a Black Hole", Anat Talshir & Zadok Yechezkeli, *Yedioth Ahronoth*, 20.4.2004 (H)

"Cheryl Bentov – The Agent Who tempted Vanunu and brought him to Israel", *YNET*, 20.4.2004 (H)

"Wendy Robbins: As a Jewess I could not Understand how Vanunu was Capable to Betray Israel", Yael Arava, London, *Maariv NRG* 6.10.2006 (H)

Interview with Danny Yatom by Michael Bar-Zohar and Nissim Mishal

Chapter 19   Linda – The Day the Ramsad Wept
Interviews with "Linda" by Michael Bar-Zohar

Chapter 20   Dina and Sammy: A Night in Teheran
"The Movie about the Iranian Archive will be named: Cohen and the Braves", Yossi Melman, *Maariv* 5.5.2018 (H)

"How did the Mossad get the nuclear documents from a neglected storage in Teheran", Ran Dagoni, *Globes*, 1.5.2018 (H)

"Iran is Covered and Buried in Snow", Foreign agencies, YNET 28.1.2018

"Armed Forces Ordered to Help in Relief Operations after Heavy Snowfall", *Teheran Times*, 28.1.18

"How the Iranian Archive was Smuggled", Ronen Bergman, *Yedioth Ahronoth*, 1.5.2018 (H)

"The Target is 5 Nuclear Bombs of 10 Kilotons on Shahab 3", Ronen Bergman, *Yedioth Ahronoth*, 6.9.2018 (H)

"Israel Defense Prize to the Mossad Unit which broke into the Iranian Archive", Eli Faibelzon, *Hidabrut*, 27.5.2019 (H) https://www .hidabroot.org/article/1125339

"In the Middle of the Night with Torchers," *Haaretz*, 15.7.2018 (H)

"More Details about the Operation in Iran", *Srugim*, 2.5.2018 (H) https://www.srugim.co.il/252660

"New Data about the operation in Iran", YNET 15.7.2018 (H)

Benjamin Netanyahu's speech, YNET 30.4.2018 (H)

"Breaking In – in the Middle of Teheran", "Real Time" (Zman Emet), Documentary, TV *Series, Chap. 16*, 2 episodes, *Channel 11* (H)

"The Nuclear Archive – Only 5 People knew its Location", Shlomo Zezna, *Israel Hayom*, 1.5.2018 (H)

"A Missile Exploded in Iran in a launching attempt", YNET, 29.8.2019 (H)

"The Big Exercise: Iran Launched Surface to Surface Missiles, one of them was Shahab", Dudi Cohen, YNET, 28.6.2018

"The Shahab-3 Missile Target – is Israel", YNET, 3.10.2002 (H)

"What is so Dangerous in the New Iranian Satellite?", Nizan Sadan, *Calcalist*, 9.5.2020 (H)

"How Israel, in the Dark of Night, Torched Its Way to Iran's Nuclear Secrets", David E. Sanger and Ronen Bergman, *New York Times*, 15.7.2018.

"Was Israel Behind a Deadly Explosion at an Iranian Missile Base?" Karl Vick, *Time Magazine*, New York, 13.11.2011.

"Iran Missile Architect Dies in a Blast. But was the Explosion a Mossad

Mission?", Julian Borger and Saeed Kamali Dehghan, *The Guardian*, London, 14.11.2011.

Epilogue

Cohen Yossi, Head of the Mossad, Speech in Herzliya Convention, 1.7.2019 (H)

https://www.idc.ac.il/he/whatsup/pages/herzliya-conf-day2.aspx

Interviews

Kfir Moti, Ninio Marcelle, Shavit Shabtai, Yatom Danny, Ben-Barak Ram, Moriah Sami, Olmert Ehud, Mizrachi Ilan, Prado Tamir, Cohen-Kishik Shula, Levanon Itzhak, Harel Isser, Eitan Rafi, Braverman Malka, Meidad (Mio) Yaakov, Shweizer Ora, Prof. Segre Dan, Sharett Yakov (Kobi), Yael and John, Magen Aliza, Harari Mike, Gershoni Yariv, Sendler-Klein Orna, "Liat", "Linda", "Daniel", "Rina", "Liron", "Sigal", Pedro family (Eilon and Asaf Kaplan, Ruthy Aner), Limor Dani Gal Mirla, Reitman Yolanta, Waxman Gila, Peretzman Ilana, Shein Sima, Erlich Yochi, Elron Sara, Caroz Yaacov, Sherf Aharon and many others who asked to remain anonymous.

Books

Golan Aviezer & Pinkas Dani, *Shula: Code Name the Pearl*, Kinneret Zmora Bitan, Tel Aviv, 1980

Yachin Ezra, *The Song of Shulamit, The Story of a Zionist Spy*, Yachin Ezri publisher, Jerusalem, 2000

Lapid Ephraim, *Secret Warriors, the Israeli Intelligence, a look from within*, Yedioth Sefarim, 2017

Avneri Arie, *Lotz the Spy on a Horse*, Y. Gutman publishers, Tel Aviv 1968

Lotz Wolfgang, *A Mission in Cairo*, Maariv, Shikmona, Tel Aviv, 1970

Oren Ram with Kfir Moti, *Sylvia, The Life and Death of a Mossad Warrior*, Keshet, Tel Aviv, 2010

Oren Ram, Kfir Moti, *Sylvia Rafael: The Life and Death of a Mossad Spy* (Foreign Military Studies) The University Press of Kentucky, 2014 (Kindle edition).

Palmor Eliezer, *The Lillehammer Affair, an outsider's diary*, Carmel, Jerusalem, 2000

Mass Efrat, *Yael, The Mossad Combatant in Beirut*, Hakibbutz Hameuchad, Tel Aviv, 2015

Sandler-Klein Orna, *The Woman Among the Shades*, Gaya Tel Aviv, 2015

Aaron Klein, *Mike Harari, The Master of Operations*, Keter, Jerusalem, 2014

Jakonte Amnon, *Meir Amit the man and the Mossad*, Yedioth Sefarim, 2012

Melman Yossi & Raviv Dan, *The Imperfect Spies*, Maariv Tel Aviv, 1990

Melman Yossi & Raviv Dan, *Spies Against Armageddons*, Yedioth Sefarim, 2012

Melman Yossi, *Imperfect Spies*, Tchelet Publishers, 2020

Shavit Shabtai, *Head of the Mossad*, Yediot Sefarim, 2018

Man Peter, Dan Uri, *Eichmann in my Hands!*, Masada Tel Aviv, 1987 (Hebrew)

Dan Uri, *Terror Incorporated*, Masada, Tel Aviv, 1976

Caroz Ya'acov, *The Man with Two Hats*, Defense office publishing House, Tel Aviv, 2002

Bar-Zohar Michael, Mishal Nissim, *Mossad*, Ecco, HarperCollins, New York, 2012

Bar-Zohar Michael, Haber Eitan, *The Quest for the Red Prince*, William Morrow, New York, 1983

Bar-Zohar Michael, *100 Men and Women of Valor*, Magal and Defense Office publishing House, 2007

Bergman Ronen, *Rise and Kill First*, Random House, New York, 2018.

Malkin Peter Z., Stein Harry, *Eichmann in My Hands!* Grand Central Pub., April 1991 (Kindle edition).

Bird Kai, *The Good Spy: The Life and Death of Robert Ames*, Crown Publishers, Broadway Books, New York 2014, (Kindle edition)

Navoth Nachik, *One Man's Mossad*, Zmora, Kinneret-Bitan, Tel Aviv, 2015